Dave Mann and Ron Main

Motorbooks International
Publishers & Wholesalers

This book is dedicated to Steve McQueen
—Dave Mann

Thanks to all and especially my teenangel, Vanessa, for making life wonderful.
—Ron Main

First published in 1994 by Motorbooks International Publishers & Wholesalers, PO Box 2, 729 Prospect Avenue, Osceola, WI 54020 USA

Library of Congress Cataloging-in-Publication Data

Mann, Dave.
Races, chases, and crashes/Dave Mann.
p. cm.
Includes bibliographical references and index.
ISBN 0-87938-859-5
1. Motor vehicles in motion pictures. I. Title.
PN1995.9.A85M36 1994
791.43'656—dc20 94-939

On the back cover: George Barris, the king of the kustoms, poses with his legendary Batmobile.

Printed and bound in the United States of America

Contents

ACKNOWLEDGMENTS

This book is to provide automotive and motorcycle enthusiasts with the most complete compilation possible of movies with English dialogue that feature hot rods, race cars, sports cars, motorcycles, trucks, racing, outstanding chase scenes, crashes, and anything that is directly related to the automotive industry. Movies are listed alphabetically according to title, followed by their date of release and a description/review of the movie.

These lists were compiled by watching the movies and researching titles listed in a wide variety of sources.

How did I become a motorhead? The first car I can remember that really got my attention was a teacher's powder blue 1955 Chevy two-door sedan. I loved the look of that car. I was 5 years old. When I was around 9, I was watching "77 Sunset Strip," waiting to get a glance of Kookie's wild T-bucket hot rod (the first of its kind, built by Norm Grabowski). By age 10, I had learned enough about hot rods to talk my way into a ride in a hopped-up 1959 Corvette that was owned by an acquaintance. With the top off and the headers uncorked, we hit an indicated 150mph on the highway. It was the kind of thing you always remember.

Another memorable motorhead experience was walking down to the end of the old drag strip outside Winnipeg, Manitoba, in the mid-sixties, and lying down as close as I could get away with to the Top Fuel cars as they screamed through the lights at the end of the quarter mile at close to 200mph. That's another experience you never forget. A series of old Harley-Davidsons and early Fords soon followed. I currently have a scratch-built Harley-Davidson Sportster cafe racer project in the works, and am currently building up a 1940 Ford Deluxe sedan delivery street rod with three things my ideal hot rod should have: a four-speed, gray primer, and a roll cage.

And even if I could afford to finish both of them, I'd still be disappointed that I couldn't afford a first-class Top Gas Harley-Davidson drag bike with billet cases, Ron Trock barrels, and aftermarket four-valve heads in a chrome-moly chassis; a perfectly restored 1939 Harley-Davidson Knucklehead; a pair of Ducati twins (a 1973 Super Sport, and a 1994 916); a 1932 Ford Victoria built by John Buttera and powered by a strong 351 Cleveland; a pair of restored Jaguar coupes (a cream XK-120 and a red early XKE); a British Racing Green V-8 Morgan; an alcohol-burning big-block Chevy-powered drag boat with a nice lowered 1994 Ford Econoline van to tow it; a mint 1970 1/2 Z/28 Rally Sport Camaro (gotta be a four-speed, with a black interior); a 1962 Corvette with modern suspension and powertrain; a Jaguar XJ-12 (rain car); and a street-legal 1994 NASCAR Winston Cup Thunderbird stock car set up for the Talladega Superspeedway and the Bonneville Salt Flats. And a pony.

Regardless of your particular area of interest in the world of motorsports, there are probably a few movies that deal with what you like. Before we get into talking about the movies, let's put things into perspective here.

There really haven't been many movies made featuring race cars or motorcycles that could be considered superb motion pictures. You have to try to enjoy these movies for what they are: entertainment. If we start looking for flaws with these movies, we won't have to look too hard, but we won't get much fun out of them either. You might say they're all we've got.

No single book could ever list every movie that has something of interest to car and motorcycle nuts. You may know of movies not listed here. Please share those titles with us by dropping me a note in care of the publisher so that later versions of this book can be more complete.

I would like to again thank the people who suggested some of the movies that are listed here, and for helping me to come up with some of the information about them. Movie guides by Leonard Maltin and Steven Scheuer were often used to dig up some of these movies, as was Raymond Lee's book, *Fit for the Chase*.

Before getting underway, a few words about my own personal biases would be in order to help you draw your own conclusions about these movies. After all, my opinions are just my opinions, nothing more. Your mileage may vary.

Of all of these movies, my favorites are mostly from the age when producers didn't need dozens of people for stunts; when you didn't have to throw millions of dollars at a movie in order to be competitive in the marketplace; when you didn't have to toss in a token "love" scene to get people to want to see it; when cars did not explode and shoot skyward when they got a flat tire; and where people with original personalities and real talent took the place of models with some acting lessons.

"I *knew* Lee Marvin, Senator Cruise, and I can assure you you're no Lee Marvin."

Dave Mann
Phoenix, Arizona
May, 1994

INTRODUCTION

Some of the earliest motion pictures ever made will be of interest to automotive and motorcycle enthusiasts. There were numerous films that featured cars or motorcycles in a significant role, back in the days when gasoline engines and talking pictures were both still novelties.

Let's take a brief look at how films evolved.

The Jazz Singer starring Al Jolson was released in 1927 and is historic because it was the first "talkie," a movie with its own soundtrack. Due to the combined work of Bell Labs and the Western Electric Company, talking pictures were first widely produced in the early thirties. A typical first-class early theater might have contained two 6-foot-tall racks for the preamplifiers, power amplifiers, and their power supplies. Every piece had a duplicate, and in case of an equipment failure, the projectionist could just flip a switch to kick in the backup unit with no interruption of the picture. The power companies of the time were not nearly as reliable as today, so theaters in the early thirties commonly had a basement filled with tons of batteries to provide backup power. In fact, looking after the battery room took up a lot of the projectionist's time.

The power amplifiers used in these earliest theaters would have used Western Electric triode output tubes, for either 5 or 30 watts of output power, depending on whether they were used separately or in a pair. This was more than enough power to do the job. The industry-standard Western Electric speaker systems used massive electrodynamic magnets and they were so efficient they easily could fill a theater with a single watt of power!

It should go without saying that all of the early movies listed in this book (say, 1917-1953) were made in black and white with a mono soundtrack. Bell Labs conducted experiments with stereo as early as 1927, but it wasn't introduced into the motion picture industry until 1953. You shouldn't let this steer you away from some of these classic early movies. Modern technology is not always needed to capture excitement.

As for motor racing itself, it was extremely dangerous in the thirties and forties due to the lack of safety equipment. Almost all of the race cars that were featured in movies made before World War II were open wheel cars. The early racers never had any seat belts or roll bars. Early crash helmets were made of leather and offered very little protection. Some of the earliest race car drivers in these movies wore their dress clothes in a race, adding only aviators' goggles. Gas tanks leaked and burst regularly. Fires were common, often with grave consequences.

Because of all the danger involved in early motorsports, the successful racers were perceived as being courageous heroes. They were almost always men, with the women in these movies inevitably either swooning with admiration or begging them to quit before they got hurt.

Some of the appeal of this period is the innocence of the characters, reflecting a time when values were simpler. You're safe in considering virtually all of these movies as wholesome family entertainment and entertaining for any motorsports fan.

There were several early series of comedy films that provided miles of footage featuring some of the earliest motor vehicles. These included the Bowery Boys, Charlie Chaplin films, the Keystone Cops, W.C. Fields, Laurel and Hardy, Harold Lloyd films, and the Our Gang series. It was common for the producers to use Model T Fords along with early Harley-Davidson, Henderson, and Indian motorcycles in these films. The bikes, usually ridden by police in the chase scenes, were sometimes equipped with sidecars. Thanks to some legendary stunt riders and drivers, the outcome was almost always wild and hilarious. And thanks to the current interest in nostalgia, collections of some of these early films have recently been released to the home video market. Although many of the earliest films have been lost over the years, there are now a number of sources offering them (see the appendices). *FILMFAX* magazine is an excellent source for locating suppliers of vintage and classic films on videotape. Many of these movies continue to show up on TV networks, so keep checking the listings.

The early days of film were an age of innocence. The people who drove the fast cars and rode the fast bikes in this era were real heroes to all who saw them run. These people were the thrilling daredevils of courage and speed.

You may have noticed that so far there been no mention here of hot rods, teenagers, street racing, drinking, fighting, or outlaws on wheels.

Hide the children, and read on.

The Golden Age of B Movies, 1954-1972

Not long after the end of World War II, America underwent many changes that resulted in the birth of the beloved B Movie.

First, we had the American soldiers returning home from the service with money in their pockets, looking for a way to put their technical and mechanical skills to use into something that enabled them to be creative and have some fun. The outcome of this was the birth of an entire new generation of companies and backyard mechanics who began building hot rods, race cars, and speed equipment. A number of organizations were formed, most notably the National Hot Rod Association (NHRA) in 1951, and the Southern California Timing Association (SCTA). Drag strips evolved from blocked-off back roads to new, purpose-built facilities with proper safety and timing equipment. The Bonneville and El Mirage dry lake beds also provided a way for an incredible variety of creativity and ingenuity to be put to good use to see whose engineering was the fastest.

1952 was the year that drag racing became properly organized, first in the Southern California area. This enabled many competitors to race without having to travel all the way out to the salt flats at Bonneville or El Mirage as in the past.

Those same people who fought for our right to freedom and cold beer also put their skills toward another cause. Shoulder harnesses, roll cages, and fire-retardant clothing came along, later followed by fuel cells that wouldn't burst in a crash like common steel gas tanks. The sport of motor racing entered into a new era where race sanctioning bodies took the safety of their drivers more seriously.

With motorsports so much safer than in previous times, this meant that if Hollywood was to play off the "danger" aspect as it had done in the past, street racing was the avenue to exploit. And there was a bit of racing happening on those old streets; there just weren't enough race tracks to go around.

These were happy and affluent times. When you could pick up a Deuce roadster or a Model A for a week's pay, any Joe could afford some wheels and hop-up goodies. Later, when the 1949 Mercury was a new car, customizing reached a new state of sophistication and class. Hot rodders began to divide themselves up into two basic categories—the "posers" who went for the smooth looks, and the "outlaw speed demons" who went for go, not show.

And then there were the teenagers. Society's shift toward instant gratification was well underway. A new world of technology and opportunities had arrived. With the combined threat of the atom bomb and the Cold War never far from America's consciousness, the kids had new reasons to party.

Drive-in theaters have all but vanished today, but they were at their peak in the fifties. A new type of motion picture came along to draw the teenagers into the drive-ins. Today they're commonly called J.D. (juvenile delinquent) movies or teen exploitation flicks. But back then, they could have been called garbage that was destructive to the minds of the leaders of tomorrow—or harmless fun, depending on who you asked.

The movies of this era are full of memories for those of us lucky enough to have been there when it all happened.

The Modern Era, 1973-1994

By the time the early seventies arrived, the novelty of the familiar themes had, to a great extent, worn off. There was still some demand for the motorcycle outlaw movies, which continue to be made occasionally today. But it was going to take some new excitement to lure patrons into the theater.

The technology that made classic films like *Goldfinger* starring Sean Connery in 1964 possible continued to evolve into even more of a sensual experience.

First came 70mm film, which enabled unprecedented detail. Theaters had subwoofer systems installed to handle the low-frequency energy in most modern movies. Later the Dolby surround sound system was introduced, and then Tomlinson Holman developed the THX sound system. The California-based Industrial Light and Magic made the greatest contribution to modern film special effects technology.

These new techniques and equipment allowed new realism that began to reach the homes of more than just the eccentric. In the mid-eighties it became fairly common for people to have a stereo VCR, with the audio outputs connected to their stereo system. The price of consumer-grade surround sound equipment came down as the demand increased. Today, a good home theater system is becoming a dream come true for thousands of us. The VCR and the video rental companies led to all kinds of neglected movies being brought back to market again.

Once the country had finished with the sixties and had a few more years for it to sink in that those years really were over, Hollywood had some new avenues for commentary and exploitation. People spoke nostalgically with more frequency and in some cases a sense of loss. When you look at them as a group, there is a different kind of energy in the movies of this era.

Motorcycle Movies: The Bad, The Bad, and the Real Bad

When Marlon Brando rumbled onto the screen back in 1954 in *The Wild One*, that was one of the first (and the most famous) of dozens of Hollywood's sensational exploitation pictures portraying motorcyclists as being Real Bad Guys. But almost all of the movies themselves were pretty bad, too. Nobody would ever call most of these movies serious attempts at creating accurate documentaries. This stuff was meant to appeal to and entertain the restless youth of the day. These were the movies most of our parents didn't want us to see. Looking at them now, they had a point.

Many of the "best" of these bad movies were created by American International Pictures (AIP), which practically invented the juvenile delinquent exploitation pictures in the mid-fifties. Many of them featured alienated teenagers with nothing better to do than getting loaded and raising hell. A few of them featured both bikers and hot rodders, and sometimes a monster or two to attract as many ticket buyers as possible.

Motorcycle Squad, from 1937, is one of the earliest movies made where motorcycles played a key role. In this film, a motorcycle cop is dishonorably discharged in order to "join" a gang of crooks. There were lots of even older movies that used bikes, such as the silent Keystone Kops series, which often had motorcycles in chase scenes. The 1939 film *Daredevils of the Red Circle* has an exciting scene where one of the heroes of the movie, on an old flathead Harley V-twin, tries to out-race a wall of water pouring through a subway.

Among more modern films, *The Great Escape* included Steve McQueen's excellent chase scene aboard a Triumph 500 Trophy. McQueen did virtually all of his own riding in *The Great Escape*. And before his untimely death, he had put together one of *the finest* collections of original and restored American motorcycles.

The Irish film from 1986 titled *Eat The Peach* was based on a true story about a pair of unemployed motorcycle enthusiasts who became professional stunt riders. They built a giant wooden barrel in which they rode, just like the old-time carnival daredevils. I can clearly remember seeing this done at the Royal American Shows in the early sixties. These tired, battle-scarred veterans with their stripped-down, rigid-frame flathead Harley 45s and KRs had a combination of tattoos and limps you just couldn't miss. Seeing them ride no-hands around the 80-degree banking at the top of the barrel is something you never forget. Those guys were the first real motorcycle outlaws I ever saw, and I miss them.

Hollywood is fascinated with the Hell's Angels, and includes "Angels" in many a film title, even though the Angels rarely appear. The club has certainly influenced the movies, including *The Wild Angels; Devil's Angels; Hell's Angels On Wheels; Angels From Hell; Run, Angel, Run; Angels Unchained; Hell's Bloody Devils; Angels Die Hard* ("Chopper outlaws riding their hot throbbing machines to a brutal climax of violence!"); *Bury Me An Angel; Angels Hard As They Come; Angels' Wild Women*; Sandy Alexander's movie *Hell's Angels Forever;* and *Hellriders*.

The plots in some motorcycle movies can be pretty wild. Check out *Viva Knievel!*, for example. Evel Knievel is the unknowing victim of a plot to kill him by exploding his back tire while he's making a big jump in Mexico, so the bad guys can smuggle dope into the States in his coffin.

But back to those old B Movie motorcycle cult classics. The titles alone can be pretty entertaining now. *Dragstrip Riot* features the heroic good-guy hot rodders setting the bad-guy bikers straight at a weekend drag meet. And check out the cult classic *She-Devils On Wheels* ("Guts as hard as the steel of their hogs!"). Big, bad biker babes in black leather tie up their old men with chains and drag them behind their bikes. (It's happened to me a few times, and it's a real nuisance.)

We have to bear in mind that the key to enjoying most of these movies is to not expect too much from them. Most of them are just entertainment, as commercial as it gets. Enjoy them for what most of them are: Bad Movies.

And if you are put off by the fact that almost every motorcycle movie ever made gives motorcyclists a bad name, remember that money is the only thing stopping you from making a major motion picture showing some of the really good things motorcyclists do.

Documentaries

There have been a few attempts to tell the inside story of a particular aspect of the automotive industry over the years. Some claim to factual, although the accuracy of most of them could be debated. You'll find several such movies in the main directory, including:

On Any Sunday, On Any Sunday 2, Evel Knievel, Hell's Angels Forever, and *God Rides A Harley* are among the documentary films that focus on various aspects of motorcycling, from real-life gang activities to racing to stunt jumping. *Dirt*, which features Parnelli Jones and Rick Mears, is about playing around off-road, in dune buggies and on motorcycles.

Steel Arena and *The Devil at Your Heels* are documentaries about stunt drivers, and *Smash-Up Alley* (also released under the title of *43: The Richard Petty Story)*, and *Greased Lightning* profile historic stock car racers.

Inside Detroit, Final Offer, Ford: The Man and The Machine, Tucker—The Man and His Dream, and *Roger and Me* offer a wide variety of historical looks at the automotive industry and some of its influential leaders.

Some Movies for Kids

"Car movies" for kids are usually pure fantasy, and many seem to revolve around cars that can fly. The cars used in these movies always seem to be either Model T Ford touring cars or Volkswagen beetles. You'll find several such movies in the main directory, including:

The Absent-Minded Professor, Son of Flubber, The Gnome-Mobile, Chitty Chitty Bang Bang, The Love Bug, Herbie Rides Again, Herbie Goes to Monte Carlo, Herbie Goes Bananas, and *Pee-Wee's Big Adventure.*

Movie Directory

Movie descriptions and reviews were written by co-author Dave Mann (—DM), except those specifically credited to co-author Ron Main (—RM) or contributors Steve Gray (—SG), Michael Dregni (—MDr), and Michael Dapper (—MDa). In the cases where more than one author or contributor had reviewed a film, multiple reviews appear so readers can see the variety of opinions a movie can generate.

It wasn't all that daring for the producers of *American Nitro* to boast in ads, "The Greatest Funny Car Movie Ever Made!" That might be a more striking claim if it weren't just about the *only* funny car movie ever made. *Ron Main Collection*

The Absent-Minded Professor

(1961) This Disney story shows how the professor, played by Fred MacMurray, develops a way to make rubber fly. This enables him to make his 1915 Ford Model T phaeton (touring car) fly, too. The cast also includes Nancy Olson, Keenan Wynn, Tommy Kirk, Ed Wynn, Leon Ames, and Elliott Reid. Disney followed this success with *Son of Flubber*.

Adventure Beyond Belief

Take one English wild man, Nick Pratt (Sklar Cole), and send him off across four continents on a Harley with Tina Tidy (Jill Whitlow), a fugitive from a naughty girls school. Mix in all manner of villains and one would presume to have an *Adventure Beyond Belief*.

It all comes to naught, however, through tedious sight gags, cute quips, and the casting of too many people you thought were dead. Ms. Tidy was not up to any comprehensive naughtiness, and violence was confined to such silliness as gluing Mr. Pratt into a bathtub and leaving the water running.

Hopes were raised when Pratt was buried to the head in a field where motorcycle polo was then played, but a cute escape was in order.

What was "Beyond Belief" were the Big-Name stars: *F Troop* legend Larry Storch, slurring and reeling his way through a throw-away role; a sullen, disheveled John Astin; Elke Sommer, reduced to a broad, stupid accent to get this part; and finally, both Edie Adams and Stella Stevens—I think they were on life support. Why the hell did they make this movie? It was a release of the Sony Video Software Co. Of course! A way to use up tape, plus maybe make the odd $2.12 off the unwary renter. My unhappiness extended to opening the cassette and licking the tape, then letting it broil in my glovebox for a full day before returning it.—SG

The Adventures of Buckaroo Banzai Across the Eighth Dimension

(1984) Here's the story of a guy who drives a rocket-powered car, in addition to being a rock star, a physicist, and a neurosurgeon. A lot of people love this movie, which stars Peter Weller, John Lithgow, Ellen Barkin, Jeff Goldblum, and Christopher Lloyd.

American Graffiti

(1973) This one has a lot to offer. It's a warm look back at a summer in the sixties, where cars are a necessity for dating and the world is changing. The people in the movie drive some neat stuff, including a fenderless 1932 Ford five-window coupe street rod, a 1949 Mercury lead sled, a '58 Impala, a nice '55 Chevrolet, and a baby T-Bird. Directed by George Lucas, the cast includes Ron Howard, Paul LeMat, Cindy Williams, Charlie Martin Smith, Richard Dreyfuss, Mackenzie Phillips, and Candy Clark. It's a good one to watch again.

American Nitro

"The Greatest Funny Car Movie Ever Made!" "Spectacular Crashes!" according to *Car Craft* magazine. Racers starring in this one as themselves include Don "The Snake" Prudhomme, Tom "The Mongoose" McEwen, "TV" Tommy Ivo, and Bob

Let's hope Tyne Daly has a copy of *Angel Unchained* on file. These days, she might have a considerably harder time trying to fit on the back of a bike. But she was bitchin' in *Angel Unchained*, and that's how we choose to remember her. *Ron Main Collection*

Here's another ad for *Angel Unchained*, this one with the copy that says you make the Slaughterhouse Run alone "when you've cut yourself off from the Pack to go flat out against the Freaks and the Straights who rule this cozy corner of HELL!" *Ron Main Collection*

Correll. You're going to see some of the best ground-pounding action ever caught on film. Tommy Ivo always told me that he did the best crashes in the movies, and he does some great ones here!—RM

Angel on Wheels

(1960) This is a fantasy about a guardian angel who is sent to look after a jilted race car driver. It stars Romy Schneider, Jean Paul Belmondo, and Henri Vidal.

Angels Die Hard

(1970) Tom Baker stars along with William Smith, Connie Nelson, R.G. Armstrong, Beach Dickerson, Rita Murray, Dan Haggerty, Bambi(!) Allen, Michael Stringer, and Gary Littlejohn. Here the Angels are the good guys, when they pitch in to help at the scene of a mining accident.

Michael Dapper's review of Angels Die Hard:

The video box proclaims that the Angels' motto is "Kill the Pigs!" and a photo on the box shows an Angel flipping someone off. Count me in. The film wasn't as stirring as hoped, but it was an archetypal late-sixties biker flick produced on no budget with two cameras, a couple of flood lights (or car headlights), and bad sound equipment. The Angels portrayed here would have left dumpy Whiskey Flat, California, alone if a local hadn't killed gang member "Seed" just outside the county line. The Angels return to town to bury him (with some hilarious funeral procession footage) and get some revenge. They save a boy from a collapsed mine (z-z-z-z-z-z), yet the locals still try to stomp them just because they think the Angels have the sheriff's daughter Nancy. Lots of genuine late-sixties choppers (some monstrous forks) and constant second-rate rock/protest music of the era. Worth seeing but keep your expectations under wraps.—MDa

Angels From Hell

(1968) This one stars Tom Stern, Arlene Martel, Ted Markland, Stephen Oliver, and Paul Bertoya. When a decorated veteran returns home from Vietnam he puts some of his training to use by starting an outlaw bike gang. They end up taking on another club and the police in this violent story.

Angels Hard As They Come

(1971) This classic was co-written by Jonathan Demme (*Philadelphia*) and directed by Joe Viola.

It stars James Iglehart, Gilda Texter, Gary Busey, Charles Dierkop, Gary Littlejohn, Larry Tucker, Sharon Peckinpah, and Scott Glenn. This was Gary Busey's movie debut, and it's either pretty good or terrible, depending on who you ask. The Angels take on the Dragons M.C. in the tiny town of Lost Cause, resulting in Harley-Davidson drag racing, fights, and revenge.—DM

Steve Gray's review of Angels—Hard As They Come:

Well, this time we are promised "Big men with throbbing machines... and the girls who take them on! Loose women, fast cycles and gang vengeance!" Whew! This New World picture is unusual in its exceptional camera work and use of real actors, notably Scott Glenn and Gary Busey. It suffers from the usual cheapy desert location and by having the director and producer write the damn thing, presumably while filming it. The cast improvises well, though, mostly by repeating "Man—can you dig it?" and "Wow, man, some (insert one: acid; scooter)!"

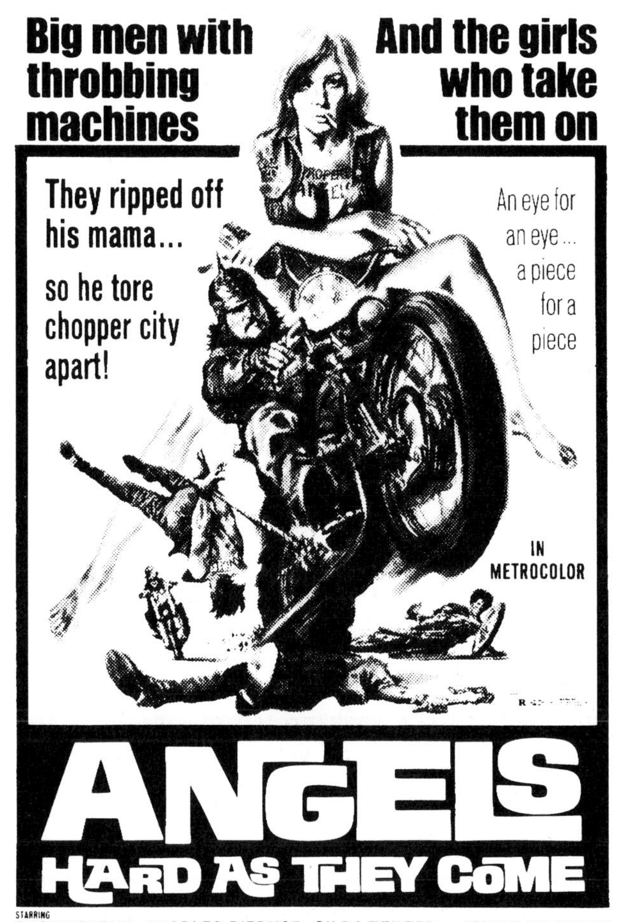

When director Jonathan Demme is being interviewed, you have to wonder if the director the 1993 hit *Philadelphia* voluntarily mentions early films on which he worked, films such as *Angels Hard as They Come.* Somehow, we doubt it. And that's a shame, because Scott Glenn starred as a biker who, well, "they ripped off his mama... so he tore chopper city apart!" *Ron Main Collection*

An early plot line involving a big acid deal is forgotten when Angels Long John, Monk, and Juicer are invited to a Dragons ghost town blow out. Things get ugly fast, progressing through chopper polo with human balls, culminating in the Big Party, where bikers on acid run riot, punching and urinating on each other. The high point is a brief but naughty biker chick vs. hippie strip-off. The rest of the Angels finally show up and dispense some chain-and-pool-cue justice.

1972 means Hogs with z-bars, peanut tanks, and imaginative exhausts. Cameos by two Triumphs and a Honda four. Good period soundtrack by "Carp." Worth the two bucks? Hey, it *did* contain loose women, fast cycles, and gang violence—in small amounts, maybe, but so is two bucks.—SG

Ron Main's Review:

"Big men with throbbing machines and the girls who take them on!" That was what the film's ad said. Now for the sensitive and tender highlights: In a rocket-paced motorcycle race, Scott Glenn sees Gilda Texter get dragged into a church, where she is brutally gang-raped and killed by candlelight (really!). The motorcycle gang holds rat

Publicity for *Army Bound* reported that $50,000 worth of automobiles were used in the filming of this late-forties movie. At today's prices, that would provide enough for a one-car race. *Ron Main Collection*

court and the offenders are sentenced to "chopper polo," a brutal game where the victims are placed—with their hands tied—in the middle of a field. You see, *they* are the balls for this polo match! The gang splits up and tries to drive the "balls" over the goal lines with "chain mallets." (Does ABC Sports know about this?) The rest of the film is your everyday torture, strip tease, giving LSD to the cops, and Charlie Dierkop plunging his pointed helmet into someone's chest.—RM

Angels Unchained

(1970) This Angels flick has the bikers teaming up with the hippies to take on a bunch of repressive rednecks. The cast includes Luke Askew, Larry Bishop, Tyne Daly, Aldo Ray, and Bill McKinney.

Angels' Wild Women

(1972) The film stars Kent Taylor, Regina Carroll, Maggie Bemby, Ross Hagen, and Vicki Volanti. This was also released as *Rough Riders,* and was actually created under the title *Screaming Angels.* Film maker Sam Sherman set out to make another picture along the lines of *Easy Rider* which portrayed bikers as being good people who were just misunderstood. For a gimmick he had the women split from the guys they were with and start their own gang, and just to make sure it had mass appeal they filmed it at the Spahn ranch where Manson and his group had lived.

The result is disappointing, with perhaps the best thing about *Angels' Wild Women* being the poster that yells: "HOT, HARD and MEAN... Too Tough For Any Man!! They'll BEAT 'em, TREAT 'em and EAT 'em alive!"

American Graffiti* was a classic. It presented a great picture of fifties teen lifestyles, combining cars, kids, rock 'n', roll, romance, and time to kill. As this ad shows, the film was later rereleased with some additional footage added to give it a second life. It was successful and profitable in the theaters and on video. *Ron Main Collection

The Angry Breed

(1969) Here is another really bad biker movie, starring James MacArthur, William Windom, Jan Sterling, Jan Murray, Murray McLeod, Lori Martin, and Melody Patterson. Remember James MacArthur, who played Danny on "Hawaii Five-0?" Would you believe MacArthur playing the leader of a gang of bikers who all ride dressed in full Nazi uniforms?

A young Vietnam veteran who has written the script for a movie is walking along the beach when he spots a beautiful girl being hassled by MacArthur and some other bikers. He fights them off, and she takes him home to meet the family. Her father just happens to be the owner of the biggest movie studio in Hollywood. But MacArthur wants to star in the picture, and he also wants revenge. The bikes range from the mid-sixties Honda 305 Super Hawk and Yamaha Big Bear scrambler to chopped Harley-Davidson Big Twins. All of the clichés are here—the unbelievable, corny story, the cheesy fuzz-tone guitar, and the evil bikers. Funny stuff.

Another 48 Hours

(1990) This Nick Nolte-Eddie Murphy sequel to *48 Hours* features bikers portrayed as murdering drug dealers in a boringly stereotypical way. The critics essentially disliked the movie, and the bikers hated it. Don't just ignore this one—boycott it.

Army Bound

Stanley Clements, Karen Sharpe, Steve Brody, and Gil Stratton, Jr., star in this racing movie from the late-forties. It's a great little film about the king of the midget racers who gets drafted into the service but tries to get free on leave for the big race.

Saugus and Culver City speedways were used for filming. The only bad point is that there's not enough racing. But you learn a new way to meet girls: Let your car roll off the trailer and run them down.—RM

Back to the Future

(1985) Christopher Lloyd (Doc Brown) creates a time machine out of a Delorean. He says the car with its stainless steel body is perfect to handle the 1.21 jigowatts needed to spark time travel. Steven Spielberg directed this film that starred Michael J. Fox (Marty McFly) and includes the bizarro Crispin Glover.

Back to the Future Part II

(1989) This sequel included considerably more action set in the future than the first film, so the producers rounded up practically every futuristic-looking car they could get their hands on. That's why several of the cars in the film also appeared in one or more other movies over the years. (See *Blade Runner, Sleeper, Garage A Go-Go* and *Condor*, too.) *BTTF Part II* also had a Pete Brock-bodied car mounted on VW chassis. The car first appeared in *Ice Pirates,* and later appeared in "The Flash," a dreadful short-lived TV show. There was also a *BTTF Part III*, but it was set predominantly in the old west.—MDa

Banzai Runner

(1986) Here is a bad car chase movie, starring Dean Stockwell, John Shepard, and Billy Drago. See if the plot makes sense to you:

Stockwell is a cop whose brother is killed in a highway accident. He decides to get even and has

George Barris, the true king of the kustomizers, stands in front of one his best-known works, the Batmobile. The car was created for the popular sixties "Batman" TV series, and was also used in the 1966 movie that starred much of the TV show's cast, including Adam West as Batman and—Holy costar, Batman!—Burt Ward as Robin. The Batmobiles (more than one was built) have logged thousands and thousands of miles making appearances at car shows and events year-round. ***Courtesy George Barris***

a mechanic friend with a chopped, lowered 200mph Chevy pickup (yes), put a turbocharger on his Plymouth four-door highway patrol cruiser. The goal is to get it capable of hitting 180mph so he can catch those crazy Californians in their sports cars. When he takes a drive in the pickup and gets clocked at 200mph (yes) he gets fired. He then becomes a vigilante, and ends up with a 200mph De Tomaso Pantera (yes), and he not only locates his brother's killer, he sets him up for a cocaine bust and then lets him drive off the road (with the mandatory Hollywood explosion and death)—and he ends up with the dealer's money, to pay off the finance company that's been after him about the mortgage. Okay?

The other cars in the movie include a second-generation Camaro, a Lotus Esprit, a Ferrari, a nice black Lamborghini Muria, and a couple of Porsches. For a chase movie the pace is slow, except in the blurry chase scenes, where the film speed looks like it's been tripled.

Batman

(1966) This is the original movie about Batman and Robin, a spin-off of the popular TV series, included here because of the Batmobile that appears throughout the movie. The original Batmobile was based on a 1955 Lincoln show car called the Futura, which was originally built as a styling exercise. Master car kustomizer George Barris turned it into the wild thing we saw in the movie. Adam West and Burt Ward play Batman and Robin, with Burgess Meredith as the Penguin, Cesar Romero as the Joker, and Frank Gorshin as the Riddler.

Regarding the movie's Batmobile: Barris has built five. Replicas have Ford chassis and Holman & Moody modified big-block engines. Barris also built Batcycles, some with a sidecar for Robin, and one for Batgirl.

Batman

(1989) Two were Batmobiles built for these most recent *Batman* movies, again by kustom king George Barris. Michael Keaton gets to pilot the trick, mean-looking Batmobile in this flick and in *Batman Returns* (1992). The cars for these latest movies were built from 1967 Chevy Impalas found in a London junkyard by special effects supervisor (and set builder) John Evans. They were given a 114in wheelbase—nearly 20ft long—and used

The 1989 movie *Batman* was dark and violent, a far cry from the lighter 1966 effort. Michael Keaton starred as Batman in the film (and its 1992 sequel), and his dark presence was enhanced by this mean, no-flash, strictly business Batmobile, which was created by George Barris. A legendary creator of vehicles for Hollywood, Barris has also appeared in and helped produce several motion pictures. *Courtesy George Barris*

Critics be damned! There's no way you can bad-mouth *Bikini Beach*, or *any* film that features Keenan Wynn sporting sideburns the size of Rhode Island as well as Don Rickles—with some hair!—as a character named "Big Drag." *Ron Main Collection*

327ci V-8 engines mounted 12in lower than normal. Rolls-Royce Olympus Spey engines were used to form the nose cones on the cars' hoods, and Harrier fighter jets donated the turbine blades up front. The cars, which were stretched 30in, cost $5,500 total before customizing.—MDa

Beach Party

(1963) This epic starred Frankie Avalon, Annette Funicello, Bob Cummings, Dorothy Malone, Harvey Lembeck, Jody McCrea, John Ashley, Morey Amsterdam, Candy Johnson, and Eva Six. The notorious American International Pictures wanted to poke fun at Marlon Brando's performance in *The Wild One*, so they had Harvey Lembeck come up with the classic character Eric Von Zipper. He was the leader of the Rats Motorcycle Club, who bumbled their way through most of the series.

In chronological order, *Beach Party* was followed by: *Muscle Beach Party* (1964), *Bikini Beach* (1964), *Pajama Party* (1964), *Beach Blanket Bingo* (1965), *How to Stuff a Wild Bikini* (1965), and finally *Ghost in the Invisible Bikini* (1966).

The Beverly Hillbillies

(1993) Back in 1962, King of the Kustoms George Barris had created the old jalopy truck for the *Beverly Hillbillies* TV show. For this film, he created a new truck (based on a 1921 Oldsmobile chassis, with a 4.0L engine, brakes all around, and fiberglass wheels) as well as a monster truck for Jethro (20ft high, 8tons, with an Olds 528ci en-

"TV" Tommy Ivo, one of the all-time showmen of the drag strip, was among the stars of *Bikini Beach*. Tommy made his name as a child star on TV, and spent plenty of his earnings on fast cars—including classic rails like this one—when he grew up. The consummate showman, Tommy had a transporter built with glass sides so his cars were always on display, even when they were on the road. *Ron Main Collection*

gine). The new truck looks like a heap but rides like a dream. Starring in this box office hit were Jim Varney ("Jed Clampett"), Cloris Leachman ("Granny"), Lily Tomlin ("Miss Jane Hathaway"), Dabney Coleman ("Mr. Drysdale"), Erika Eleniak ("Ellie Mae"), and Diedrich Bader ("Jethro Bodine"). —MDa

The Big Bus

(1976) This is a dubiously successful satire on disaster movies, revolving around a nuclear-powered Trailways bus. (Well, you wanted *all* the movies!) The cast includes Joseph Bologna, Stockard Channing, René Auberjonois, Lynn Redgrave, and Ruth Gordon.

The Big Wheel

(1949) One of Ron Main's favorite race movies: This one had Mickey Rooney playing an Indy Car driver, with Tom Mitchell co-starring. Some racing fans think it's too corny, but I enjoyed it and recommend it if you haven't seen it. Rooney shines as an incredibly gritty and determined racer, especially when he's racing at Indianapolis.

Bikini Beach

(1964) Frankie and Annette are back rockin', surfin', and drag racing! The bulk of the action takes place at the drag strip run by "Big Drag" (played by master thespian Don Rickles). Tommy Ivo was the film's technical advisor and the racing sequences were shot at the Pomona Drags. Harvey Lembeck (as Erik Von Zipper), Martha Hyer, John Ashley, Jody McCrea, Candy (Wow!) Johnson, and all the babes are back. The rock 'n' roll is provided by Little Stevie Wonder, The Exciters, and the great surf band, The Pyramids (they're all bald!). Oh, if we could only keep that summer going forever!—RM

Black Angels

(1970) This was also released as *Black Bikers from Hell*. The title gives the gimmick away, as the producers decided to exploit two groups of minorities at once this time. Des Roberts, John King III, Linda Jackson, and James Whitworth are among the cast. The following text, from the videotape's liner notes, says it all: "God forgives, the Black Angels don't. Bike gangs fight for supremacy and consume civilized society and all who stand in their way. The gangs of "Mad Max" are a bicycle club by comparison. Is there anyone who can stop them on their mad rampage?"

Black Moon Rising

(1986) This is the only movie in here that I know of that has anything to do with a race car that's built for the Bonneville Salt Flats. Robert Vaughn is cast as the thief who steals the Black Moon, with Tommy Lee Jones, Linda Hamilton, Bubba Smith, Richard Jaeckel, Lee Ving, and William Sanderson appearing.

There is some fine cinematography and good use of special effects here. The film features the custom car called Concordia II, black and red with racing wheels and huge rear-deck lid spoiler. Sort of a flying saucer-shaped car.

The Black Rider

(1954) Clyde Earl offers this vintage classic in his video catalog. Don't expect to find it at the corner video store. It's a black-and-white flick with a plot built around some British espionage, and lots of classic British iron is used and shown throughout.

Blackboard Jungle

(1955) A great classic. Rampant with juvenile delinquency and with "Rock Around the Clock" by Bill Haley and the Comets as the theme song. It was the first movie to feature rock 'n' roll music, and the film did more than any other to spread the word of rock 'n' roll mania. Glenn Ford stars as the teacher, "Mr. Daddy-O." Students act more like prisoners. A shocking film of the era. Vic Morrow, in his film debut, beats up Ford, then threatens his wife (Anne Francis), and with the help of cool Sidney Poitier, life as we know it goes on.—RM

Blade Runner

(1982) Ridley Scott directed this film that stars Harrison Ford, Rutger Hauer, Sean Young, Edward James Olmos, and Daryl Hannah. It's set in the 21st century and includes the spinner cars, one of which is owned by the Miami Beach Police Museum while the other was sent to a Japanese museum. The car still in the States was repainted and reused in *Back to the Future Part II*.

The Blonde Comet

(1941) Indy Car champion Barney Oldfield costars in this story about a woman race car driver (Virginia Vale) who tries desperately to win the big race so she can save her father's tire company. As Ron Main says: "It's true blondes do have more fun with the help of the great Barney Oldfield and her own race car. Lots of racing [footage shot at] Ascot, Oakland, and Indy."—RM

Blue de Ville

(1986) This one was made for TV and was the pilot for a series that went unsold. A group of free-wheeling young people head off for adventure in a 1959 Cadillac, with entertaining results. The movie has a charm to it, and would have had a following as a series. *Blue de Ville* was directed by Jim Johnson, with Jennifer Runyon, Kimberley Pistone, and Robert Prescott starring.

Blues Brothers

(1980) A comedy classic with an all-star cast led by the late John Belushi. The Bluesmobile featured in the movie was a 1974 Dodge Monaco. Dodge built just 4,900 1974 Monaco Specials for police use, and it seemed like at least that many were destroyed in the film. Dan Aykroyd (Elwood Blues) said to John Belushi (Jake Blues): "It's got a cop motor. A 440 cubic inch plant. It's got cop tires, cop suspension, cop shocks. It's a model built before catalytic converters so it'll run on regular gas. What do you say? Is it the new Bluesmobile, or what?"

Universal Studios build eight identical Bluesmobiles for use in the film, all badged as former Chicago Police Department cars. Dozens more were used as extras and crash vehicles in the film, especially during the downtown Chicago chase scenes. Seven of the Bluesmobiles were destroyed

Sure-fire, fool-proof, 100-percent guaranteed way to attract hordes of young movie goers to a flick? Insert in the ad for your movie: "Recommended for mature audiences." Young teens will either think they're pulling one over on their parents by going to see the film, or they'll be banned from seeing it—which really guarantees that they'll sneak out of the house to go see it. "Deborah, you are not going to see that *Born Losers* movie!" "Oh, no, mom, we're going over to the church youth center to play games and enjoy the wholesome company of other young teens." ***Ron Main Collection***

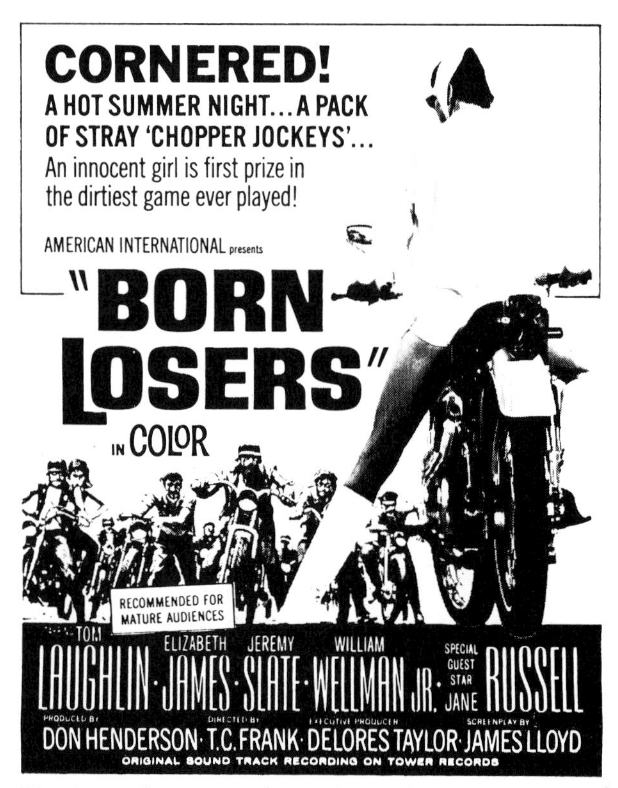

Here's another *Born Losers* ad, one that shows the rider in the foreground in full view. Uh-oh, it's an "innocent girl" who's been cornered by the "chopper jockeys." Things look bad for her, which is why it's appropriate that only mature audiences view this motion picture. ***Ron Main Collection***

during filming, and the last is owned by a retired police sergeant, Sgt. Jim Post, who was president of the Police Car Owners of America. Post received authenticity papers from Universal so he can prove the car is actually from the movie. It's complete with six steel eyelets in the roof and snow tires all around.—MDa

Bobby Deerfield

(1977) Here is a love story that makes a token attempt to deal with race car driving, but it's a waste of time. Al Pacino and Martha Keller wasted their talent in this boring story about the glamorous Formula One Grand Prix racing world. It's more a story about the relationship between them, with the race cars serving as an incidental backdrop.

Bonnie and Clyde

(1967) This old warrior stars Warren Beatty and Faye Dunaway as the legendary gangsters. Lots of thirties-style cars on the roll and in big chases. A Barris-built car was actually riddled with bullets fired from a .45caliber Thompson sub-machine gun for an authentic look for the final scene. The real B & C death car was most recently owned by Gary Primm of Whiskey Pete's Casino, on Nevada's southern state line. He paid $250,000.—MDa

Born Losers

(1967) This film stars Tom Laughlin, Elizabeth James, Jeremy Slate, William Wellman, Jr., and Robert Tessler. "Kitten on wheels with her bike, her boots, and her bikini" (who writes this stuff?). Tom Laughlin is "Billy Jack," a half-Native American who single-handedly takes on a wild gang of motorcycle outlaws as they launch a program of destruction, murder, rape, and pillaging (what, no jay walking?) in a small town. Shapely Elizabeth James is almost always in a revealing bikini and riding a motorcycle. But it you're looking for a more mature-looking gal, how about exotic Jane Russell? This film marks her return to the screen following a too-long absence; she plays Miss James' mother. This was the first of the Billy Jack films, and was directed by Laughlin, who used the name "T.C. Frank" in the credits.—RM

Born To Race

(1988) This one's a disaster. How's this for a story? A brilliant, beautiful, single, available, interested young woman has designed a revolutionary new racing engine and she takes it to a stock car track to use it in NASCAR Winston Cup racing. Okay, I know that happens all the time. But the engine has four valves per cylinder! You can't run four valves per cylinder in NASCAR! See, it was almost totally realistic and believable, but with this one little detail they spoiled the movie.

Born to Ride

(1991) Here's one about a young Harley-Davidson racer who chooses serving in the Army over jail time and joins a team of motorcycle scouts. It stars John Stamos, John Stockwell, and Teri Polo. The movie has lots of (actual) Harley-Davidsons from the forties in it, mostly the old WLA 45 army bikes.

In the opening scene and in other parts of the film, John Stamos rides a blue and white Harley-Davidson Knucklehead that looks completely stock (not stripped-down, as you would expect an old racer's bike to be). There is a fair amount of parade-style exhibition riding throughout the movie. *Born to Ride* is a decent movie, recommended for any fans of classic Harley-Davidsons.

Born to Speed

(1947) This is another one of those old racing movies that's really hard to find, and not in most movie guides. It stars Johnny Sands and John Castla, and plays up the daredevil aspect of driving race cars. Prime Sports network affiliates televise it once in a while.

Breaker! Breaker!

(1971) It's a big 10-4 that this one starred Chuck Norris as a trucker whose younger brother lands in jail, and big bro wants to spring him. The cast includes George Murdock, Terry O'Connor, and Don Gentry. Unfortunately, even if you're a Norris fan, this one was pretty bad.

Breathless

(1983) This heavy breather has Richard Gere on a Harley-Davidson being chased by the police. Valerie Kapriski, Art Metrano, John P. Ryan, William Tepper, and Gary Goodrow also star in this remake of the original *Breathless* from 1959.

Buck Privates Come Home

(1947) Abbott and Costello smuggle an orphan into the country after the war, and they need someone to adopt her. Joan Fulton is their choice, and her fiancé is a midget car racer who is certain to win the upcoming big race. Lou Costello accidentally starts the race and leads the police and immigration types on a mad-cap cross-country race that became one of the most memorable in film history. Racer Roy Simmons' car is used in all the stunts, and Louis Tomei was behind the wheel.—RM

Bullit

(1968) *Bullit* is a classic motion picture in a number of ways. Anything with Steve McQueen and wheels is a classic in itself, partly because he performed virtually all of his own driving, riding, and stunts. Here we are treated to some fine acting, some real tension and suspense, an excellent sixties "cool jazz" soundtrack, and the chase scene that many feel remains the standard of excellence to this day. McQueen plays a detective assigned to protect a key witness who's slated to testify in a court case. When the witness is murdered, McQueen hunts down the killers—who are also hunting him since only he knows they're guilty.

The film costars: a dark green 1968 Mustang fastback with a 390 engine and a four-speed, driven by McQueen; and a deadly, black, big-block four-speed 1968 Charger piloted by hit man Bill Hickman (who appeared on film in the non-speaking role of the driver and who actually drove during the chase scene filming). We get our first glimpse of the Charger at 59 minutes into the movie, sneaking along after McQueen, who's in a cab. At the 65-minute mark, the stage has been set for one of the finest chase scenes in history. McQueen's Mustang rumbles along through the Mission District of San Francisco, tailed by the Charger, which is occupied by the two mob heavies and

Burn 'em Up Barnes **was actually a serial, a series of episodes, each of which was loaded with action. There was plenty of car racing, chasing, crashing, and motorcycle action in the Barnes films.** ***Ron Main Collection***

one Winchester pump shotgun. The action that follows revolves around tight city streets, those famous hills, lots of corners, and a winding highway.

I could find faults with the movie if I had to, but there doesn't seem to be any reason to. (Well, okay—during the chase scene in the streets of San Francisco, there's a yellow Volkswagen bug that you can spot in at least at least four shots. And, thanks to the way the film was edited, the Mustang that McQueen drives seems to have a twenty-speed transmission.)

Bullit is one of a handful of movies in this book that is a true classic every motorsports fan should see at least once.

It's also one of the few in this book that is available on laserdisc. Video quality is a bit pale in places but it's very crisp—a surprisingly good transfer to disc. Audio quality is very clean, having been re-mastered in CX-encoded stereo. You may want to add a bit of bottom end; and mind your tweeters during the chase scene. If you're playing this back at the level it deserves, the tire screaming might call for your amplifier to put out more power than it really can, toasting your tweeters.

Bullit is an absolute must for all fans of muscle cars, chase scenes, or McQueen.—DM

Ron Main's review of Bullit:

This is *the best* and most famous car chase ever filmed—Period! Through the hills of San Francisco, Steve McQueen in his 400hp '68 Mustang and the Dodge Charger driven by stunt driver Bill Hickman take you on a roller coaster ride you will never forget. One of the many dangerous stunts was when McQueen forces the Charger into the gas station to its fiery death. This stunt was done by "tow and release." McQueen's car is actually towing the Charger with two dummies inside. He then pulls a release lever and the Charger heads off to the gas station. Steve McQueen did his own stunts and would ride or drive anything on wheels. And it's worth noting that Hickman, an outstanding driver, also drove for chase scenes in *The French Connection*.—RM

Bundle of Joy

(1956) The Plymouth Belmont dream car appeared in this film starring Eddie Fisher and Debbie Reynolds, and the car is thought to have been in the 1957 movie *Mister Cory* with Tony Curtis. In *Bundle of Joy,* the car still has its Belmont nameplates. The car is currently in the Blackhawk Collection in California. It has been restored, but was painted red; the car was originally azure blue.—MDa

Burn 'Em Up

(1939) This is a movie about early open-wheel race car drivers. You won't find it listed in most movie guides, and it doesn't seem to show up in video stores or on TV.

Burn 'Em Up Barnes

(1934) This was originally released as an MGM twelve-episode serial and did quite well. In 1935 it was released as a full-length feature that ran 75 minutes but it did poorly, partly because so many people had already seen it. The movie is hard to find today, which is unfortunate because it seemed to devote more attention to early Indy Car racing than any other film of the era.

Burn 'Em Up O'Conner

According to Ron Main, this is an incredible (as in unbelievable) old-timer about a racer who goes blind prior to the film's climactic big race. Prudent judgment might have him skip the race, but no, he is behind the wheel and gunning it around the track. How? Well, a mechanic runs toward the corners of the track and blows a whistle, which O'Conner interprets as the signal to turn. We'll just let that image sink in and leave you with your thoughts.—MDa

The Burning Hell

(1974) The was made by the Nashville-based June and Ron Ormond, and marked a turning point in their career together. For years they had produced a series of classic B movies and supplied them to many of the exploitation-oriented theaters throughout the South. Their films always did well, with titles like *White Lightnin' Road*, the tasteful *Monster and the Stripper* ("WARNING!! Unless you can stand Vivid Realism... IT MIGHT SNAP YOUR MIND!"), and *Girl from Tobacco Row* ("a girl wilder than a peach orchard hog").

When they were on their way to the opening of *Girl from Tobacco Row*, their single-engine Beechcraft plane lost power and crashed in a field. Although their son Tim was not hurt, they both had back and rib injuries that put them in the hospital for six weeks. They felt they had been spared from death, and decided to give something back.

The Burning Hell is about two motorcyclists, one of whom is played by Tim Ormond. They are out riding one day when by chance they find themselves stopping in at the home of a minister. He tells them about salvation but they're not interested and they go back out on the highway. One of the riders goes down hard in a crash and is killed, leaving Tim in shock. He heads back to see the preacher, who is in the middle of a sermon, and Tim experiences salvation.

Burnout

(1977) Have you ever tried to describe the sound of nitro-burning top fuel dragsters? Don't even try! Show 'em *Burnout* instead. Mark Schneider, Robert Louden, and our man, Big John Zenda of the NHRA star in this one. Big John also drives for Mark and Robert (while wearing a fire mask). It's a great story as the Master (Big John) and the young bull (Schneider) drag it out. It was filmed at the Irwindale Raceway, Indy Raceway Park, and the Orange County International Raceway. Gary Beck, Frank Bradley, Carl Olson, and Carl Denshan play themselves. Big John still uses nitro in his hair.—RM

Bury Me An Angel

(1971) Here's a biker movie with a twist, with the story coming from a woman's perspective. It was directed by Barbara Peters, and stars Dixie Peabody, Terry Mace, Joanne Jordan, Clyde Ventura, Dan Haggerty, Stephen Whittaker, Gary Littlejohn, and Beach Dickerson. The story is about a

The 1970 *Angel Unchained* had star Don Stroud as a biker who joins a hippie commune and then finds himself in the midst of a conflict between dune buggy drivers and the hippies. Stroud's got a way to settle that: Call in the bikers. *American International/ Ron Main Collection*

murdered man and the snarly sister who's out for revenge.

Bye Bye Birdie

(1963) Delightful, this movie has it all. Bobby Rydell is in his first movie, singing and rocking. You'll see singing idol Conrad Birdie (Jesse Pearson) on his Norton Atlas motorcycle with his gold lame suit. This Elvis-like rock idol wears the kookiest clothes. The typical teen is portrayed by young Swedish bundle of beauty Ann-Margaret (incredible in the sweater-changing scene). Dick Van Dyke's love is the ever-hot Janet Leigh, and with help from Paul Lynde and Mary La Roche, chemistry will never again be the same. This movie has Ed Sullivan, too. It's a honey! After you see this one, you'll know you've gotta lotta livin' to do.—RM

Cadillac Man

(1990) This comedy has Robin Williams playing a car salesman who gets involved with some wild situations in his personal life and at the dealership. The performances are good, the story is decent and there's a mixture of comedy (due to Williams) and suspense.

The California Kid

(1974) This was made for TV and it doesn't turn up too often. It's the story of a hard-core local sheriff (Vic Morrow) who comes down hard on speeders. His approach to justice sometimes includes sideswiping offenders rather than stopping them for the usual ticket or trip to jail. The stars include Martin Sheen and the wild, full-fendered 1934 Ford three-window coupe built by Pete Chapouris. The film makers spotted the car on the cover of *Hot Rod* and said they just had to have it for the movie. During filming, it was driven good and hard, thus requiring some touching up and repair, but it looks great in a good film. Filming took place in Piru, California, and in the Soledad Canyon area, 45 miles north of Los Angeles. The car burned up a new set of tires in three days of filming. The car is an all-time classic, and the movie is worth watching just to see it. Michelle Phillips and Stuart Margolin also appear.—DM

Ron Main's review of The California Kid:

Your heart will start pounding when Martin Sheen smokes into town in Pete Chapouris' "The California Kid." This flamed '34 coupe must take the dangerous Clarksberg curve at over 90mph, something no other car can do, so he can get his revenge on "Baddy" Sheriff Vic Morrow, a psychotic killer who nerfed seven speedsters to their death. Nick Nolte and Michelle Phillips help "Da Kid" and the stunt driving was left up to Gerry Summers, while Hal Needham, doubling for Vic Morrow, handled the sheriff's car. We all love "Da Kid." A must-see.—RM

California Straight Ahead

(1937) Roll 'em! This one stars John Wayne as a trucker who's doing his best to show that trucks can compete with the railroads by racing across the country. Louise Latimer, Robert McQuade, Theodore Von Eltz, and Tully Marshall costar. *California Straight Ahead* is a good action movie.

Cannonball

(1976) This was also released under the name *Carquake*. It is very similar to *Gumball Rally* (which was released earlier in 1976) but nowhere near as good. David Carradine, Veronica Hamel, Bill McKinney, Gerrit Graham, Judy Canova, Carl Gottlieb, and Belinda Balaski star; Paul Bartel directed. See *Gumball Rally* instead.

Cannonball Run

(1981) This film stars Burt Reynolds, Dom DeLuise, Farrah Fawcett, Dean Martin, Sammy Davis, Jr., and Roger Moore. It's loosely based on the real Cannonball Run, which at that time was a flat-out race across the nation's highways. This could have been excellent but unfortunately it ends up being pretty juvenile and forgettable.

Cannonball Run 2

(1984) They're at it again. This is a sequel about the cross-country roadrace, and again it fails to be worth watching. About the only thing that's good about movies like this (other than the great cast, which went to waste here) is that they create employment.

The Car

(1977) This film stars James Brolin, Kathleen Lloyd, John Marley, and John Rubenstein. The plot: a car with no driver is possessed by the devil and drives itself around, killing people. Well, it's more believable than some of the stuff in here.—DM

Michael Dregni's review of The Car:

(1977) This is one of those movies you walk out of halfway through with no regrets. The plot: a car that looks like a Pro Street Lincoln Continental with deeply tinted windows is possessed by Satan and drives itself around, terrorizing a town and killing the denizens. Poker-faced James Brolin does his best taking it all seriously in saving the town and swinging co-star Kathleen Lloyd in her skin-tight leather jeans that could only have come from the seventies. Also stars John Marley and John Rubenstein. Well, thinking about it, the plot *is* more believable that some of the stuff here. *The Car* itself was a Barris kustom job that weighed about three tons and had its fenders raised 18in to make it look more menacing. Too bad George Barris couldn't have helped the script as much.—MDr

Carquake

(1976) See: *Cannonball.*

Car Trouble

(1986) Here is a British comedy about a middle-aged couple, the husband of which decides to indulge in his fantasy of owning a Jaguar XKE. He buys a used red E-type coupe from a car lot, and both of their lives change completely—ultimately for the worse. This is better than most of the contemporary automotive comedies, and it's a must for all XKE fans (even if the car gets totaled). Ian Charleson and Julie Walters are the couple, with David Greene, Vincenzo Ricotta, Stratford Johns, Hazel O'Connor, and Dave Hill also starring.

Oh, that Broadway Joe! He was a total stiff as an actor, a regular man of wood, but he was good-looking, could be portrayed as a tough guy, and his name was extremely marketable in 1970, when the film was released. After all, he was endorsing products as unlikely as women's panty hose at the time, just because of his mass-market appeal. Teaming him with Ann-Margaret, a talented actress as well as a young sex kitten, certainly didn't hurt. *Ron Main Collection*

The Cars That Ate Paris

(1971) This one can also sometimes be found under the title *The Cars that Ate People.* It's from France, and is about a Volkswagen bug with huge spikes all over it that, well, eats a lot. This one is as weird as it sounds.

Car Wash

(1976) A wild comedy with stars such as Richard Pryor, Ivan Dixon (from TV's *Hogan's Heroes*), George Carlin, Prof. Irwin Corey, the Pointer Sisters, and Garrett Morris. The action centers around a wild L.A. car wash and the people who frequent it. Not great, but just seeing the hair and fashions of the era is a gas. And there just aren't enough curb feelers around these days.—MDa

Casino Royale

(1967) This was a James Bond spoof with David Niven as a 007 who is—gasp!—afraid of women. There's some neat cars but overall this is a Bond flick to be missed.—MDr

Catch Me If You Can

(1989) Here is an extremely contrived movie that was made for teenagers. A kid becomes the town hero by street racing a red 1957 Chevy two-door sedan to raise money for the local high school. Lots of swearing doesn't help its excitement value. This one stars Matt Lattanzi, Lori Locklin, and Grant Heslov, and it's really bad. If you enjoy it and you're over 12, you might get yourself checked out.

C.C. and Company

(1970) This one stars Joe Namath, Ann-Margaret, William Smith, Jennifer Billingsley, Teda Bracci, Greg Mullavey, Sid Haig, Bruce Glover, and Wayne County & the C.C. Riders. It's the story of the (relatively) clean-cut Namath against Smith the wild biker, with the real interest provided by the chopped Harley-Davidsons they ride and Ann-Margaret's cleavage.—DM

Ron Main's review of C.C. and Company:

Joe Namath woos and wins beautiful Ann-Margaret. Broadway Joe never made a pass like this with the Jets! For the film, a half-mile motocross track was constructed near Tucson. Namath rides against John De Soto and about two dozen of America's top motocross pros. They roar across steep hills, sand traps, and over water jumps. The outlaw motorcycle gang led by William Smith kidnaps Ann (who wouldn't?). This leads to the climactic chopper flat-track race staged in the University of Arizona football stadium! This two-man, sudden death duel has the bad guy getting destroyed while the hero rides off with the girl. Ann-Margaret had fourteen costume changes, but the best-remembered one of all didn't cost a penny! For her big lovemaking scene with Joe, Ann wears no costume at all!—RM (Also look for it on video entitled *Chrome Hearts.*)

The Challengers

(1969) This film was made for TV, with Darren McGavin, Sean Garrison, Nico Minardos, Anne Baxter, Richard Conte, and Farley Granger. It's a poorly done story of Formula One drivers fighting over a lady.

The Charge of the Model Ts

(1979) Here we've got stars John David Carson, Louis Nye, Arte Johnson, Herb Edelman, and Carol Bagdasarian. It's a disappointing comedy about a German spy with a modified Model T Ford during the first world war.

Checkered Flag

(1989) This one was an ABC TV series pilot that absolutely stunk. We in the racing community heard it was coming, and we were led to believe it was going to tell the real story about driving an Indy Car.

It had a revoltingly ridiculous story line. We knew we were in trouble when in the first minute of the movie one of the drivers is testing a state-of-the-art Indy Car at a paved oval. He cuts a tire, smacks the wall, explodes like a bomb, and dies.

It looks like the producers were afraid that a series about racing wouldn't sell, so they had the two remaining racers spending most of their time fighting over a girl. It was a mistake to have made a movie with a story like this, and it's a good thing nobody bought it.

There's trouble in that smirk. Sure enough, Arch Hall, Jr., was in plenty of jams in *The Choppers*, a 1961 release. *Ron Main Collection*

Checkered Flag or Crash

(1977) Look out! This one has Joe Don Baker (of the *Walking Tall* films), Susan Sarandon, Larry Hagman (Who Shot J.R.?), Alan Vint, real racer Parnelli Jones, and Logan Clark starring. The story involves a 1,000-mile off-road race run in the Philippines.

Chitty Chitty Bang Bang

(1968) This United Artists flick stars Dick Van Dyke in a disappointing movie on a now-familiar theme involving a car that flies. The cast includes Sally Ann Howes, Lionel Jeffries, Gert (Goldfinger) Frobe, Anna Quayle, and the late British TV comic Benny Hill. The film was based on a book by Ian Fleming, author of the James Bond stories. The imaginary flying car was named after an actual series of racing cars. Count Louis Zbrowski built the three airplane-engined CCBB race cars, completing the first one in 1921 with a Mercedes body and a 23liter Maybach engine.

Chopper Chicks in Zombietown

(1989) This is a laughing look at horror movies, with a gang of girls on Evolution Sportsters battling some scary monsters. The cast includes Jamie Rose, Catherine Carlen, Kristina Loggia, Don Calfa, and MTV's Martha Quinn.

Police officers today must want to weep as they find themselves climbing into tasteless blobs such as Chevrolet Caprice Classics. Oh, for the days when the police drove cars worth desiring, such as these '59 Chevys that were used in the 1961 release, *The Choppers. Ron Main Collection*

The Choppers

(1961) Here is another teen exploitation flick, about a young country gang who operate a chop shop for stolen cars and raises hell with the locals. Arch Hall, Jr., Marianne Gaba, and Bruno Ve Sota star in this low-budget teen classic.

Christine

(1983) A car movie with a twist. A teenager buys a very neglected 1958 Plymouth Fury and patiently does a good job of restoring it. The car turns out to have powers of its own and ends up driving itself with tragic results. Stephen King wrote the story, which is directed by John Carpenter, starring Keith Gordon, John Stockwell, Robert Prosky, Alexandra Paul, Harry Dean Stanton, Christine Belford, and Roberts Blossom. There are better examples of King's talent, but *Christine* has a lot of fans. This movie is suspenseful and well-done.

Chrome and Hot Leather

(1971) Yet another biker movie with William Smith, Tony Young, Michael Haynes, Peter Brown, and Marvin Gaye. This time, a gang of bikers kills a woman, whose fiancé is out for revenge. The best thing about *Chrome and Hot Leather* is the title.

City Limits

(1985) Here's one about a future society where disease has reduced the population, and several motorcycle gangs are fighting to the finish. It was directed by Aaron Lipstadt and stars Darrell Larson, John Stockwell, Kim Cattrall, Rae Dawn Chong, John Diehl, Don Opper, James Earl Jones, Robby Benson, Danny De La Paz, and Norbert Weisser.

Cobra

(1986) Sylvester Stallone is a rebel with a cause when his cruiser is a kool 1950 Mercury Custom hot rod. He and his super Merc must protect sexy Brigitte Nielsen from hundreds of bikers, psychopaths, and axe murderers. His custom Merc does 360 spins, smashes through buildings, catches on fire, and jumps off a two-story parking garage in a stunt you must see to believe. Four custom Mercs were built by Eddie Paul of Los Angeles for the film. All were nosed and decked, had custom hoods and grilles, and were chopped 2in. To keep up with the Italian Stallion, the cars used blown Chevy engines with nitrous oxide good for 140+mph and 0-60 in 4 seconds flat!—RM

Code Two

(1953) This film was the first to use the "cop on a Harley-Davidson" theme. The cast includes Ralph Meeker, Sally Forrest, Keenan Wynn, Robert Horton, Jeff Richards, and Lee Marvin. Marvin gives a good performance here, and this movie is worth looking out for although it doesn't turn up too often.

Condor

This little-known flick includes an appearance by the Tedham Car, which was built by a Phoenix man who sold it to Fantasy Cars. The vehicle was also in *BTTF Part II*. It started life as a 1956 Lincoln Continental originally owned by news commentator and actor Alex Drier of Chicago. It had a push-button bubble roof, vertical grille, four bucket seats, TV, phone, stereo, and fur carpets.

Convoy

(1978) Well, good buddy, this one stars Kris Kristofferson and Ali MacGraw in another story

Teens, car thefts, car stripping, chicks, cops, fights. That's what you'll get from *The Choppers*, and that's a heap of action, mister. *Ron Main Collection*

about the independent trucker, along with Ernest Borgnine, Burt Young, Madge Sinclair, Franklyn Ajaye, and Cassie Yates. There's some debatable acting here but there's lots of action and laughs. Directed by Sam Peckinpah.

Cool as Ice

(1991) Yo! This one stars rapper and former motocross racer Vanilla Ice, more or less playing himself. The function of this movie seems to be more for promotion of the star than anything else. It reportedly did poorly in theaters, and has received some bad press in motorcycle magazines. For the record, Ice rides a Suzuki GSX-R and does a fair amount of stunt riding. Interestingly, Ice has claimed to have been a motocross racer on the national circuit, but there was no record of his competing at any level higher than regional events within his home state of Florida, where he has raced personal watercraft in recent years. All of which is more than we probably need to know about Vanilla Ice.—MDa

The Cool Hot Rod

(1953-54) Talk about buried treasure. I thought I would never find this award-winning film that honestly told the true story of hot rodding in the fifties. Bill, the new kid in school, figures he

The Bowery Boys made a large number of extremely popular movies and serials that were shown in theaters and later aired on television (and they're still being shown today). They got their start playing the Dead End Kids in the 1937 film *Dead End*, and were featured in several movies in the early forties before becoming The Bowery Boys in 1946. They starred in Bowery Boys films through 1956, with Leo Gorcey and Huntz Hall attaining considerable fame. *Allied Artists/ Ron Main Collection*

will show them all how cool he is by driving all over them with his outlaw '29 Ford roadster. But luckily, the local car club takes him out to the drags, and he learns his car is a slug around here. Your heart will start pumping when you see the "Bean Bandits" 142mph rear-engine roadster and a host of other great cars. *Hot Rod* magazine, the Inglewood Police, Rambling Rods, and 1,320 car clubs helped make this Sid David classic, and it was shown in high schools all across the country. And so began the dreams of thousands of teenage boys with their first hot rods. This one's a 10+!—RM

Corky

(1972) "Corky's coming, smell the rubber burn, hear the women scream." Bobby Allison, Donnie Allison, Buddy Baker, Richard Petty, and Cale Yarborough play themselves and participate in the racing sequences in this film. Robert Blake plays Corky, a great Grand National driver who abandons his wife (Charlotte Rampling) for his only true love, stock car racing. Breathtakingly filmed in Dallas and Atlanta. Exciting racing plus a demolition derby highlight this film. Patrick O'Neal and Ben Johnson costar in this film, which has some good race scenes and a strong cast. A 1967 Plymouth Barracuda used in the film also appeared in several commercials and the "Knight Rider" TV series. (While it could have been titled "We Interrupt This Marriage to Bring You the Racing Season," the film was actually originally called *Lookin' Good.*)—RM

Corvette Summer

(1978) This is a movie about a kid who buys a wrecked Corvette and "fixes it up" with his classmates into what is sure to be the ugliest custom Corvette you're ever likely to see. The cast here is Mark Hamill, Annie Potts, Eugene Roche, Kim Milford, Richard McKenzie, and William Bryant. Even if the Corvette had been nicely done up, this would still have been a terrible movie.—DM

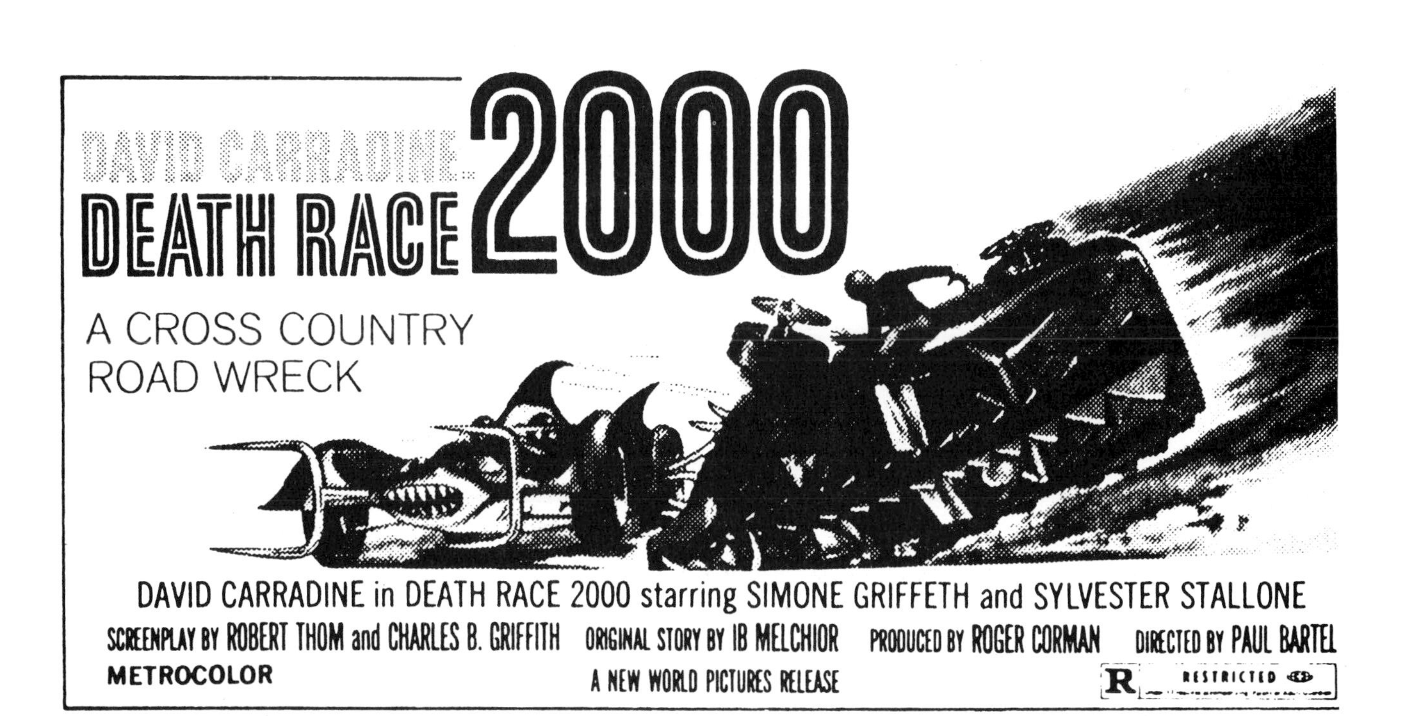

Death Race 2000* was the fifth feature film in which Sylvester Stallone appeared, and he got strong billing. This 1975 film became a hit, as did his 1976 career-maker, the original *Rocky* movie. *New World Pictures/ Ron Main Collection

Ron Main's review of Corvette Summer:

The star of this movie was created by art director James Shoppe and built by customizer Richard Korkes. It exhibits some of the most radical changes ever made to a Corvette. It even has right-hand drive, the better to eye the young girls on the sidewalk, my dear! One of the great scenes was shot on Van Nuys Boulevard, which, for years, was the famous stretch of road where hot rods and custom cars from all over southern California cruised. Getting this fabulous phenomenon on film posed mammoth problems in car casting and traffic control. The end result is guaranteed to bring a smile to the face of anyone who has ever been there! Now, back to the story: Mark Hamill (Luke Skywalker) built the dream machine, but the 'Vette gets stolen. He falls in love, but the girl's a would-be hooker. The real beauty in this film is Annie Potts in her rolling bordello van. She comes to Vegas with delusions of making it big in the world's oldest profession. Annie's a sheer delight and Mark needs a degreasing! Lots of fun for everyone!—RM

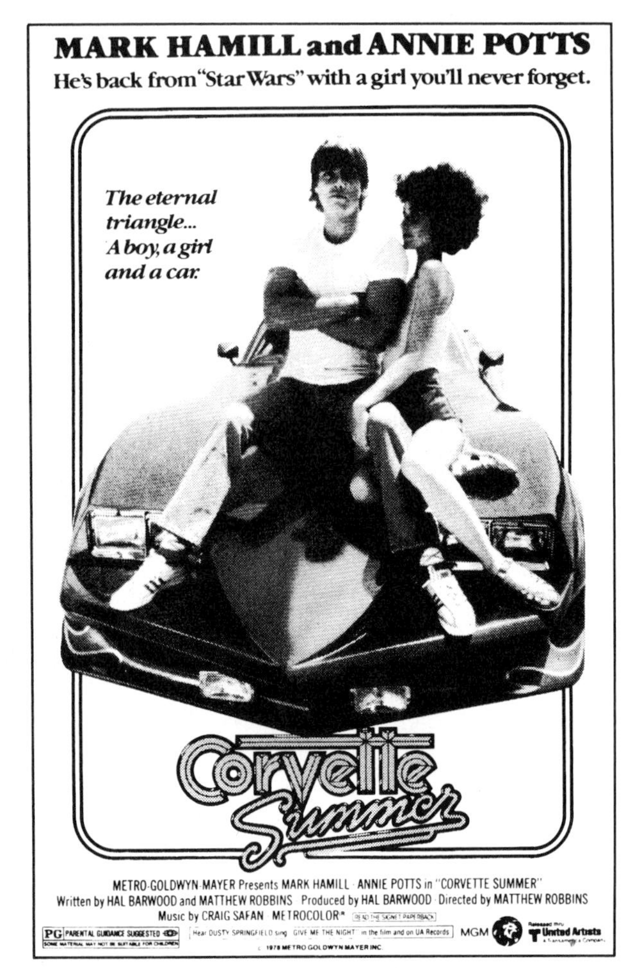

Annie Potts was one of the stars of TV's "Designing Women" who left the series amid some flak. We doubt, though, whether anyone in the production company had the gall to bring up the fact she starred as a wanna-be hooker opposite Mark "Use the Force, Luke" Hamill in MGM's *Corvette Summer. Ron Main Collection*

Coupe de Ville

(1990) This flick has several brothers sent to drive a 1956 Cadillac convertible across the country so they can deliver it to their mother as a surprise. This is a good family movie, starring Patrick Dempsey, Arne Gross, Daniel Stern, Annabeth Gish, Rita Taggart, Joseph Bologna, and Alan Arkin.

Crash Drive

(1959) Here's one about a race car driver who gets messed up badly in a big wreck and ends up paralyzed and depressed. The movie stars Dermot Walsh and Wendy Williams.

Crossing the Line

(1989) This film has a young motocross racer spending more time and energy battling his family and enemies than racing. It's a decent movie, with a bit of good riding scenes, fairly typical of the stuff that's created for today's teenagers. (That means it's sensational, contrived, and corny.)

The Crowd Roars

(1932) A very good picture, with James Cagney starring as a race car driver. This one provides excitement and good entertainment, as did any Cagney picture I've ever seen. The other stars here are Joan Blondell, Frank McHugh, Eric Linden, Ann Dvorak, and Guy Kibbee.

This is a classic to search for, but don't confuse it with the 1938 boxing movie with the same name. It's still televised occasionally.

Cycle Savages

(1969) Our stars here are Bruce Dern, Melody Patterson, Chris Robinson, Maray Ayres, and Scott Brady. This movie is a real piece of junk. An artist's talent offends an insecure greaseball biker, who sticks the guy's hands in a vise and then goes and gang-rapes...hey, this is junk. So what's the point?—DM

Ron Main's review of Cycle Savages:

"Roaring through the streets on chopped-down Hogs! They steal women... initiate them into the pack... and then sell them!!" Bruce Dern is the vicious leader and Melody Patterson is the beautiful and shapely model who poses nude(!) for our artist, Chris Johnson. Unfortunately, he not only captures Melody's charms, but also the gang in their perverse customs such as men slashed and stomped to a bleeding mess, and women kidnapped for sadism and that night's orgy. Melody has come a long way since she was "Wrangler Jane" in the TV series "*F Troop*."—RM

Cyclone

(1987) This one stars Heather Thomas and Jeffrey Combs. The story revolves around a very special futuristic motorcycle Combs has built as a top secret government project, and the bad guys that try to steal it from him. The bike has bulletproof aerodynamic bodywork and a turbocharged 400hp engine with nitrous oxide injection.

There is nothing remarkable here—in fact the stunt work by the legendary Dar Williams is one of the few things that might make this movie worth watching. You may wonder why a 400hp motorcycle can't outrun a stock 1974 Oldsmobile station wagon. So did I.

Dakota

(1988) The cast here includes Lou Diamond Phillips, Eli Cummins, and Dee Dee Norton.

James Cagney stars as an intense racer in the 1932 film *The Crowd Roars*. Legendary Howard Hawks directed the film, which was remade years later and released as *Indianapolis Speedway*. *Ron Main Collection*

Phillips is cast as Dakota, a talented young mechanic whose father is a long-time car buff. Phillips is asked to enter the Great American Race, a cross-country event for speedsters from the teens. There is a scene where Phillips rides a stock Honda Nighthawk through a field to impress the girl he's after (including some stunt riding), but there isn't enough riding for this to qualify as a motorcycle movie. In fact, this movie is like tens of thousand of love stories, with cars and the bike added to make things interesting.

The Damned

(1962) Here is a British film that was later released as *These Are The Damned*. It stars Macdonald Carey (who went on to become a soap opera legend), Shirley Anne Field, Viveca Lindfors, Alexander Knox, Oliver Reed, and James Villiers, and is about a violent rocker motorcycle gang.—DM

Michael Dregni's review of The Damned:

An eccentric movie, *The Damned* centered around an unusual love story among the prototypes of the British rockers, the "Teddy boys." Mounted on good British single-and twin-cylinder motorcycles, they strut their stuff and talk tough. And then, halfway through the film, the plot takes the oddest twist you could never prepare yourself for and becomes a kind of "Twilight Zone" episode. Very odd, very quixotic.

The cast included Oliver Reed, Macdonald Carey, Shirley Anne Field, Viveca Lindfors, Alexander Knox, and James Villiers.—MDr

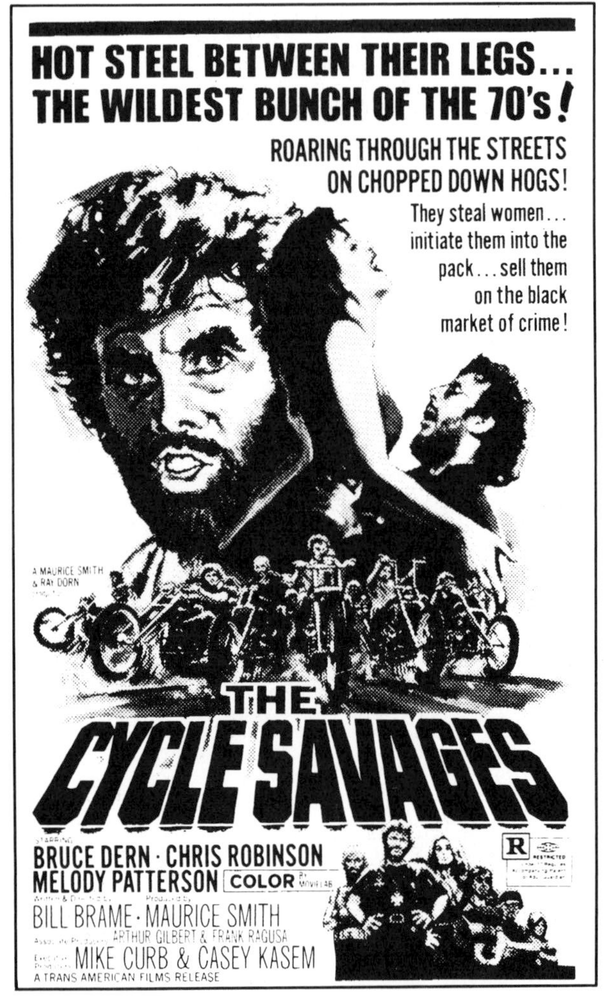

We'd call them capitalists, not savages. After all, the *Cycle Savages* "steal women, initiate them into the pack [then] sell them back on the black market." Our only question is why bother with the initiation? Just sell 'em back and go out and buy some nicer bikes. *Ron Main Collection*

Danger on Wheels

This is an early racing classic that's entertaining. We know we're in for some fun right at the beginning of the picture when we read:

"We dedicate this picture to "Lucky" Teter and his stunt drivers, in appreciation of their many feats of daring and indomitable courage—men

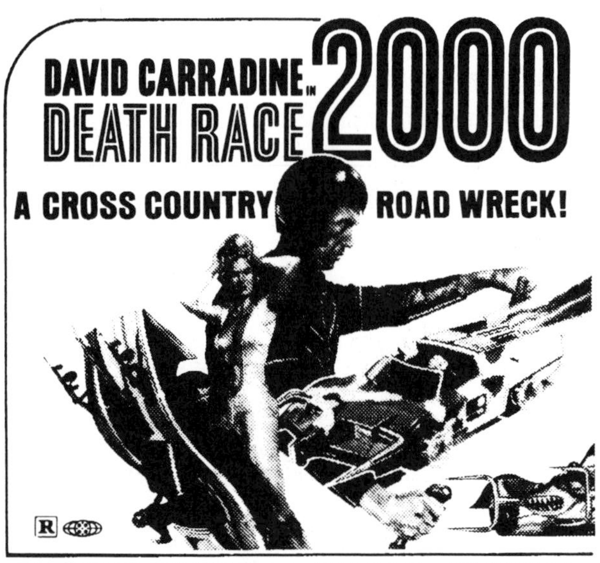

Death Race 2000* costar Simone Griffeth probably wishes that her movie career had gone on to be as Rocky as that of a young actor named Sylvester Stallone. Sorry for her, but we've hardly heard from her since this 1975 film. This was one of Roger Corman's New World Pictures classics, even though he produced but did not direct the film. *Ron Main Collection

Here's the full-sized ad for *The Devil's Hairpin.* There's trouble in paradise in the inset photo of the woman who's scolding the man by telling him: "For what you did to your brother in that race, you are as guilty as Cain!" Wow. Maybe it's time to move out into an apartment of your own, fella. *Ron Main Collection*

whose actual work it is to scientifically advance those principles that make automobile driving safer each year."

Richard Arlen stars as "Lucky" Larry Taylor, the best test driver the Atlas Motor Company has ever seen. Andy Devine plays "Guppy" Wexel, Lucky's mechanic, who builds an open-wheel sprint car, with an engine than runs on oil, for a race at the local fairgrounds.

When the big day arrives, the show begins with a demonstration of stunt driving, where Lucky jumps over a row of cars and performs a series of rolls. Lucky then drives his dependable Atlas sedan through a wall of fire to the delight of the crowd. The track's announcer proclaims, "Lucky Taylor is now about to laugh in death's face, as he hurtles himself through flaming barriers at 80 miles per hour!" Fifteen minutes into the picture, three motorcycles are also ridden through a wall of fire, although this is the only scene with bikes in it.

Would somebody please tell Cornel Wilde to take a break. That workaholic not only co-wrote *The Devil's Hairpin,* but he also produced and directed the film, and—incredible!—he starred in it as well. His failure to receive an Oscar for this effort is unforgivable. *Ron Main Collection*

The Grover County Speed Classic is for sprint cars that look like thirties-era Indy Cars, run on a dirt oval track. Lucky is asked to enter as driver of the Atlas Motors Special. Remember, the safety equipment used back in the thirties consisted entirely of a pudding-bowl helmet and goggles—no harnesses, roll cages or fuel cells. There are several violent wrecks in the race where drivers are thrown from their cars, and champion driver Eddie Dodd is killed.

If we don't deal with the obligatory love interest, or the drama involving another engine builder, there's still enough to hold your interest. The high point of *Danger on Wheels* comes around three-quarters of the way through this one-hour film. Lucky pilots a car powered by a prototype engine to a controversial finish. Speeds here top 120mph, with some good nostalgic racing footage.

Most of the "Atlas" cars look like modified Pontiacs, although they use a 1938 Ford one-ton truck on the proving grounds, and the boss's daughter drives what looks like a modified Cord boat-tailed convertible. This movie is harmless fun for the whole family.

Danger Zone

(1987) Look out! This one stars Robert Canada and Jason Williams. Available as a 90-minute videotape, the story is about dope-dealing bikers who encounter six young women on their way to Las Vegas.

Danger Zone II

(1988) They're back! Here's one about a biker who gets released from prison on a technicality and goes after the undercover cop who set him up. There are some good chase scenes here.

Danger Zone III—Steel Horse War

(1990) Now we've got Jason Williams starring as a renegade cop on a Harley. From the videotape cover notes: "West of Hell the gold was buried. Out of Hell came an army of bikers to find it. Into Hell rides one man,who will bury them all."

Danger Zone IV

Danger Zone IV is yet another film by Jason Williams, a man not widely known outside of the soft-core sex/violence/low-budget genre. Mr. Williams not only produced this film, but wrote it and starred in the lead role along with other luminaries such as Deenie Decker and "Amerika." He knows what his audience wants and delivers. No background, plot development, or subtleties; just straight to violent, scantily clad women.

Williams plays "Olsen," an ex-cop with a knack for killing drug dealers in a variety of violent ways. He is bundled into the trunk of a Mercedes by a group of biker women who want vengeance for their dead or imprisoned old men. They take him to the desert, strip him to his underwear, and stake him spread-eagled in the sun. The bulk of the movie is spent as the young women take turns trying to arouse Olsen while telling what he had done to their old men. This is shown in a series of flashbacks of bikers being blown up, knifed in the groin, set afire while in a sleeping bag, etc. They also detail how they plan to kill him, my personal favorite being the miss in the garters and bustier who shows him the Bernsomatic she plans to roast his privates with. Olsen eventually turns one of the women to his cause and gets chased around the desert by scantily clad ladies with large handguns. He turns the tables on them and drives off in the Mercedes with his new friend and a big pile of drug money.

Darn good fun, and if the plot and acting aren't enough to keep things from getting serious, the complete lack of continuity sure is. Bits of the movie seem to be missing everywhere, as if they just tossed out the parts they screwed up rather than reshooting. The soundtrack is a heavy-metal lead fronting a drum machine. Highly recommended for the inattentive or as background noise at parties.—SG

Dangerous Curves

(1988) This one is directed by David Lewis and stars Tate Donovan, Danielle Von Zerneck,

Frank Gorshin, you are no fool. You apparently know how to treat the women right so you have them hanging all over you and your hot rod in the classic *Dragstrip Girl. Ron Main Collection*

and Grant Heslov, with appearances by Robert Stack and Leslie Nielsen. The story involves a couple of young guys who are given the job of delivering a red Porsche 928 to a new owner. The trouble starts when they have to get the car back after it gets stolen. It's a decent comedy but it's not outstanding; only in here because of the 928.

The Daredevil

(1972) This film has George Montgomery playing a race car driver who becomes a driver for some dope dealers. Terry Moore, Gay Perkins, Cyril Poitier, and Bill Kelly star in this strange action picture.

Daredevil Drivers

(1937) Beverly Roberts and Dick Purcell star in this rare MGM film. Dick ("Wild Bill") in the Klein 7 Special wins the Indy 500, only to be suspended for rough driving. So it's off to the outlaw tracks. On the way, a bus totals his Indy car, and this is our story. Lovely Beverly battles the sinister bus line for the city contract. There's a great scene in which Wild Bill must catch the runaway bus, and chases it down the changing grade in his roadster. There are some great Indy crashes in the film's opening, and Bill races his Indy Car through town to get the city contract!—RM

Daredevils of the Red Circle

Here's a film all about the old-time motorcycle stunt riders and how they risked their lives in their performances. This one has recently been released to the home video market.

Darktown Strutters (Get Down and Boogie)

(1975) Remember Roger Corman, producer of *Wild Angels* and dozens of other drive-in epics? He had a substantially less talented brother named Gene, and this movie is Gene's legacy. Released in 1975 as *Darktown Strutters*, it later had five minutes cut out and was re-released as *Get Down and Boogie*. It stars Trina Parks, Edna Richardson, Bettye Sweet, and Shirley Washington as four black disco-inspired biker women. The plot, which involved Trina's search for her mother, kidnapped by a deranged Col. Sanders look-alike, could be taken for a spoof of black and white stereotypes. Motives aside, the movie consists mostly of bad slapstick sight gags and heavy-handed shtick like Klansmen on dirt bikes. The movie's only redeeming feature is the soundtrack, credited to STAX, which had such things as the Dramatics doing "What You See Is What You Get," and a Curtis Mayfield sound-alike doing "Motorbike Queen." I like to think that Curtis Mayfield himself had better things to do. Not recommended, except as a reminder of how bad the seventies were at times.—SG

Date Bait

(1960) This film has one of the best titles in the book. This is one of the two movies that were produced and directed for Filmgroup by O. Dale Ireland. (The other was *High School Caesar*, also in 1960.)

The story involves teenagers, heroin, fights, knives, an MG-TD roadster, and some good chase scenes. *Date Bait* stars Richard Gering, Marla Ryan, Gary Clarke, Chad Williams, Steve Ihnat, Jon Lindon, Carole Dawn, and Michael Bachus.

Days of Thunder

(1990) Our stars here are Tom Cruise, Robert Duvall, Randy Quaid, Michael Rooker, Nicole Kidman (who later married Cruise), and Cary Elwes.

The stock car racing community awaited the release of *Days of Thunder* with more anticipation than any other movie in history. This was supposed to be *the* one movie that portrayed professional stock car racing accurately. For months, we NASCAR racing fans heard about the care, the attention to detail, the research, the consultants and the stars who were creating the definitive stock car racing movie. ESPN Home Video even released a video called NASCAR Goes Hollywood: The Making of *Days of Thunder*.

Days of Thunder was released on June 27th, 1990. What we ended up with, despite all the money that was poured into it, was some great camera work and effects, with some exciting NASCAR racing footage. But as far as the plot goes, we got something so utterly unbelievable, corny, and downright silly it could be thought of as just more sensational Hollywood escapist mind candy.

This is more of a story about a driver than one about racing. Tom Cruise plays the part of Cole Trickle, race car driver and miracle worker. We are to believe that a driver with a solid Indy Car racing background has no knowledge at all of how race cars work or anything about setting them up—he doesn't even understand tire wear. And his very first time in a stock car, he runs quick enough to qualify on the pole at the Charlotte Motor Speedway. After a few races, one of which he wins, he gets caught up in a big wreck and is hospitalized. His doctor turns out to be female, very intelligent, very beautiful, available, and interested. Would I spoil it for you if I told you that shortly after that, Trickle wins the Daytona 500, with her—having apparently forgotten about her obligations as a doctor—following him around like a starving pup?

NASCAR drivers are portrayed here as being violent hillbillies. Winning Winston Cup rides aren't built in barns. NASCAR officials are shown ignoring the constant, deliberate ramming and smashing on the racetrack, as if to imply that it's all in the game. This may make for a sensational movie, but it is simply not the way it is out there. Thirty-four people were used for the stunts in *Days of Thunder*, and close to a million dollars' worth of race cars were badly torn up or wrecked.

If they wanted to do a movie that really did justice to NASCAR racing, more attention should have been paid to the spirit of family that helps make Winston Cup the great sport that it is. This is an aspect of NASCAR Winston Cup that anyone who is actually involved in it would have included.

Robert Duvall did an excellent job playing the role of the car builder and crew chief, with a very strong resemblance to the NASCAR legend Harry Hyde. As evidenced in virtually every other movie in this book, Hollywood just doesn't know about the technical side of racing. More care could have been taken here making sure that the script made sense. There is a scene where Duvall is alone in his shop, talking to the Daytona-bound race car chassis under construction there. He says "I'm going to give you an engine, low to the ground, an extra big oil pan that will cut the wind from underneath you, that will give you 30 to 40 more horsepower." Aerodynamics don't mean a thing on the dyno.

Even the use of the word "Thunder" in the title of an automotive- or motorsports-related movie is a cliché now. First we had the fifties B movie called *Teenage Thunder*, then *Thunder Road* in 1958, *Thunder in Carolina* in 1960, *Thunder Alley* in 1967, *Track of Thunder* in 1968, followed by *Thunder and Lightning* in 1977, *Thunder Boat Row* in 1989, and finally, *Days of Thunder* in 1990.

Oops! Perhaps we spoke too soon about Frank Gorshin's treat-'em-right manners. This is not going to make you popular with the girls, Frank, but that probably doesn't matter to you as one of the hot rodding wildmen in *Dragstrip Girl. Ron Main Collection*

And what about the racing fans? They're what keeps the sport going. Their support of the sponsors' products enables the sponsors to help keep the teams operating. We all know that without the fans there would be no big-time professional racing. This movie just uses the fans for a background in a few scenes, taking them for granted the rest of the time, focusing on Mr. Cruise and his costars.

NASCAR drivers Neil Bonnett, Harry Gant, Rusty Wallace, and Greg Sacks all make appearances in the film, with Sacks doing some of the driving. ESPN pit reporter Dr. Jerry Punch plays himself, and the voice of ESPN commentator Bob Jenkins is heard in the movie as well. With talent like this involved in this production it's unfortunate for those of us who really love the sport that *Days of Thunder* ended up being so largely unrealistic and completely unbelievable. NASCAR Winston Cup stock car racing is exciting, spectacular, and thrilling in itself. None of it needs to be exaggerated or sped up.

Why am I so critical of *Days of Thunder*? Based on the pre-release publicity, most of us thought that we were finally going to get just one stock car racing movie that shows why the sport is so popular, without it being phony. Any NASCAR Winston Cup race that's telecast live on ESPN does a vastly more credible representation of Win-

Looking for some classic hot rod action? Check our *Dragstrip Girl*, which included plenty of these classic rods, not to mention plenty of teen trouble. *Ron Main Collection*

ston Cup racing, and it's a lot more exciting because it's real.

See it for yourself. If you don't follow the sport, you may find more to enjoy here than I did.

Ron Main's review of Days of Thunder:

This one is destined to become a classic. From the engine roar and the fever pitch of stock car racing, it explodes with the most spectacular racing action ever captured on film. They needed twelve on-board cameras to capture the riveting race shots! Tom Cruise plays driver Cole Trickle, whose talent is surpassed only by his burning desire to win. Robert Duvall is the legendary crew chief named Harry (guess who?). It has got to be the best Hollywood racing film ever made. You die-hard fans will notice some boo-boos, but fasten your seat belt and prepare to take the ride of your life. It comes off just like thunder!—RM

D.C. Cab

(1983) If you think I'm going to criticize a film that featured Mr. T, you're crazy. I don't need his gold-laden fist pounding on my door in the middle of the night as he pays a visit to a critic. Not unlike *Car Wash*, this is a loose comedy built around a car-related business, in this case a Washington, D.C., cab company. There's some good work by comedians and actors such as Paul Rodriguez, Marsha Warfield, Max Gail, Irene Cara, and Gary Busey. And to fend off great bodily harm, permit me to say this: Why Mr. T didn't get an Oscar for his performance, I'll never know!—MDa

Deadman's Curve

(1978) The Jan and Dean story featuring thirteen hot sounds from the sixties ("Surf City," "Little Old Lady from Pasadena," "Wipe Out," etc.). Things were cool, chicks were hot, waves were groovy, and cars had real muscle. Richard Hatch, Bruce Davidson, and Mike Love of the Beach Boys star. See what really happened to the Corvette at Deadman's Curve!—RM

Here's step one in producing a lobby card or poster for a movie. The film we'll use in our example is *Dragstrip Girl.* A promotional photo is taken that shows the cast and a prop like this hot rod. The photo may be poorly lit and slightly out of focus, but Hollywood is the capital of enhancing images, as you'll see in the next illustration. *Ron Main Collection*

Death Race 2000

(1975) Vrooom! This flick's about the future sport of using cars to run people down. The cast includes David Carradine, Simone Griffith, Sylvester Stallone, Louisa Moritz, Mary Woronov, Don Steele, and Joyce Jameson. Of all the movies in here I've been able to see, this is the worst. It's so incredibly bad it's scary. I bet you can't watch the whole thing. Leave it alone. The Monster Gator Car and Bull Car: Both were also seen in *Earth Girls are Easy*, commercials, and videos.—DM

Ron Main's review of Death Race 2000:

In the year 2000, hit-and-run driving has become our national sport! It's the spectacle of the future: The annual transcontinental death race, in which every pedestrian is fair game and the winner is determined by fast time and the highest body count! David Carradine (named "Frankenstein" here) is our champion. Previous races and miraculous surgery have left him half-man and half-machine. Sylvester Stallone is great as vicious Machine Gun Joe Viterbo. Their famous cars, which are endowed with deadly accessories such as claws, bayonets, steer horns, and machine guns, were conceived and constructed by Lee James Powers and Dean Jeffries. This film has some of the most eye-popping stunts ever captured on film—RM

The Death Wheelers

(1971) This cycle movie was also released under the name *Psychomania*. Selling their souls to the devil pays off for a bad-tempered British mo-

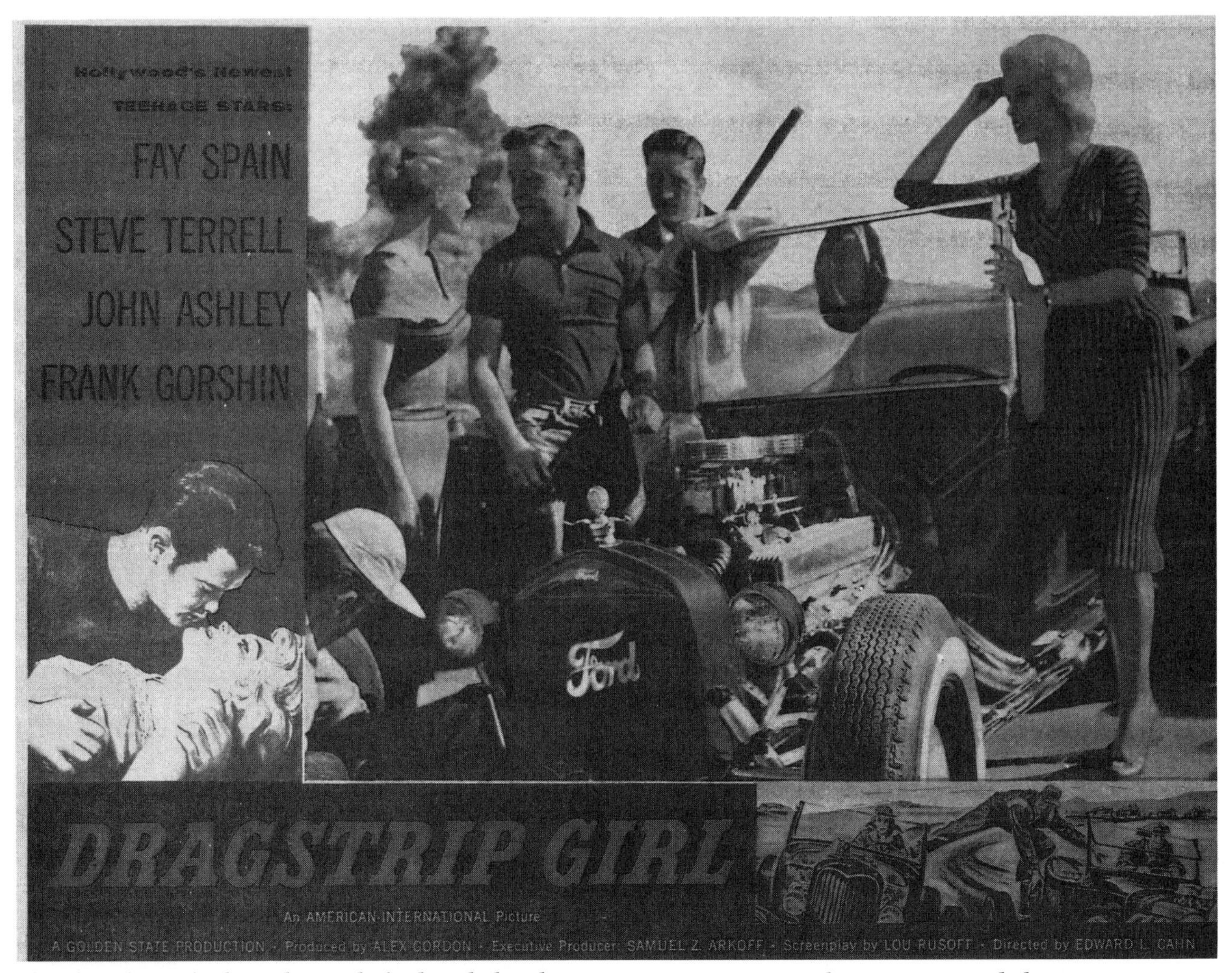

The photo image is cleaned up, colorized, and placed on a lobby card that lists some cast members and includes illustrations to hype the action. You learn from this *Dragstrip Girl* lobby card that there will be some steamy make-out scenes and also a car-to-car jump sequence in the middle of a race. *Ron Main Collection*

torcycle gang. Its gets a second chance to really terrorize and deliver its own, special brand of mayhem. George Sanders, Nicky Henson, and Mary Larkin star in this rough-and-tumble one.—MDa

Ron Main's review of The Death Wheelers:

You will not believe this one! "The dead still ride and the living will howl in terror!" What is George Sanders doing in this motorcycle film? Beryl Reid and Nicky Henson also star.—RM

Deathsport

(1978) This New World Pictures release, produced by Roger Corman, stars David Carradine, Claudia Jennings, and Richard Lynch. It was billed as the sequel to Carradine's 1976 *Deathrace 2000*, and was shot the same year he did *Boxcar Bertha*. The late Claudia Jennings (best known as Playboy's Miss November 1969) did *Deathsport* as a follow-up to 1974's *Truckstop Women* and 1976's *Gatorbait*.

The setting is "A thousand years from tomorrow, after the great neutron wars." Carradine and Jennings are "Ranger Guides"—nomadic warriors in briefs and nancy-looking capes taking plastic swords to the townies (who ride dirt bikes with bad fairings, open-face Bucos with fins on top) and possess the ultimate cheapo special effect weapon—a hand-held coffee can which makes people vanish.

The ranger guides are bushwhacked and kidnapped to face certain defeat in gladiatorial combat with the bikers, for "the people must believe that riding a death machine will make them as powerful as gods."

Our heroes grab a couple of bikes and despite never having been on them before, prove to be stunningly fast dirt riders. After a brief tiff with cannibal mutants they reach the showdown, where bad guy Lynch disses Carradine's mom and gets his head whacked off.

While all the bikes in this film are identical big dirt singles with really stupid fairings, there are a lot of them to blow up with real abandon; Star Wars-type explosions with little flaming globs of crap raining down.

The soundtrack is truly spacy: synthesizer music by "Blue" Gene Tranny, with guitar credit to Jerry Garcia, who must have been going through a bad period, as he only gets a few minutes in. Recommended for Carradine/Jennings fans.—SG

Demo Derby

(1964) Jim Pike produced this documentary that was filmed at the Norwood Arena near Boston. It follows young Don MacTavish of Dover, who later became the national champion of destruction. Arthur Korb composed a great crashing score. They even pressed the record "Demo Derby" and on the flip side was "Kathy," the love theme by the Rondels. That record would be a sure collectible today.—RM

Demolition Man

(1993) Sylvester Stallone is a cop chasing bad guy Wesley Snipes in this action thriller set in the year 2032. To make the vehicles fit the era, the film's producers procured some eighteen concept cars from General Motors, including the Ultralite, of which a dozen copies were produced (in whole or part) for use and abuse in the flick. The GM cars were worth an estimated $69 million, and were provided to the filmmakers by Trakon Show and Display. Sly also chases Snipes in a 1970 Olds 442. Three such cars were built through restorations that took just seventeen days before filming. When you're on a Hollywood budget and schedule, that's how long your resto projects take.—MDa

The Devil at Your Heels

(1981) Here is a documentary about the Canadian stunt driver Ken Carter. It tells the story of the five years of preparation that went into Carter's us-

Fay Wray, the star of the original *King Kong*, stars as the mother of the new sports car stud in town in *Dragstrip Riot*. Let's hope she doesn't get mixed up in the "Train Drag." It's one contest where losing can be fatal. *Ron Main Collection*

ing a ten-story ramp to jump over the Saint Lawrence River. *The Devil at Your Heels* was made by Canada's National Film Board and stars Ken Carter with narration by Gordon Pinsent.

Devil on Wheels

(1947) This film was written and directed by Crane Wilbur, and stars Mickey Rooney, Noreen Nash, Darryl Hickman, Jan Ford, and Sue England. It's one of the original hot rod movies where you'll learn that speed kills! See dad speed his new Buick convertible. See dad hit the judge, see young Mickey Rooney build his first hot rod roadster, see Mickey smooching, see teen love, see back road drag racing with five cars running at once. "What's the use of hopping up a car if you can't give her the gun?" Exactly! It's so true! This movie is great.—RM

This 1976 movie about action at a Texas drive-in made attempts to catch the coattails of popularity of the 1973 film *American Graffiti. Ron Main Collection*

Devil's Angels

(1967) This is more of the same, this time starring Daniel Haller, John Cassavetes, Beverly Adams, Mimsy Farmer, and Leo Gordon. When Leonard Maltin says the movie is "lurid and cheap" it makes you want to see it, right?

The Devil's Hairpin

(1957) This film stars Cornel Wilde, Jean Wallace, and Jean Astor. It's the story of a reckless race car driver who accidentally injures his brother in a wreck.—DM

Ron Main's review of The Devil's Hairpin:

Cornell Wilde, Jean Wallace, Mary Astor, and Arthur Franz star here. Cornell will stop at nothing to win, but this reckless sports car champion comes to learn fair play on the track. The racing scenes are great in this classic. Scenes were shot on a mountainside track along treacherous curves, and were then edited with footage from an actual 200-car race that attracted over 80,000 spectators. The Sports Car Club of America awarded Wilde with an honor in recognition of the excellence of this race film.—RM

Diamonds Are Forever

(1971) A British-produced James Bond flick with Sean Connery as 007 (thank goodness) and lovely Jill St. John costarring as Bond's conquest of the week. For vehicles, look for a wacky moon buggy-type ride, and lots of Fords (a supplier to the production company), including a 1971 Mustang that Bond puts up on two wheels to squeeze through an alley during a chase scene.—MDa

Diamonds on Wheels

(1973) This one is another Disney fantasy, about some kids who come across an old sports car. They take it home and start working on it, and later discover that some thieves have hidden their loot in the car. The cast includes Peter Firth, Patrick Allen, and George Seawell.

Dirt

(1979) No, not the story of Pigpen. This one features Parnelli Jones and Rick Mears among dozens of others. It's all about playing around in the dirt or off-road, in dune buggies and on motorcycles. *Dirt* opens with footage of an early sand rail with a V-8 and a drilled-out Model A front axle. There's a segment that shows the roots of dirt-track racing with film of some of the first race cars (along the lines of a stripped-down Model T), and then some USAC midgets from the fifties. We see enduro riding, motocross, and hill-climbing. We go to the sand drags at Bakersfield, and then out to the sand dunes, where there's all kinds of home-built machinery running around. Pike's Peak gets some coverage, with the Unser family, Rick Mears ,and Parnelli Jones shown blasting up the legendary mountain road. Then it's off to an AMA motocross race for the Women's National where a field of young enthusiasts provides a bit of talking and a lot of dicing. There's a segment on swamp buggies and a good one on hill-climbing on dirt and on snow. The climb in the snow is the Skyline Snow Rally, and it comes down to two brothers in the final. Then we see Parnelli getting ready for the Baja race, and there's coverage of the Mint 400. They also show tractor pulling and a Willys Jeep rodeo.

It could have been better, and longer, but if you are a fan of off-road racing of any kind you're bound to get something out of it. *Dirt* was created by Mike Heummer and Jim Deckard, produced by Michael Loen and Roger Riddell, narrated by Clarke Gordon, and is distributed by Pacific Films.

The Dirt Bike Kid

(1985) Peter Billingsley plays a kid with a little Yamaha who's up against a sleazy banker trying to appropriate the land he runs his hot dog stand on, and against a gang of bikers. Heard enough?

The Dirt Gang

(1972) This is another movie about a motorcycle gang that is not very good, with Paul Carr, Michael Pataki, Lee DeBroux, Jon Shank, Nancy Harris, and T.J. Escott.

Dirty Mary, Crazy Larry

(1974) This one stars Peter Fonda as a "little guy" local race car driver who wants to race on the national level. The only thing in his way is a lack of money, so he and a friend pull a holdup and then it's car-chase time. The cast also includes Vic Morrow and Susan George.—DM

Michael Dregni's review of Dirty Mary, Crazy Larry:

This one stars Peter Fonda of Easy Rider fame as Crazy Larry, a "little guy" local race car driver who dreams of racing in the big time. The only thing standing in his way is financing, so off he goes looking for it the illegal way. He meets up with Susan George—Dirty Mary. They pull a heist and then it's car-chase time. Since Larry's a racer, he can out-corner, out-accelerate, out-squeal, and out-fox all of the local constabulary. After lots of daring-do, the duo outrun the law only to meet their destiny head-on. The cast also includes Vic Morrow.—MDr

Ron Main's review:

Peter Fonda, Susan George, and Adam Roarke star as a trio of wild fugitives who out-race the police in this crash-a-minute, top-speed, spectacular cross-country chase. This film has eighteen separate car crashes, a head-on collision with a train, a drawbridge jump of over 50ft, a crash through a billboard, a backward skid into a canal, a helicopter slamming into a car, innumerable rollovers, and a truck collision. Stockton, California, is the main site for the action, with areas around Sonora, Clements, Jamestown, and the walnut groves around Linden providing the racing areas for the

Maybe you *can* take the kids to see *Dirty Mary*... Publicity for the film said: "With all the mechanical mayhem, however, there is no brutal violence in the film, none of the horror and blood-spilling generally shown in action motion pictures." *Ron Main Collection*

cat-and-mouse, 100-mile-plus chase. Fonda is the speed-crazy "racing driver" who steals $150,000 to finance a race car. Vic Morrow leads the manhunt after our fleeing outlaws in their yellow 1968 Dodge Charger. It's one of the greatest chases in film history.—RM

Diva

(1982) Here is the story of a French mailman who tapes an opera diva on a bootleg recording machine and is then chased down by underworld thugs who want his tape—all very existential for some reason. The crowning moment is the motorcycle chase through the Paris subways, an action classic. This beautiful film was directed by Frenchman Jean-Jacques Beineix.—MDr

Doc Hollywood

(1991) Not a serious car movie, but the story *does* hinge around the Porsche 356 that young doctor Michael J. Fox crashes in rural South Carolina, stranding him there while it's being repaired in a local rube's garage. Fox resists, but gets adopted, in a way, by the people of small town where he's stuck. His original destination was Hollywood, but he ends up staying put, even after one visit to L.A., and especially because his car gets crunched a second time near the film's end. Julie Warner is the fetching romantic lead, and her first scene—in which she's topless!—seems highly incongruous to the rest of this PG-13 flick. Bridget Fonda and Woody Harrelson are only mildly interesting, and tanning god George Hamilton has a nice scene. We especially liked the local mechanics, who do such an efficient job of getting the Porsche running that they've even got lots of parts left over.—MDa

Dorf Goes Auto Racing

(1989) Tim Conway will give 200mph laughs in his own style when he goes from golf to grease with the help of racing superstars Richard Petty, Kenny Schrader, and the late Neil Bonnett.—RM

Dragstrip Girl

(1956) This flick was directed by Edward Cahn and stars Fay Spain and Steve Terrell. When Fay's

It might not sound like much when you learn that producers of *Eat My Dust!* spent $12,000 building Ron Howard's race car for the film. But you have to consider that the film's director, Roger Corman, was used to producing an entire film for that budget, so it was an outlandishly large expense for him to approve. *Ron Main Collection*

Hollywood has long been in the habit of reusing movie titles. The original *Excuse My Dust* was an old Red Skelton comedy that included all the action hyped in this ad as well as "hit songs by Broadway's famed *tunesmiths* Arthur Schwartz and Dorothy Fields." *Ron Main Collection*

boyfriend is unable to drive his fenderless 1927 Model T turtledeck roadster at the drags, she drives it for him, and she becomes the Dragstrip Girl.

Dragstrip Riot

(1958) This was the first film produced by O. Dale Ireland. To promote the movie, American International Pictures sent out a press kit that contained the following message:

"Once again American International Pictures brings to the screen an all-new combination that is aimed at the teenagers of this modern day. Heading this all-new teenage program is *Dragstrip Riot*, which stars Yvonne Lime, Gary Clarke and Connie Stevens. Varied excitement controls the screen as motorcyclists and hot rodders encounter each other, fighting with spear guns at the rate of 100mph. Drag races on railroad tracks as a locomotive train comes within inches of destroying both cars and occupants. All of this is shared with some lighter moments as pretty Connie Stevens abounds with a few rock and roll numbers."

This was the last movie Fay Wray appeared in. The cars in *Dragstrip Riot* are all Corvettes from 1955 to 1957, and the bikes are Triumph twins.

Dragstrip She-Devil

(1956) This is another old low-budget, hyped-action hot rod movie.

Dream Machine

(1991) Well, this one stars Corey Hain, Brittney Lewis, and Evan Richards. When a rich woman gives her Porsche 911 whale-tail roadster to a college fraternity, they discover her husband's body in the trunk.

Drive a Crooked Road

(1954) The stars here are Mickey Rooney, Dianne Foster, Kevin McCarthy, Jack Kelly, and Harry Landers. It would be considered too sentimental by today's standards, but it's a lot of fun. It's also a treasure of old sports cars. In the first ten minutes of the film we see Jaguar XK-120, MG-TD, and Porsche 356 roadsters, and a beautiful early Aston Martin coupe.

Mickey Rooney gives an enjoyable performance as Eddy Shannon, a "sweet kid" who's an exceptional mechanic and race driver. He works during the week in a shop that specializes in servicing sports cars, and races an XK-120 successfully on weekends. Despite his automotive talents, he is shy and awkward around women. The plot revolves around Eddy being set up by a smooth-talking bank robber named Steve Norris. Steve uses his pretty girlfriend to lure Eddie into agreeing to drive a getaway car down nineteen miles of country road after the heist he is planning. Eddie is provided with a 1940 Ford Deluxe Fordor sedan to build up into a "sleeper" getaway car in the evenings. He begins work on it by pulling the stock engine and then drops in a hot twin-carb Flathead with finned aluminum heads.

Most of the automotive-related scenes are in the first half of the film, with the latter part devoted more to the drama that unfolds after they pull the job. *Drive a Crooked Road* is fun for the whole family, whether you like 1940 Fords, vintage sports cars, or corny drama. For me, it's a classic.

Drive Hard, Drive Fast

(1969) This is another movie that was made for TV. It's a forgettable movie about murder, with

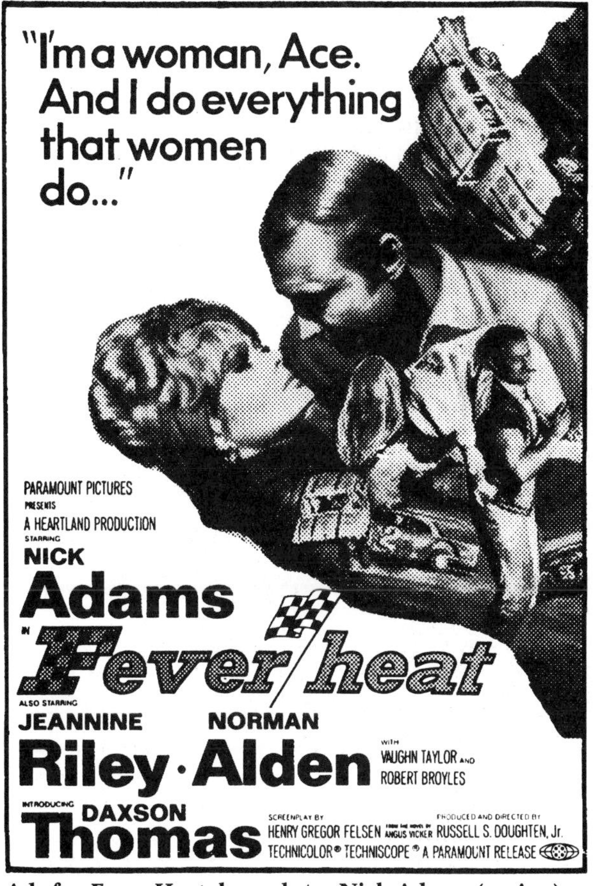

Ads for *Fever Heat* showed star Nick Adams (as Ace) wrapped up with foxy Jeannie Riley, who was telling him, "I'm a woman, Ace. And I do everything that women do..." Makes us think that if we get a bad haircut, dress poorly, and drive hobby stock junkers at a third-rate dirt track, we, too, might get some girls. ***Paramount Pictures/Ron Main Collection***

professional race car drivers as the stars. The cast includes Brian Kelly, Joan Collins, Henry Silva, Joseph Campanella, Karen Huston, and Todd Martin.

Drive Like Lightning

(1992) This film was made for television and stars Steven Bauer, Cynthia Gibb, and William Russ. It's about a stunt driver and a country singer who head out on the road in a car that belongs to a rival daredevil. The car looks like a late Camaro, with a rocket engine and a roll cage. This is an unremarkable movie that you need not bother with.

The Driver

(1978) This under-appreciated film stars Ryan O'Neal as the getaway driver and Bruce Dern as one of the cops chasing him. Isabelle Adjani, Ronee Blakley, Matt Clark, and Felice Orlandi also star in one of the best car-chase movies ever.

Duel

(1972) This was an early Steven Spielberg film that was made for television, starring Dennis Weaver, Tim Herbert, Charles Peel, and Eddie Firestone. The plot involves Weaver in his rented Plymouth Valiant and an 18-wheeler that pursues him for reasons Weaver cannot figure out. You never get a good look at the truck's driver. There's some good camera work and stunts here—look for it.

Easy Rider

(1969) By now almost all of you have probably seen this movie, so you don't need somebody to describe it for you. But for those of you who forgot all about it because you saw it when you were on drugs, here's a quick recap.

Easy Rider was the big movie that rode the wave of the chopper craze in the summer of 1969. Peter Fonda, Dennis Hopper, and Jack Nicholson starred in what became the most publicized and

There was lots and lots of car action in this 1974 hit, which featured a strong cast. Besides Peter Fonda and Susan George, the cast included Adam Roarke, Vic Morrow, and Roddy McDowall. ***20th Century Fox/ Ron Main Collection***

controversial motorcycle movie of the sixties. The three ride across America on a pair of chopped rigid-frame Panhead Harley-Davidsons, and meet up with adventure that leads to trouble. Fonda's ride is the more radical, with a wild rake and an extended Wide Glide front end, ape hangers, lots of plating, good detailing, and a teardrop tank painted with the American flag. (You remember the bike, don't you?)

This movie manages to do a good job of capturing the non-violent, open-minded mood of the sixties. It's also significant in its portrayal of people who ride custom Harley-Davidsons as being decent human beings. The acting in *Easy Rider* is good (outstanding for a biker movie) and the story is timeless. In addition to Fonda, Hopper, and Nicholson, the cast includes Karen Black, Luke Askew, Luana Anders, Robert Walker, and Phil Spector. *Easy Rider* was directed by Dennis Hopper, with photography by Laslo Kovacs. See it again.

Easy Wheels

(1986) This is a satirical "comedy" of biker movies, directed by David O'Malley, who did the *Evil Dead* series. This is very bizarre stuff that may appeal to some, I suppose, but it wasted my time and I didn't want to see the whole thing. Eileen Davidson, Barry Livingston, and Mark Holton are the stars. Next.

Eat My Dust!

(1976) Cough! This is a comedy that has Ron Howard as one of a pair of drag racers. There's lots of good racing action in this movie. The cast also includes Christopher Norris and Warren Kemmerling.

Eat The Peach

(1986) Here is an Irish film that is based on a true story about a pair of unemployed motorcycle enthusiasts who decided to become professional stunt riders. They built a giant wooden barrel to ride their bikes around in, like the old-time daredevils did in exhibitions.

I can clearly remember seeing this done at the Royal American Shows from Florida in the early sixties. These tired, battle-scarred veterans with their stripped-down rigid-frame flathead Harley-Davidson 45s and KRs had a combination of tattoos and limps you just couldn't miss. Seeing them ride no-hands around the 80-degree banking at the top of the barrel is something you never forget.

Those guys were the first real motorcycle outlaws I ever saw, and I miss them.

Eegah!

(1963) This was a classically terrible movie about a prehistoric monster, played by Richard Kiel, who falls in love with a teenager, played by Marilyn Manning. *Eegah!* was one of the first movies to feature a dune buggy, although the one here was a far cry from the Meyers Manx (which most dune buggy body manufacturers copied around 1962). This one looks like it might have started out as a 1936 Ford, but the only bodywork that's left on it is the cowl and the windshield. Later in his career, Kiel was the villain with a mean bite in James Bond movies.

Electra Glide In Blue

(1973) This film has Richard Blake as a cop with an attitude problem and a Shovelhead Harley-Davidson. Not a comedy, but it's powerful and the movie says something that needed to be said. Besides Blake, the cast includes Billy Green Bush, Elisha Cook, Jr., and Mitchell Ryan.

Evel Knievel

(1971) Here is a documentary about the legendary motorcycle stunt rider, starring George Hamilton. As you would expect, there is a lot of excellent footage of Evel in action, performing some of the wildest jumps in history. And thankfully there's no distracting and needless plot to spoil the real story. Evel feels this is the best of the movies that have been made about him. *Evel Knievel* was directed by Marvin Chomsky, and costars Sue Lyon, Burt Freed, and John Cameron.

Every Which Way But Loose

(1978) A far cry from the world of Dirty Harry, this film stars Clint Eastwood, with some fast driving scenes that are well done.

Excuse My Dust

(1951) This was a comedy that featured Red Skelton, who develops a new kind of car back when they were a novelty. The cast includes Macdonald Carey (later a TV soap opera star), and Sally Forrest.

The Fast and the Furious

(1954) This film is historically significant in that it was the first picture that was released by American Releasing Corporation, which went on to become American International Pictures. You remember American International Pictures—they brought us lots of really neat movies our moms didn't want us to see, like *Devil's Angels*, *Hell's Angels on Wheels*, *Motorcycle Gang*, *The Wild Angels*, and the exquisitely tasteful *Dragstrip Girl*. As for the plot (which was not really A.I.P.'s greatest strength) of *The Fast and the Furious*, it's about a guy who's wrongly accused of murder, so he borrows a friend's sports car and runs. The cast includes John Ireland, Dorothy Malone, Iris Adrian, Bruce Carlisle, Jean Howell, and Larry Thor. Producer Roger Corman and other crew members had to drive in the race scenes because the budget didn't allow for paying professional drivers. There's lots of good chase scenes, but the American International Pictures crew hadn't yet mastered the all-important cleavage shots.

Nothing like a sock in the jaw to settle a dispute between a couple of racers. Who needs attorneys? An extremely rare bit of memorabilia is a record on which Dick Strout interviews the stars of *Fireball 500*. The records were distributed to theater owners who were supposed to provide them to their local radio stations. *Ron Main Collection*

Fast Charlie, the Moonbeam Rider

(1979) Here's a film about a soldier who quits the army in World War I to become a motorcycle racer, where he attempts to fix the outcome of a long-distance race he enters. The cast includes David Carradine, Brenda Vaccaro, L.Q. Jones, R.G. Armstrong, and Jesse Vint.

Fast Company

(1978) *Fast Company* is a Canadian film that was produced in 1978 and released in 1979 by Quadrant Films, starring William Smith, John Saxon, Claudia Jennings, Don Franks, and Nicholas Campbell. Lonnie "Lucky Man" Johnson had crashed his race car once too often, but his sponsor convinces him to return to competition. He ends up in a disagreement with the sponsor, and the climax of the movie is the chase scene between them. Don't confuse this *Fast Company* with the two other movies with the same name. One is a mystery from 1938; the other about horse racing from 1953.

The Fast Lady

(1962) This one's a British comedy that stars James Robertson Justice, Leslie Phillips, Stanley Baxter, Kathleen Harrison, a young Julie Christie, and Eric Barker. The story is about Baxter learning to drive an antique Bentley roadster, and chasing the lovely Christie in the process. This one is good family entertainment.

Here's another ad for Fireball 500. This one says the boys will "take a curve...any curve!" It was common for a wide variety of ads to be produced for each film of the fifties and sixties. Theater operators received ad mats containing ads of varied sizes and with different features promoted, whether they be cars, music, women stars, or men stars. *Ron Main Collection*

FastCo

According to a former NHRA Funny Car driver, *FastCo* is a movie that was made about NHRA drag racing with lots of Funny Cars and Top Fuel dragsters. It's hard to find.

Faster, Pussycat! Kill! Kill!

(1966) Meow! This flick has Tura Satana, Haji, and Lori Williams cast as go-go girls who like to hop in their sports cars and beat up guys. The promotional poster for the movie includes the line "Go-Go for a Wild Ride with the Action Girls!" Once again the great director Russ Meyer shows his mastery of film making, providing the two necessary requirements for a top-quality motion picture—squealing tires and serious cleavage.—DM

Steve Gray's review of Faster Pussycat Kill! Kill!:

This is a mid-sixties release from the prolific trend-setter Russ Meyer, also known for *Beneath The Valley of the Ultra-Vixens, Common-Law Cabin*, and *Mondo Topless* (Honest!). *Faster Pussycat Kill! Kill!* follows three go-go dancers on a fast, brutal road trip: Varla, their twisted, man-hating leader; Rosie, the sultry Mediterranean with the hots for Varla; and Billie, the bimbo who just plain loves to dance. Driven to violent vengeance by prolonged exposure to their leering, taunting audience, they head for the desert, driving fast, looking for kicks.

The kicks turn ugly fast and the violence gets out of hand, consuming Billie, then Rosie, and eventually Varla herself. I found that *FPK!K!* only really failed on one count: There are absolutely no motorcycles of any type whatsoever in this movie. But is this one flaw enough to keep *FPK!K!* from

Funny Car Summer* gave viewers a good look inside funny car racing. It showed quite a bit of detail on the cars and also contained a good deal of race footage.** ***Ambassador Releasing/Ron Main Collection

being a proper biker movie? Let's examine the major elements:

Mean, crazy characters; cheap desert locations (gas station and ranch); lots of meaningless violence (Varla screams with laughter as she runs over an old man in a wheelchair); everyone they meet is really screwed up; complete lack of plot development; bad rock and sax lounge music; and everyone dies in the end.

With this much going for it, I maintain that *Faster Pussycat Kill! Kill!* can attain biker movie status without bikes.—SG

Ferris Bueller's Day Off

(1986) This John Hughes-directed film starring Matthew Broderick is no car movie, but it involves a Ferrari California 250 Spyder that today is found in a most unusual parking spot. As part of his zany day of cutting high school classes, Bueller (Broderick) motors around in the Ferrari. As a sign that the apocalypse is upon us, that Ferrari now hangs from ceiling of the glitzy Planet Hollywood restaurant at the Mall of America in Bloomington, Minnesota.—MDa

Racer Jim Dunn gets ready to strap himself into his car before a race sequence in *Funny Car Summer.* *Ambassador Releasing/Ron Main Collection*

Fever Heat

(1968) This rare, low-budget film is about the small local dirt tracks and the everyday wannabe heroes who spend their time, money, and sometimes even their lives on the rough Iowa race circuit. Nick Adams is "Ace Jones" with the urge to kill, and Jennine Riley (remember Billie Jo on *Petticoat Junction*?) is the young woman left widowed by racing. The book and screenplay, which center on the old Pioneer Speedway in Des Moines, Iowa, are by Henry Gregor Felsen—yes, the same writer who thrilled young and old with *Hot Rod*, *Ragtop*, and *Street Rod* in the fifties and sixties. They used no sound stages, so what you see and hear at the Stuart and the Oskaloosa tracks is for real. Speedway champion Matt Moro said Nick was great when he took his turns around the track.—RM

52 Pick-Up

(1986) This film was built around the story by novelist Elmore Leonard (another adaptation of the story was released as *The Ambassador* two years earlier), and is gritty and somewhat difficult to watch as it dwells on the low-life scum of the criminal element. There is a thrilling sequence in which a Series II E-Type roadster makes a high-speed run through the mountains. Later in the film, the car is blown to bits. The cast features Roy Scheider, Ann-Margaret, Vanity, Doug McClure, and Clarence Williams III (Linc Hayes from TV's "Mod Squad").

The Final Alliance

(1990) Here is another mediocre, phony, stupid, stereotypical portrayal of motorcyclists as dumb violent bad guys. It has enough fights and explosions to qualify it as an action movie, but dumb violent outlaw bikers on dirt bikes? It stars David Hasselhoff, Bo Hopkins, and John Saxon, and has enough swearing in it to get an R rating but forget about it.

Final Offer

(1985) This is a Canadian film that tells the story of how the members of the Canadian Auto Workers Union broke away from the United Auto Workers in 1984. It was produced by the CBC and the National Film Board and has been shown in Canadian theaters.

Fireball 500

(1966) *Fireball 500* starred the clean teen idols Frankie Avalon, Annette Funicello, and Fabian. Frankie plays a stock car racer here, who gets tricked into hauling some moonshine.

This one is pure, sensationalist fun for people who are, or used to be, white teenagers. The star car in the movie started life as a 1966 Plymouth Barracuda, then underwent a makeover by George Barris. The car had a 424hp, 426ci Hemi, and 40 coats of hand-rubbed lacquer called Fireheat, which consisted of multi-color blends, leaving the car with an incredible glow.

Firebird 2015 A.D.

(1981) This film is set in the time when the earth's oil supply has almost run dry, and even if you can find some gas, the only people who are allowed to drive are the police. (So far, this sounds just like Mad Max.) The difference is that people aren't even allowed to own cars at all. A man who has seen this day coming has hidden a 1981 Firebird in a barn, and he decides to show his young son how much fun a healthy V-8 can be. There lots of performance driving and the movie is enjoyable if unusual.

The tires of the Dunn & Reath Special buckle as Jim Dunn accelerates at the start of a race in *Funny Car Summer. Ambassador Releasing/Ron Main Collection*

Ford: The Man and The Machine

(1987) This Ford profile is a made-for-TV movie that aired on NBC in two parts. Cliff Robertson played the part of Henry Ford convincingly, and it's quite a story. If you can find this movie, you will see lots of Model A Fords and some early V-8 models throughout as you would expect, along with some good footage of the early production lines that revolutionized the automotive industry.

The early part of the film his some memorable scenes showing the young Henry Ford in his tiny workshop with his partner, developing their new engine design. The film deals with some aspects of Ford's personal life that are not fun at all to contemplate. In fact, the further the story progresses, the less happy the man. Henry's son Edsel, played here by Michael Ironside, is all too often subjected to Ford's stubborn and bitter nature, with Edsel's progressive ideas in the thirties and forties being

The Dunn & Reath Special is a fog machine as it burns away from the line in *Funny Car Summer,* which provided viewers with a good feel for drag racing. If the theater could have simulated the heat and smell of the track, it would have been a complete viewing experience. *Ambassador Releasing/Ron Main Collection*

ridiculed.

Still, the combination of the importance of the story, the quality acting and production, and the wide variety of interesting vintage Fords in the movie makes for something that would interest any fan of American cars. Hope Lange, Heather Thomas, R.H. Thomson, and Chris Wiggins joined Cliff Robertson and Michael Ironside in this highly recommended film.

The French Connection

(1971) Clear the shelf for Mr. Oscar. This classic film won five Academy Awards, including Best Picture, Best Actor (Gene Hackman), Best Director (William Friedkin, who also directed *The Exorcist*), Best Screenplay (Ernest Tidyman), and Best Editing (Jerry Greenberg). The editing was especially spectacular in the film's key scene, a car chase in New York City. You'll find yourself holding your breath and shutting your eyes. Hackman, who played detective Popeye Doyle, is terrific. Among the stunt drivers was Bill Hickman, who drove the Charger in the legendary chase scene with Steve McQueen in *Bullit*. There was also some good chase action in the 1975 sequel, *The French Connection II*, in which the action shifted to Europe.—MDa

Funny Car Summer

(1973) Here is a movie that seems to have disappeared, which is too bad since there haven't been many movies made about professional drag racing.

Gangway for Tomorrow

(1943) This is an unusual picture about life during World War II. While it's not really about racing, one of the film's three segments is devoted to a race car driver and his life on and off the track during the war. This movie is not much fun, but the segment about the driver is interesting. It is televised occasionally on A&E, starring John Carradine, Robert Ryan, Amelita Ward, William Terry, Harry Davenport, James Bell, Wally Brown, Charles Arnt, and Alan Carney.

Garage A Go-Go

This little-known epic starred the unlikely duo of Tom Jones and Walter Brennan. It featured the Turbo Sonic, a three-wheeled futuristic race car built by George Barris. The car also appeared in *Back to the Future Part II*. The car had a 1000hp turbine engine, but it was stolen while the car was in storage.—MDa

Gas-s-s-s!

(1970) Here's an American International Pictures release produced and directed by budget-film master Roger Corman. The young counterculture crowd finds itself in a future world with no older generation against which to rebel. There is some car action, some motorcycle gang members, and even those gang members motoring around in golf cars. Country Joe and the Fish provide music, and Bud Cort, Talia Coppola (Shire), Ben Vereen, and Cindy Williams star.

Gas

(1981) This is a Canadian movie about the way a perceived gas shortage affects a supposedly typical American city. There are lots of car crashes in this movie that tries to be funny while making a statement, and it's best forgotten about unless you are a fan of Howie Mandell and that kind of comedy.

Perhaps only Russ Meyer could give us a film with the title *Faster, Pussycat! Kill! Kill!* The Bostweeds performed the hit title track, and as usual with a Russ Meyer film, women of ample proportions were the rule. "Superwomen! Belted, Buckled and BOOTED!" *Russ Meyer Associates/Ron Main Collection*

Gator

(1976) Here is the sequel to *White Lightning* (from 1973), with more moonshine running and wild car chases. Burt Reynolds, Lauren Hutton, and Jerry Reed star. In one of his better performances, Reynolds plays the role of Gator McLusky, working undercover to go after the corrupt Sheriff Connors.

Genevieve

(1953) *Genevieve* is a British comedy that tells the story of two couples who like to work on very old cars and then enter a cross-country race with them. The cast includes Dinah Sheridan, John Gregson, Kay Kendall, Kenneth More, Geoffrey Keene, Joyce Grenfell, and Michael Medwin. It's well-done, although the humor is dry slapstick and the cars are mainly in the movie to provide laughs by breaking down.

The Getaway

(1972) This is another movie that's practically one big chase scene. Directed by Sam Peckinpah, the cast includes Steve McQueen, Ali MacGraw, Ben Johnson, Sally Struthers (of TV's "All in the Family"), Al Lettieri, and Slim Pickens. When McQueen is involved in robbing a bank something goes wrong, so the rest of the movie has McQueen and his wife Ali MacGraw on the run. It's a classic. Do *not* confuse this original with a remake released in 1993 that starred Don Johnson and Melanie Griffith; you'll regret it if you pick the dreadful late-model version off the video shelf.

Getting Gertie's Goat

(1921) A vintage comedy short that features some zany motorcycle riding scenes, including some involving sidecars. This is a silent film with sub-titles.

Ghostbusters

(1984) Ecto I was name of modified 1959 Cadillac in this film and the 1989 sequel. The first film was funny, but the second was more typical of

Campy, funny teen action complete with hot rods and drag racing made American International's *Ghost of Dragstrip Hollow* a fun flick. *American International/Ron Main Collection*

a Hollywood sequel: made to capitalize off the success of the first effort. Bill Murray, Dan Aykroyd, and Sigourney Weaver star. Ivan Reirman directs.

The Giant Gila Monster

(1959) Would you fill your deuce roadster with nitro and charge a rear-projected gila monster? Great rock music and teen hot rodders in this one, which has a lot of heart and a laughable monster.—RM

Girl on a Motorcycle

(1968) This flick was also released under the title of *Naked Under Leather*, and had Marianne Faithful playing a biker chick in serious heat.

The Glory Stompers

(1968) Ouch! This one stars Dennis Hopper, Jody McCrea, Chris Noel, Jock Mahoney, and Lindsay Crosby. This is another incredibly bad movie about biker gangs, with the classic line from biker chick Chris Noel "I just want something better than being a Stompers girl."—DM

Ron Main's review of The Glory Stompers:

"Straddle your hogs and ride, man! In the deadliest cycle war ever waged." Cool Dennis Hopper is the leader of the Black Souls cycle gang in this pre-*Easy Rider* bomb. Jody McCrea and blonde beauty Chris Noel head the rival Glory Stomper gang. It's the old story: The Black Souls beat up Jody and leave him for dead. The gang

Well, things are getting just a little bit wacky here, now aren't they. The inspector was simply trying to ask a few questions in this scene from *Ghost of Dragstrip Hollow*, and the next thing you know, there's a chick dancing on the front end of the dragster. Crazy, man. *American International/Ron Main Collection*

plans to rape Chris and then sell her to the Mexican outlaws. Meanwhile, Jock Mahoney (a former Stomper) finds Jody and they set out after Chris. They are tipped off at the nude swimming hole that everybody is heading for the big love-in and orgy at the dome. It's so bad, it's a scream! The music featured Davie Allen and the Arrows. Hopper says, "Man" at least 900 times in this gem.—RM

The Gnome-Mobile

(1967) Here is another Disney fantasy. This one features a 1932 Rolls Royce town car. This film has some outstanding special effects and is probably the best movie in this chapter. The cast includes Walter Brennan, Mathew Garber, Karen Dotrice, Richard Deacon, Tom Lowell, Sean McClory, and funny man Ed Wynn.

God Rides A Harley

(1984) This is a Canadian film about some of the members of the Christian Riders M.C. and how they have gone from booze, dope, and despair to new freedom through Christ. Some of these guys have some pretty grim stories to tell, and it's a wonder they survived. There's not much here that will crack you up, but this movie has a very strong following (kinda like the guy who inspired it). *God Rides A Harley* was produced by Stavros Stavrides and is distributed by Arto-Pelli Motion Pictures, Inc.

Goldfinger

(1964) *Goldfinger* qualifies for this compilation because of the outstanding Aston Martin DB-5 that costars along with Sean Connery. You've probably seen it, but it was fitted with an array of entertaining accessories that helped it to evade the bad guys. This one is a real classic, and many feel it was the best of the James Bond series. It's worth seeing again. Gert Frobe is the evil title villain and Harold Sakata plays Goldfinger's martial arts expert assistant; watch out if he tries to toss you his hat.—DM

Michael Dregni's review of Goldfinger:

This was the third James Bond movie but it was the first to star a car and set a trend that all Bond fans came to expect from the later gaggle of 007 flicks, good and bad (and there were probably more of the latter). *Goldfinger* was preceded by *Dr. No* (1962) and *From Russia With Love* (1963) (which starred the Orient Express train), both classic Bond flicks but lacking in four-wheeled fun.

Goldfinger starred Sean Connery as 007 and costarred a fabulous Aston Martin DB5. This wasn't your typical DB5—either in real life or in celluloid fantasyland. In the real world, the Bond DB5 was actually a DB4 Vantage that had been reworked as the prototype for the new DB5 model that made its debut at London's Earls Court car show in 1963. After its show premiere, the prototype was further developed before subsequently winning a role in the Bond flick, which was a major promotional coup for Aston Martin and the new DB5 model.

In the film, the DB5 has been further souped up by Q, the secret agent techno freak also responsible for pen guns, radio transmitters built into shoe heels, and many more goodies. Q must have studied all those American moonshiner accessories because he added a score of gadgets to the Aston Martin that would have made Junior Johnson green with envy. In *Goldfinger* and the subsequent *Thunderball*, the DB5 is fitted with non-dealer-installed options from a bulletproof rear shield and passenger ejector seat to machine guns and rocket launchers. Just the things for getting rid of pesky bad guys, whether they're Russian spies or Revenue agents. Oh yeah, and the plot's pretty exciting, too.

You've probably seen *Goldfinger* once but it's always worth catching again.—MDr

Editor's Note: For more on the Aston Martin DB5, other cars used in James Bond movies, and gadgets used in the Bond movies, see the book: *The Most Famous Car in the World*, by Dave Worrall, (Solo Publishing, 1993; available from Motorbooks International).

Gone in 60 Seconds

(1974) Kabloom! This is a classic motorhead movie. A professional thief who specializes in exotic sports cars takes some wild rides while he's at work. In case you're wondering what the yellow mid-engined sports car with the gull-wing doors is, it's a Manta. Built by Brad Lovette in California in the early seventies, this was a kit car that was inspired by the old McLaren Can Am cars. The Manta featured small-block Chevy power, a tube frame, fuel cells on each side, and your choice of an inverted Corvair or racing ZF transaxle. They're still available from a company in Washington state. This is the only movie in the book that features one.

The cast includes Toby Halicki (who also produced the film), Marion Busia, James McIntire, George Cole, Jerry Daugirda, and Indy Car drivers Parnelli Jones and Gary Bettenhausen.

In August of 1989, a sequel to *Gone in 60 Sec-*

onds was in the works when Toby Halicki was killed in an accident. The original *Gone in 60 Seconds* was one of the best car chase movies from this decade.

The Graduate

(1967) Here is perhaps the sole movie that became the name for a model of car. A classic sixties film, it stars Dustin Hoffman in his first movie role as a naive, spoiled, and undirected college graduate who is seduced by a married woman, the famous Mrs. Robinson (Anne Bancroft), and then later falls for her young daughter (Katherine Ross). The soundtrack is by Simon and Garfunkel.

The graduate is given an Alfa Romeo Duetto as a graduation present, which later inspired Alfa Romeo's US marketeers to name their base-model spyder The Graduate in the hope that proud parents would buy their graduates The Graduate—a marketing ploy that misses the whole point of *The Graduate.*

This is another great film that you'll probably enjoy more for its story than for the scenes of the Alfa Romeo.—MDr

Grand Prix

(1966) This popular film is about the personal lives and on-track action of Formula One Grand Prix race car drivers (in that order). If you like soap operas and Formula One, this is your movie. James Garner stars as one of the drivers. Excellent racing footage help make this a classic racing film. It's a very long movie, a minute under three hours; so it gives you time to take a bath or go shopping between the racing segments. Nonetheless, it's one of the better racing movies.—DM

Ron Main's review of Grand Prix:

James Garner, Eva Marie Saint, and Yves Montand star in this story of Grand Prix racing, the men, their loves, and their fears. The excitement that was captured on film was mostly due to James Garner. He underwent expensive training with former Grand Prix racer Bob Bondurant and was so good that they dispensed with the usual stationary car and rear screen projection and Garner did most of the driving himself. The insurance people found out and the production company had to film the final two months with no insurance, but we got a stunning film with sights and sounds that earned two Oscars. Garner went on to race in

Ads for the lighthearted *Ghost of Dragstrip Hollow* were different from so many B movie ads of the day. No women, no rough teens, just a hot rod, the promise of the Hot Rod Gang's presence, and the lure of a fun-filled scary flick. *American International/Ron Main Collection*

You could dance to "The Gila Monster Crawl" after seeing this 1959 epic in which a nice rod was sacrificed for something as insignificant as saving all of mankind from destruction. *McLendon Radio Pictures/Ron Main Collection*

events such as the Mexican 1000, Mint 400, and the Baja 500. He also drove the pace cars at a few Indy 500s.—RM

Grand Theft Auto

(1977) GTA stars Ron Howard (who also directed), Nancy Morgan, Marion Ross, Isacksen, and Barry Cahill. It's a comedy about a young couple being chased while running off together, resulting in lots of action and wrecks.

Grandview, U.S.A.

(1984) This one features a woman who runs her father's demolition derby business. It stars Jamie Lee Curtis, Thomas Howell, Jennifer Jason Leigh, Patrick Swayze, Ramon Bieri, Carole Cook, Elizabeth Gorcey, William Windom, and Troy Donahue.

Grease

(1978) John Travolta and Olivia Newton-John costar in this look at the fifties. The cars involved include a '49 Merc racing an early-fifties Ford in the dry river beds of California. Travolta "sings" lyrics about headers, four on the floor, and dual-quad lifters.

Greased Lightning

(1977) This film stars Richard Prior in the story of Wendell Scott, the first black driver to compete in NASCAR Grand National stock car racing. Beau Bridges plays the buddy who helps his career. The movie is probably a reasonably accurate representation of what it was like for Wendell in overcoming the attitudes that tried to hold him back.

Most stock car racing fans will enjoy the movie, and I would recommend it both from historical and entertainment perspectives.

Wendell Scott passed away in 1991 and this performance by Richard Prior gives us some good memories of a fine competitor. Pam Greer, Cleavon Little, Vincent Gardenia, and politician Julian Bond give good performances in addition to Prior and Bridges. *Greased Lightning* has some good racing scenes and is a quality picture. A&E broadcasts it occasionally.

Five of the vintage stock cars from the movie are currently owned and driven by Race Cars of Yesterday (1831 26th Street North, St. Petersburg, FL 33713).

In *The Glory Stompers,* Dennis Hopper's gang is on the lam, trying to outrun charges of murder and kidnapping. What? No drug trafficking, extortion, or running a busload of nuns off a cliff? What a bunch of sissies. *American International/Ron Main Collection*

The Great Chase

(1962) This is a compilation of classic chase scenes and stunt work from old movies that was compiled by Paul Killiam.

The Great Escape

(1963) This classic stars Steve McQueen, James Garner, Richard Attenborough, Charles Bronson, James Coburn, David McCallum, Donald Pleasence, James Donald, and Gordon Jackson. There is a famous scene where McQueen rides an old Triumph Trophy (of sixties-vintage, actually) in one of several attempts to break out of a World War II prison camp. Although McQueen normally did all of his own stunt riding (and driving) in his movies, there is a part of the scene on the Triumph where it is actually ridden by McQueen's friend, Bud Ekins. The producers insisted

Rebel With a Projector

The movie could be called "Straight-Line Rebel," or "High-Speed Outlaws." The poster would show: a streamliner tearing across the Bonneville Salt Flats; a young stud wearing blue jeans, a white T-shirt, and a rebellious sneer; and his beautiful teenangel, Vanessa.

That angry young man would be Ron Main, long-time hot rodder, veteran racer on the salt and the dry lakes, and avid collector of classic movies featuring teenage troublemakers.

It's not that Ron's a bad egg, or that he ever was as a teen, but that hell-bent-for-speed-and-thrills rebel is the archetypal lead man in many of the classic B movies of the fifties and sixties. Those are the movies Ron loves, the kind he now collects and distributes through his hobby business, Main Attractions. He comes by his affection for those flicks honestly.

"I'm basically a hot rodder. I grew up in the fifties and things were simpler. There were cars and there were girls. I wasn't too lucky when I was young with the girls, so you buy magazines on hot cars... The one key thing I've always felt is the dreams that you have when you're around 16, the things you see and want at that age will stay with you the rest of your life. That's what motivates most people to pursue their interests."

Ron's right. His interests—then and now—included hot rods, race cars, and teenage action like that depicted in the movies. As a teen, he and his pals loved the basics: Dragging Main Street, peeling rubber, and going to movies.

"Some of these movies were made in a week. They were made for pre-teens, for the people who were at the movies on a Saturday night and couldn't be out doing what's being done *in* the movies themselves."

Ron later started collecting posters, especially old movie posters, and that sparked his interest in the films.

"Seeing the posters, I wanted to see the movies. I couldn't find them at first, but as I got into it, I found it got easier to locate them."

As you can see from the ads and poster reproductions in this book, movies were sold on pure hype in the fifties and sixties. The more outlandish, outrageous, and controversial a movie sounded, the more kids wanted to see it—especially if their parents objected.

"In those days you had to sell the sizzle because there was no steak. Now, they don't advertise that way. We were so naive, really."

As Ron's film collection grew, so did the crowd at his house each week.

"I had a projector at home, and we'd show the movies on the wall or on a sheet outside. People wanted copies of the movies, and we tried to make some, but it was hard."

Until about four years ago, that is, when he found a film service that could transfer old reel film to video with impressive results. The film quality on the video benefits from enhancing done during the transfer, and it's better than if you were watching the theater reels.

Main Attractions is just a hobby, but it's one that keeps Ron busy. He and his wife Vanessa have produced catalogs listing dozens of the films they have for sale on video. (Order one of his catalogs; the film descriptions are a riot themselves.) The catalogs show his love for racing, race films, and good, old bad movies, whether they involve dragstrip trouble, good girls gone way bad, or monsters like those in Friend Without a Face, where the creatures "appear as flying brains with their spines attached."

Ron is interested in all sorts of old films, not just hot rod and teen rebel flicks. As an avid car enthusiast, he delights in seeing the vehicles in the old films.

"You watch a fifties movie and every car they used is a collector car today."

on this because of the possibility of McQueen being injured.

The Great Race

(1965). Blake Edwards directs this film, which was loosely based on 1908 New York to Paris race. The movie cost $8 million to make, lots at the time. More than $100,000—also a lot—was spent building special vehicles. Tony Curtis (Leslie Galant III) and Natalie Wood drive the Leslie Special. against Jack Lemmon (Professor Fate). Leslie Special had body of PVC plastic, while fenders, running boards and other parts are metal; loose interpretation of the Thomas Flyer. Four such cars were built, and one later appeared in *Good Guys and Bad Guys* with Robert Mitchum and George Kennedy. Hannibal 8 was an elevator car with spiked nose cone out front. Professor Fate's car was a rocket-powered rail runner that actually had Corvair engine at its base. Warner Bros.

The Great Skycopter Rescue

(1981) Here is another action movie with a token biker gang thrown in. It's got a story built around an introvert who has built a tiny helicopter, and the bikers get snarly when it impresses the babes more than their bikes.

Before the stricter "R" ratings, potentially offensive movies could be rated "M," meaning they were "suggested for mature audiences. Parental discretion advised." That meant plenty of young movie goers got in to see *Hell's Angels '69*, letting those young teens feel like they were experiencing the wild side of life. *American International/ Ron Main Collection*

The Great Smokey Roadblock

(1976) This film stars the late Henry Fonda is a trucker who can make one final run before his truck gets repossessed, hauling a load of hookers. The film was originally released under the title The Last of the Cowboys, which ran 106 minutes. This version is 84 minutes. The cast includes Eileen Brennan, John Byner, Dub Taylor, Susan Sarandon, Melanie Mayron, and Austin Pendleton. This one is worth seeing just for Fonda's performance, as always.

The Great Texas Dynamite Chase

(1977) This film was the original *Thelma and Louise* concept except the women here are nude in the bathtub and don't die! This low-budget gem had the queen of the B's, Claudia Jennings, the 1970 Playboy Playmate of the Year. Her attitude was that nice girls *do* take off their clothes, and she and her partner, the lovely Jocelyn Jones, make one sexy pair of bank robbers who outwit the cops and sweaty rednecks. Michael Pressman and Johnny "All grown up and flexing his muscles" Crawford (from *The Rifleman*) costar. The ending would make Thelma and Louise proud, as they send an exploding car into the cops and ride off into the sunset.—RM

The Green Helmet

(1961) Here is a British film about a race car driver. The cast includes Bill Travers, Nancy Walters, Ed Begley, and racing legend Jack Brabham. This is one of the few movies in here that features Jaguar roadracers.

Grumpy Old Men

(1993) This one's just getting to video, and doesn't have much for car action, but it's got some wild sprints across the frozen landscape on a snowmobile, a 1994 Arctic Cat Cougar piloted by Ann-Margaret (and her stunt driver). The film features stars Walter Matthau and Jack Lemmon as two Minnesota neighbors whose rivalry extends beyond the ice fishing world once bombshell Ann-Margaret moves into the neighborhood. Shot in the dead of a Minnesota winter, it's a good flick to cool you off in the midst of a humid summer.—MDa

Gumball Rally

(1976) This was the start of a series that did pretty well, although few seem to be proud to have been involved in them. It's based loosely on the actual Cannonball Run where drivers and their navigators raced for 2,900 miles across the highways of America, shooting for the record time of 34 hours and 11 minutes. The competitors draw to choose their vehicles, which include a Camaro, a Chevy van, a Cobra, a Corvette convertible, a Kawasaki KR-400 two-stroke motorcycle, a Ferrari, a Jaguar XKE roadster, a Mercedes-Benz 300SL roadster, a Porsche 911, and a Rolls Royce. Of all of the movies in the series, *Gumball Rally* was the best. The sequel, *Cannonball* (from 1976), which was also released under the name *Carquake*, was forgettable despite all the talent involved in it. The cast here includes Michael Sarrazin, Tim McIntire, Gary Busey, Susan Flannery, Nicholas Prior, and Raul Julia.

Handle With Care

(1977) *HWC* was originally released as *Citizens Band*, and it deals with truckers and the CB radio fad, among other things. The cast here is Paul LeMat, Candy Clark, Ann Wedgeworth, Marcia Rodd, Charles Napier, Alix Elias, and Roberts Blossom. It's funny and entertaining.

The Hard Ride

(1971) *The Hard Ride* stars Robert Fuller, Sherry Bain, Tony Russel, Marshall Reed, Biff Elliot, and William Bonner. It's a biker movie with a difference—a message for unity.

Harley

(1991) *Harley* is another forgettable drama, with Lou Diamond Phillips whining and pouting his way through the role of the Angry Youth who feels the world owes him an apology and a bike. Don't bother with it.

Harley Davidson and the Marlboro Man

(1991) This one stars Mickey Rourke, Don Johnson, and Chelsea Field. It's set in California in 1996, with Rourke and Johnson cast as a pair of Harley-riding cowboys who rob an armored car so they can save a bar belonging to a friend who has money problems. Things get crazy when the armored car turns out to be filled with drugs instead of cash. This movie did poorly in the theaters and is not one of the greats but it has some good action.—DM

Steve Gray's review of Harley Davidson and the Marlboro Man:

To quote the video box: "Renegade actor Mickey Rourke and the explosively talented Don Johnson erupt with no-holds-barred action and off-beat humor." I'll add that it seared the screen with the white-hot presence of Vanessa Williams. All that aside, *HD & the MM* is basically *Butch Cassidy and the Sundance Kid* on bikes. The plot is controlled, the dialogue stilted. Rourke, who is usually described in the industry media nowadays as "unwashed," makes a far more believable biker than Johnson does a cowboy. There are, though, a few good bike scenes and quite a bit of amusing gunplay. The best dialogue in the movie has Johnson and Rourke arguing the cost effectiveness of different caliber ammunition while in a running gunfight. Being an expensive motion picture, it looks and sounds good, and a few expensive things get shot or blown up. A good movie to run during a party or any situation where you don't plan on paying close attention. Fair amount of violence and profanity, some nudity, very loud ZZ Top-type soundtrack.—SG

Heart Like a Wheel

(1983) This is a true story, and it's an incredible story at that. You likely already know that Shirley Muldowney became the first woman in history to get an NHRA Top Fuel license, and she went on to become a legend.

Bonnie Bedelia does an outstanding job here of portraying Shirley as the hero she is. The movie costars Leo Rossi as Jack Muldowney, and Beau Bridges as Connie Kalitta. There are also appearances by Hoyt Axton, as Shirley's father, and Diamond P Sports/TNN racing commentator Steve Evans as himself.

The only real criticism I could make of *Heart Like A Wheel* is that it doesn't last long enough to go into more detail. Movies this good should last all day. There is a scene where Jack asks their son to help with the carburetor on their dragster, which has Hilborn injectors, but it is otherwise very good technically.

Fourteen minutes into the picture we see Shirley pilot her husband Jack's chopped 1949 Mercury two-door sedan to a win over a cherry full-fendered 1932 Ford roadster out on an old blocked-off street drag strip. Shortly after that, their Mercury is replaced with a red 1962 Corvette (that looks stock except for a hood scoop) in which she also wins a few. At 17 minutes in, we ar-

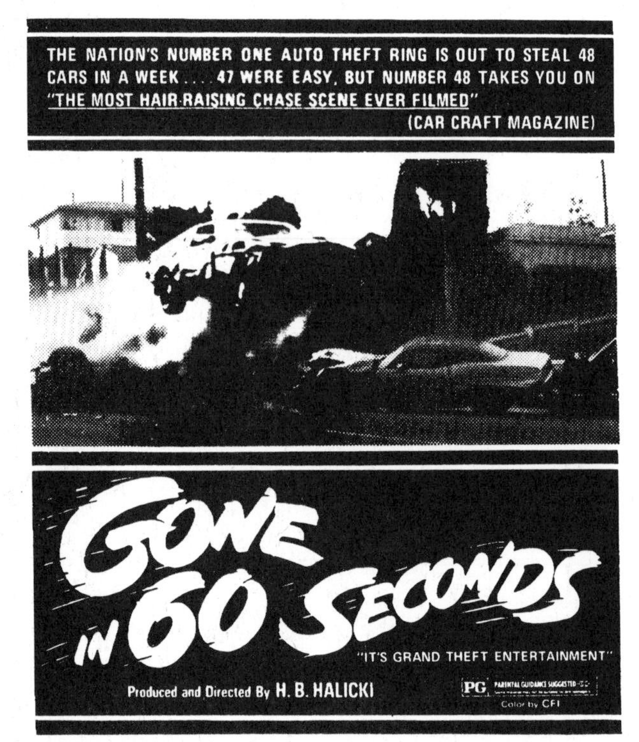

Did someone say "classic?" That's what we've got in *Gone in 60 Seconds*, a Tony Halicki creation that was short on production quality but long on car action. The highly coveted "Eleanor," a 1973 Mustang, is finally stolen by Maindrain Pace (played by Toby), and it leads police on a chase through seven south L.A. cities before the action comes to a halt. *Ron Main Collection*

Ads for *Gone in 60 Seconds* were designed from the outset with drive-in theaters in mind. The movie was perfect fare for the open air, youthful, playful drive-in scene. *Ron Main Collection*

rive at the old NHRA-sanctioned Fonda Speedway, where Don Garlits (played here by Robert Duvall), grants Shirley's request to sit in his Top Fuel dragster. At the 24-minute mark, Shirley and Jack arrive at the Englishtown, New Jersey drag strip, where she manages to get her license (thanks in part to some support from Garlits) and set a new track record with her first pass in her Hilborn-injected gas dragster. 62 minutes into the picture, Shirley and her crew arrive at Orange County International Raceway in 1972 to hold a press conference announcing her debut in a Kalitta-built Funny Car. Pomona was the scene of Shirley's horrible crash in 1973 when her Funny Car's new blower exploded, turning the car into a 200mph fireball. Due in part to Tommy Ivo's fine stunt driving, the incident is recreated with unsettling realism.

As an interesting side note, Shirley's old Top Fuel dragster that was used in the movie was later tracked down by Don Garlits, who found it on a back lot at the studio. It now can be seen in his outstanding museum, the Don Garlits Museum of Drag Racing, located at 13700 S.W. 16th Avenue, Ocala, FL 32676.

There is none of the usual Hollywood sensationalism here, just some accurate recreations of some of the many events that have made Shirley's life such a powerful and moving story. All through this movie, Shirley's character is treated with the dignity and respect she has earned. This is undoubtedly one of the very finest motorsports-related films ever made, and the most accurate and emotionally-involving one of its kind. *Heart Like A Wheel* stands as a terrific tribute to someone who has inspired and touched us all.

In *Eat My Dust*, Ron Howard played Big Bubba Jones, who earned more speeding tickets than anybody in town. Theater owners were urged to promote the movie by offering free passes to anyone who was ticketed in the previous week, but "hit-and-runs need not apply." *New World Pictures/ Ron Main Collection*

Hell Drivers

(1957) *Hell Drivers* is a British film that was released in America in 1958. It borrows heavily from *Wages of Fear*. A strong cast includes Cy Endfield, Stanley Baker, Herbert Lom, Peggy Cummins, Patrick McGoohan (who later was TV's "The Prisoner"), Jill Ireland, Gordon Jackson, David McCallum (later the star of TV's "The Man from U.N.C.L.E."), and Sean Connery ("Bond, James Bond."). The story revolves around corruption and bad roads. The original British version ran 108 minutes; the American version, 91 minutes. Recommended.

World Champion Jack Brabham costars in *The Green Helmet*, a sensationalized race movie that also starred Ed Begley, Sr. Let's hope Sir Jack could keep up with leading man, leadfoot Bill Travers. *MGM/Ron Main Collection*

The Hellcats

(1968) This film is about a girls' motorcycle gang that kills a cop, starring Ross Hagen, Dee Duffy, Sharyn Kinzie, Sonny West, Robert Slatzer, Eric Lidberg, and Gus Trikonis.

Hellcats

Approaching this movie you're promised "Motorcycle Mamas On A Highway To Hell." At least that's what the video box said, along with artwork that made me feel dirty all over for renting the damn movie. Well, the highway led to Walton's Mountain or Oral Roberts University or somewhere, but definitely not to Hell.

Hellcats, a Slatzer-Cardoza-Gemini American production, had passable acting and an actual plot. A dead narc's brother and fianceé infiltrate a bike gang to discover how "Mr. Big" is smuggling yellow jackets, reds, and bennies up from Mexico. After the usual "pretending to be bikers" foolishness, justice is served. The problem is that they managed to do it without any sex, violence, or profanity. The "R" rating was a crock. A few "hecks" and "darns", some beer swilling and a glimpse of a lady's belly button. Easily a PG rating, not what we'd consider Hot Biker action.

There were a few redeeming features. Triumphs outnumbered Hogs by far and sounded good on drag pipes. There was a classic "Biker Chain Fight" (with no injuries of course) and in an updated "trial by ordeal" a couple of guys were tied between two flathead trikes. Consistent with the wimpy nature of the movie, they couldn't get the slicks to hook up in the dirt. Goofy soundtrack by Davey Jones and the Dolphins. Worth the two bucks? Only to entertain the very faint hearted.—SG

Hell on Wheels

Recording star Marty Robbins was no stranger to NASCAR. He ran his own stocker in the summer and even ran in the Daytona 500! (He was also a pace car driver at the Indy 500.) He loved doing this film, in which he was the stock car hero and John Ashley was his misguided brother who yearns to race and get the glory. Bro falls in with bad moonshine runners to get his own stocker, and the showdown is inevitable. The gang is out to get Marty, but he's a racing, singing, and fighting son of a gun. It's pure corn. Lovely Gigi Perreau is the love interest, and songsters Connie Smith and the Stonemen are featured. Marty sings "No Tears Milady" and "Fly, Butterfly, Fly." Boy, do I miss this guy.—RM

Hellriders

(1985) Here is another biker movie, available from Trans World Video as a 90-minute videotape. This one is billed as "Action, adventure, and trouble." Isn't that what they're all about?

Hell's Angels Forever

(1983) This one was so big that it was directed by the trio of Richard Chase, Kevin Keating, and Leon Grant. The goal here was to provide some insight into what the Angels are really like and in most aspects the film succeeds. This movie is not for kids, but it's real.

Hell's Angels On Wheels

(1967) Rev 'em up. This one stars Adam Roarke, Jack Nicholson, Sabrina Scharf, Sonny Barger, Jana Taylor, Richard Anders, I.J. Jefferson, John Garwood (Gabe De Lutri), James Oliver, Jack Starrett, Bruno Vesota, Robert Kelljian, Kathryn Harrow, Bud Cardos, Tex Hall, Gary Littlejohn, along with Hell's Angels members from the Oakland, San Francisco, Daly City, and Richmond, California, chapters, as well as the Nomads M.C. of Sacramento. Some of the music (by Stu Phillips) is pretty bad and is out of place, but otherwise this remains one of the best movies that's been made about the Angels.

The movie opens with the bikers pulling into a town where they do a bit of wheelie popping and girl grabbing, and then pull in to a gas station where Nicholson works as a pump jockey. Nicholson is cast as Poet, a soft-spoken, decent guy. After a hassle with a customer, Poet quits his job and takes off on his stripped-down rigid-frame Panhead to hang out with the club. The Angels have a score to settle with a member of the Madcaps M.C. (from Bakersfield) who's messed up one of their members, and it's time for the mandatory biker movie fist fight scene. Poet shows his usefulness by hammering a guy and stuffing his head in a toilet, and is rewarded by the President who tells his old lady to ride with him instead. They all end up at a carnival, where four Navy guys catch Poet on his own and pick a fight with him. The Angels find him and tell him to split—they'll take care of it. But when they do, one of the sailors actually dies, which they hadn't counted on. From here, the club

Ann-Margaret has an all-too-willing Walter Matthau along for the ride on her Arctic Cat in *Grumpy Old Men*. The film was shot in a less-than-exotic location: Minnesota in winter. *Courtesy Arctco, Inc.*

spends its time partying and hassling with the law.

None of the outlaw biker movies are masterpieces, but *Hell's Angels On Wheels* is one of the best of them. The screenplay is by R. Wright Campbell, produced by Joe Solomon and directed by Richard Rush.

Hell's Angels '69

(1969) Here is one of the few movies made to feature some of the actual members of the Hell's Angels. Sonny Barger, Terry the Tramp, Skip, Tiny, and Magoo were all original members of the Oakland chapter of the Hell's Angels.

Hell's Belles

(1969) This is actually a remake of the 1950 western *Winchester '73*. James Gordon White, the screenwriter for the film, admits that he essentially took out Jimmy Stewart on a horse and put in Jeremy Slate on a Harley-Davidson.

Hell's Bloody Devils

(1970) What a cast! What a melee! This one stars Broderick Crawford, Scott Brady, John Gabriel, Kent Taylor, John Carradine, Robert Dix, Keith Andes, Jack Starrett, Anne Randall, and Vicki Volante. It was also later released as *The Fakers* and *Smashing the Crime Syndicate*. It's basically one big fist fight.

Herbie Goes Bananas

(1980) So long. This was the end of the road for the Herbie series. By this time Disney seemed to be running out of ideas for stories, although a TV series based on the movies followed. The cast includes Charlie Martin Smith, Steven Burns, Cloris Leachman, John Vernon, Elyssa Davalos, Harvey Korman, Richard Jaeckel, Alex Rocco, and Fritz Field.

Herbie Goes to Monte Carlo

(1977) This one finds Dean Jones playing a race car driver, when some crooks get involved

An Arctic Cat snowmobile was converted into a camera sled for the filming of *Grumpy Old Men*. The back end of the seat was made to accommodate the cameraman facing backward to shoot footage of Ann-Margaret on her snowmobile, while the hood was replaced with a large shield to help block the spray of snow. *Courtesy Arctco, Inc.*

with hiding something they stole in Herbie's gas tank. The cast features Dean Jones, Don Knotts, Julie Sommars, Roy Kinnear, and Jacques Marin.

Herbie Rides Again

(1974) This film and the two other sequels that follow, are more of the same comedy and special effects. This time the magical Volkswagen rounds up some other cars to help a fire station in San Francisco. The cast includes Helen Hayes, Ken Berry, Stefanie Powers, Keenan Wynn, John McIntire, and former Bowery Boy ("Satch") Huntz Hall.

High-Ballin'

(1978) Here is another trucking movie with

You want action? How about a van crashing full-speed into a fireworks factory? And if you don't like Corvettes, stay tuned to *The Gumball Rally* for a 'vette that gets launched through a roadblock and is demolished upon landing. *Warner Bros./Ron Main Collection*

Unlike Hollywood pretty boy Tom Cruise (who starred in *Days of Thunder*), Marty Robbins was a real race car driver who spent his weekends at the track whenever he was able. He also drove the pace car for the 1976 Indy 500. *Crown-International/ Ron Main Collection*

Peter Fonda, with him battling mobsters this time. Helen Shaver plays a lady trucker here, with Jerry Reed, Chris Wiggins, David Ferry, and Chris Longevin. Lots of action.

High Rolling in a Hot Corvette

(1978) This film was made in Australia and stars Joseph Bottoms, Grigor Taylor, Judy Davis, John Clayton, and Wendy Hughes. It's about a pair of guys who resort to crime while on the road.

High School Caesar

(1960) This movie stars Gary Vinson, John Ashley, Steve Stevens, Judy Nugent, Lowell Brown, and Dariah Massey and was directed by the great O. Dale Ireland (see *Date Bait*, above).

Although it follows the standard juvenile delinquent theme with crazed teens tearing up the roads and each other's lives, this one is a classic that's better than most of the exploitation flicks. The promotional poster for *High School Caesar* screams: "Mob Rule in High School! He had more rackets than Al Capone! She turned a Cool-School into a Hotbed of Violence!"

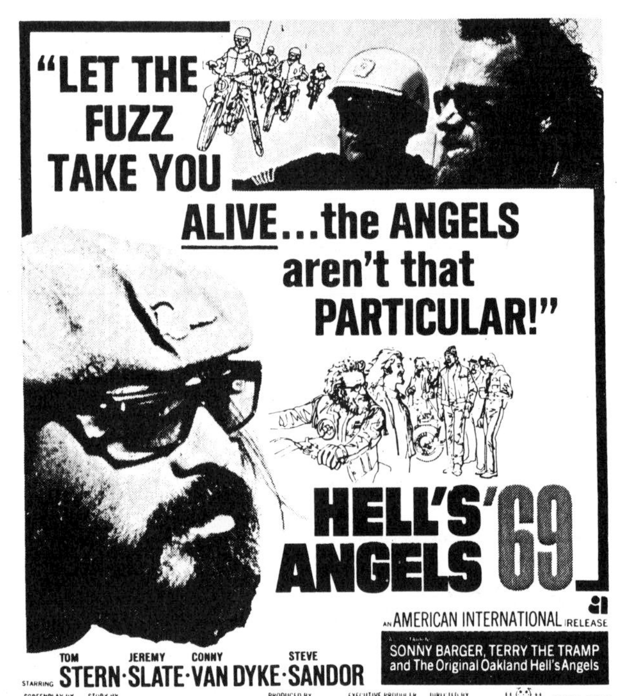

You know, we've seen Oakland Hell's Angels leader Sonny Barger's name associated with so many legitimate or respectable projects (acting in films, technical advisor for films, author or subject of books), that we want to call him a big phony and a wimp. But then again, Sonny's got a lot of friends who are a lot bigger and tougher than our buddies, so we'll just label him as one bad biker, dude. *American International/ Ron Main Collection*

High School Confidential

(1958) Wow, man, this one has quite a cast—including Russ Tamblyn, Jan Sterling, John Drew Barrymore, Mamie Van Doren, Diane Jergens, Ray Anthony, Jerry Lee Lewis, Jackie Coogan, Charles Chaplin, Jr., Lyle Talbot, William Wellman, Jr., and Michael Landon (yes, "Little Joe"). This has Russ Tamblyn cast as an undercover cop who's after a gang of dope dealers who just happen to be hot rodders.

High School Hellcats

(1958) *HSH* stars Yvonne Lime, Brett Halsey, Jana Lund, Suzanne Sydney, Heather Ames, and Nancy Kilgar. It's about a gang of delinquent girls who love to drive hot cars and raise hell.

The Highwayman

(1987) "The Highwayman" was the TV series pilot that starred Watergate conspirator G. Gordon Liddy as a shady businessman who is pursued by the trucker played by Sam Jones, along with Claudia Christian, Stanford Egi, Wings Hauser, Jimmy Smits, and Theresa Saldana. That's some truck!

Hog Wild

(1980) This is a Canadian film that stars Michael Biehn, Patti Darbanville, and Tony Rosato, produced by Filmplan International and Reindeer Films Ltd. It's "a comedy for young people" with the story of a guy returning to his home town after being away for a long time. When he goes to college he finds bikers terrorizing the campus. He makes a fuss and they start hassling him. He and the leader of the gang are after the same girl, and he decides to teach the biker a lesson—he challenges him to a race at the annual fair.

I haven't seen this movie, and I don't think I want to. This book already has more than eighty movies in it that portray motorcyclists with the negative stereotypes that were old in 1970. Did we need one sending the same message to kids?

Hollywood Knights

(1980) This film has Tony Danza making his debut in a leading role, with Michelle Pfeiffer, Fran Drescher, Leigh French, Randy Gornel, Robert Wuhl, Stuart Pankin, P.R. Paul, Richard Schaal, and Debra Feuer. The story is set in 1965, on Halloween night. Tubby's, the local drive-in restaurant that serves as the meeting place for all kinds of car enthusiasts, is about to close down against the wishes of all the customers. An abandoned A&W drive-in restaurant on Van Nuys Boulevard in California was converted to the movie set for the film. *Hollywood Knights* features a good variety of street rods and muscle cars and is one of the best of this kind of movies. Tony Nancy's 1932 Ford roadster, a Shelby Cobra, and a Porsche Spyder are among the fifty pre-1966 cars that appear.

Hooper

(1978) From an era when Burt Reynolds actually made some movies worth seeing, this one tells the story of an aging movie stunt man (Reynolds) and the young buck [(Jan-Michael Vincent (what's with the two first names, anyway?)] who tries to run him out of the business and replace him. Some wild stunt driving and motorcycle riding. Look for the rocket-boosted 1977 Pontiac Trans Am.—MDa

Hot Cars

(1956) "A stop-at-nothing blonde... A buck-hungry guy... Slam the screen head-on!" Blonde temptress Joi Lansing (she's red-hot) lures John Bromfield into a stolen car ring. The climax is great, with an incredible roller coaster ride at the finish.—RM

Hot Rod

(1979) This one is a classic in some ways, something any fan of street rods and dragsters would want to see. The plot is ridiculous and best forgotten. It's all about the Munn's Root Beer Nationals at the "Lyons" drag strip in Fremont, California, and every competitor who doesn't run a Munn's decal on their car is harassed by the cor-

Hells Angels on Wheels **was the start of a full-circle cycle for actor Jack Nicholson. As "Poet" in this film, he was beat up by a bunch of sailors. In a later film, *The Last Detail,* Nicholson was a rough MP who would have been dishing out that beating to an unkempt biker. *US Films/ Ron Main Collection***

There just aren't enough drivers playing chicken on the road anymore. But there's no shortage of chicken racing, girl grabbin', and full-throttle making out in *High School Caesar,* where you'll hear Reggie Perkins sing the title tune. *Marathon/ Ron Main Collection*

rupt local cops. But you'll see enough interesting cars to make it worth your while.

A Hot Rod Hall of Fame museum that is shown in a few scenes includes a glass-bodied turtledeck 1927 T roadster, a 1934 five-window, and several early dragsters. The star of the movie drives a 1965 Plymouth two-door hardtop powered by a 426 Hemi. Later in the movie the Hemi finds its way into a gray-primered 1941 Willys Blown Altered coupe that runs very low 11's on the drag strip. There are also brief looks at a fiberglass Bantam roadster with a Model T grille, a cherry 1956 Chevy Nomad, and lots of old Fords: Model As, several '32s (including a three-window and a five-window), a yellow 1939 sedan delivery with a 1940 Deluxe grille, and a red 1940 woody. The race cars in *Hot Rod* include a glass Fiat altered coupe, a 1948 Austin, some mid-seventies Funny Cars, some Camaros and Mustangs, and several Top Fuel cars. Too bad the plot is so embarrassing—with all that machinery it could have been a great movie. This was a made-for-TV movie that starred Robert Culp and Pernell Roberts, among other lesser-knowns. You may also find it under the title *Rebel of the Road*.

Hot Rod Action

(1966) Hats off to Robert E. Petersen of the Petersen Publishing empire for producing this one. This film chronicles racing of all types in the early sixties, capturing the cars, the people, and the action in a time capsule to be cherished. The cars include top fuel dragsters, salt flats streamliners, Craig Breedlove's record setter, 427 Cobras, sprint cars, stockers, sports cars, and Indy Cars. The people include "TV" Tommy Ivo, "Big Daddy" Don Garlits, Tom McEwen, Danny Ongais, Bobby Unser, Linda Vaughn, Dean Jeffries, Richard Petty, A.J. Foyt, and many more. As Ron Main notes, "Also dune buggies and sand rails. One of the best hot rod movies ever made of the hot sixties. What a reunion! It's got it all."—RM

Hot Rod Gang

(1958) This flick stars John Ashley, rock 'n' roller Gene Vincent, Jody Fair, and Steve Drexel.

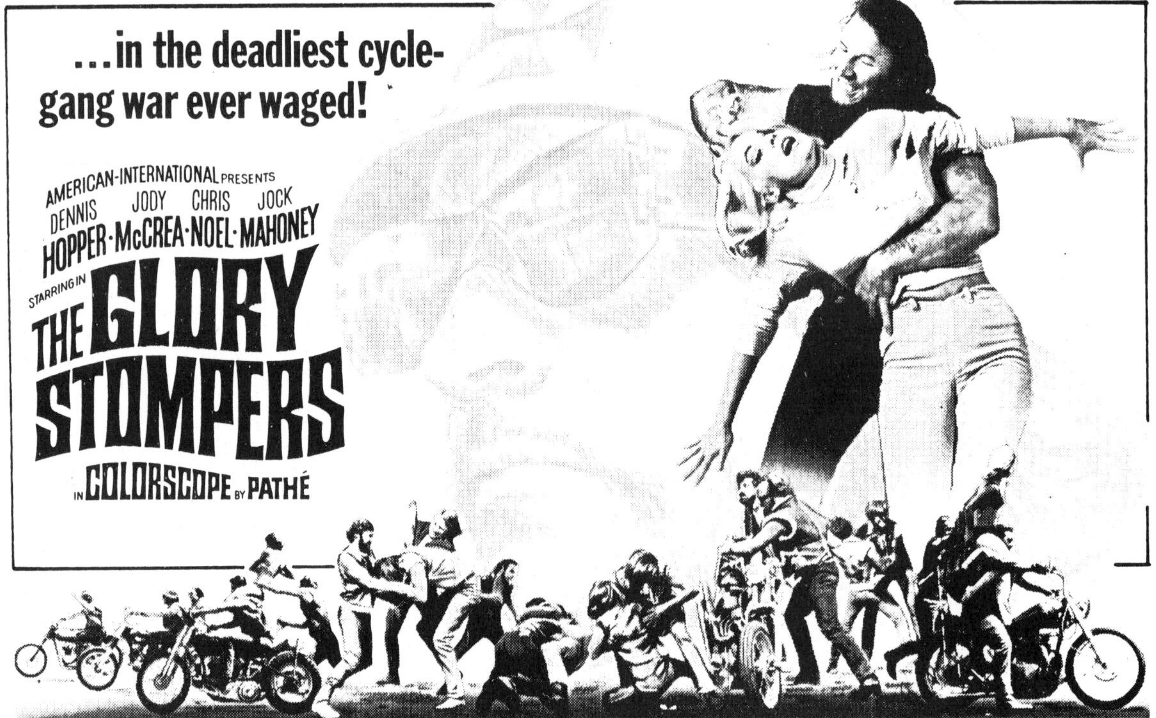

Dennis Hopper, who starred in the 1967 release, *The Glory Stompers*, has sometimes been perceived as a flake because of the wild roles he has played in many films. Yes, the real-life Hopper has had his wild moments–or years–but he is closing in on his fortieth anniversary in movies. His first film was a small bit in 1955's *I Died a Thousand Times*. *American International/ Ron Main Collection*

John Ashley plays a hot rodder who wants to run in the drags, so to raise the money, he joins Gene Vincent's band.

Hot-Rod Girl

(1956) Another film whose title combines two vital elements of any teen-age boy's reasons for existing, this one has a cast with some names that gained fame as their careers progressed. Too bad they didn't shine particularly brightly here. The cast includes Chuck Connors (TV's "Rifleman"), and impersonator (and Riddler) Frank Gorshin. The leading lady here is Lori Nelson, who tries to rein in the outlaw hot rodders who are racing on the streets. Gorshin delivers the classic line to his buddies as lawman Connors approaches: "Clam up, you squares, it's the law!"

Hot Rod Girl

(1956) *Hot Rod Girl* has June Kenney, Richard Bakalyan, John Brinkley, Robert Knapp, Jana Lund, Bruno Vesota, and Ed Nelson. The story involves a nice girl who gets mixed up with a nasty hot rodder. In one scene where she's driving a 1954 Kaiser convertible she runs into a cop and knocks him off his rigid-frame Panhead.

Hot Rod Hullabaloo

(1966) "Speed's Their Creed!" You want action? Well, once upon a time in demo-derby land, Vince smashes Eddie. He challenges Vince to a "chicken" race. Vince kills Eddie with a gun he had installed in his car! You want more? Cindy (Luke's girl) warns the Pacemakers that the good citizens are trying to close the drag strip. Vince gives Joe (Luke's older brother) a beating and tries

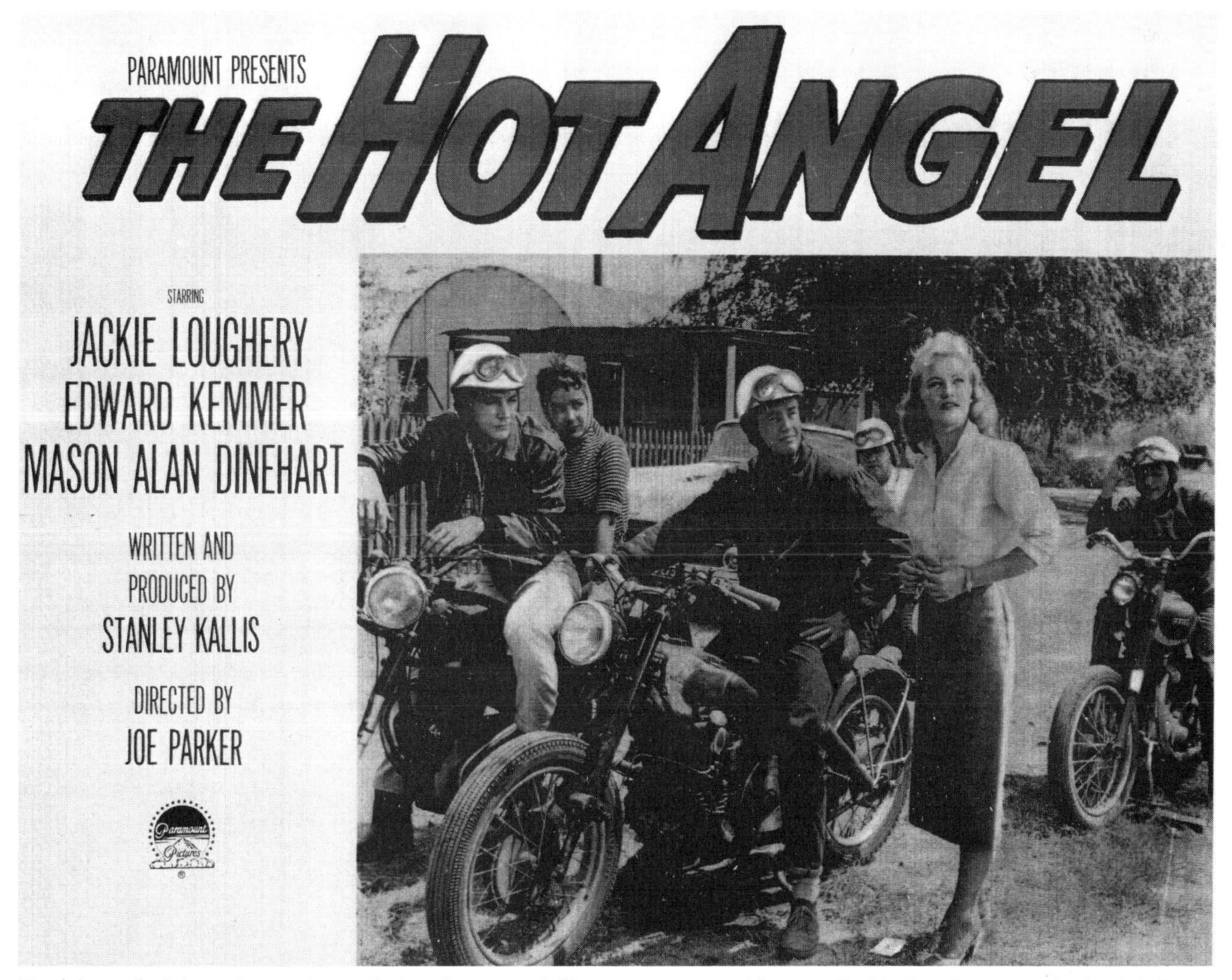

Decisions, decisions. It wasn't easy being the smart doll when you're just dying to run with a fast-livin' motorcycle gang. Jackie Loughery was the lead doll in *The Hot Angel. Paramount/ Ron Main Collection*

to crush him with the grease rack. It gets better... Luke becomes the Pacemakers' president and beats up Vince. Meanwhile, at a beach dance, Vince tries to rape Sheila, Luke's pal Frank is furious, and again Vince is challenged to a "chicken" race. Joe and Luke build a dragster—The White Monster—but it throws a rod and the Pacemakers give Luke a "heap" so he can enter the demo derby to get money to repair the dragster. Vince is also entered in the drag race, but with insurance—a gun! On race day, Cindy finds Frank at the track, and he manages to stuff a pencil down the barrel of the gun as Vince drives up to the starting line. They just don't make 'em like this anymore! This epic was filmed in and around Washington, D.C., and the nearby towns of Aquasco, Maryland, and Manassas, Virginia, where the drag strip and racetracks were located.—RM

Hot Rod Rumble

(1957) *Rumble* stars Brett Halsey, Leigh Snowden, Richard Hartunian, and Joey Forman. When a new member of a hot rod club gets accused of causing another hot rodder's death, the result is the inevitable Hot Rod Rumble. Put up your dukes, man.

Hot Rods to Hell

(1967) This was originally made for TV (titled *52 Miles to Midnight*) and was the last movie directed by John Brahm. It stars Dana Andrews, Jeanne Crain, Mimsy Farmer, and Laurie Mock. This one is really corny, but fun. When a family is driving away for a vacation, they encounter a hot-rodded, fenderless Model A roadster and an early Corvette, both filled with street racers who are headed for the same motel as the family. The family's young daughter gets turned on by the reckless thrill-seekers, and when they all arrive she goes into heat and takes a ride in a Hot Rod To Hell (almost).

"Call them punks... Call them animals... But you better get out of their way! They're souped-up for thrills and there's no limit to what they'll do!"

Ads and publicity posters for *Hot Car Girl* show a girl being tossed from a car as it speeds through a railroad crossing sign. While the girl is spit out of the raging rag top, the teenager at the wheel gives her a look like, "Gee, she's being thrown from the car to her death. So I guess I can finish her french fries, eh?" *Allied Artists/ Ron Main Collection*

The Robert Petersen publishing empire hasn't dabbled often in feature films, but it did so most successfully with the 1966 film *Hot Rod Action.* This one serves as an outstanding chronicle of racing of the early sixties. It's a racing time capsule that we wish someone would recreate every five to ten years to preserve the feel of each era in racing. *Cinerama Releasing/ Ron Main Collection*

How to Stuff a Wild Bikini

(1965) Thank goodness there's some hot rodding and some motorcycles in this flick so we can include it here. Ridiculous, but we love it! The lovely Annette, Dwayne (Dobie Gillis) Hickman, Harvey Lembeck, and Mickey (yes, he sings) Rooney star in this one. And for the girls, there's cool John Ashley, and 70-year-old Buster Keaton (Bwana) conjures up a floating bikini and then "stuffs" it with Beverly (Wow!) Adams. Music is by the Kingsmen, and watch for Brian Wilson of the Beach Boys with four Playboy playmates, including Marianne Gaba, Miss September 1959. What are you waiting for? This is the wildest and most ridiculous motorcycle race ever run.—RM

In Tandem

(1974) *In Tandem* was made for television and was later released as *Movin' On*, which led to the *Movin' On* TV series. *In Tandem* stars Claude Akins, Frank Converse, Sondra Blake, Richard Angarola, Ann Coleman, Janis Hansen, and Titos Vandis. The story is about a mismatched pair of truckers who get caught up with labor problems. There is good acting and lots of action.

Way-out, daddy! *Hot Rod Gang's* got it all: rods, customs, chicks, groovy tunes we can dig, and starlet Jody Fair. Dig, man! *American International/ Ron Main Collection*

Indianapolis Speedway

(1939) This is a Warner Brothers picture that still shows up on TV from time to time. The plot is built around a rivalry between a pair of brothers who share in interest in racing open-wheel cars around the old dirt ovals in Salinas, San Diego, and Ventura County, California, as well as Tucson, Arizona, and in Mexico. Joe Greer is played by Pat O'Brien, and his brother Eddie is played by John Payne. Joe is the successful one who tries unsuccessfully to discourage his younger brother from becoming a race driver. Prime Sports TV network affiliates run it once in a while.

Inside Detroit

(1956) *Inside Detroit* was a movie that set out to show auto workers' labor union problems. It sets out to document American auto workers struggling against the threat of corruption by the mob. The cast includes Dennis O'Keefe, Pat O'Brien, Margaret Field, and Mark Damon. The story drags along slowly and it really is a tiring picture. There is little here to interest the car buff. The cars shown are mostly from 1954-1956, with a few earlier, but it's really more about labor than the product. The movie is a very long disappointment.

It Started With a Kiss

(1959) Glenn Ford stars as a serviceman stationed in Madrid, Spain, and Debbie Reynolds is his wife in this enjoyable comedy. The couple wins an incredible car in a contest. In this case, it's a customized, bubble-top Ford Futura—whose looks greatly resemble those of the original Batmobile. Their winning the prize leads to some hi-jinx and puts them in some real jams, but all turns out well in the end. Eva Gabor, Harry Morgan, and Edgar Buchanan also star. Fun, late-fifties fare.—MDa

It's a Mad Mad Mad Mad World

(1963) You'll never see a film like this made again. Movie stars' schedules and especially their salaries and egos will never allow it to happen. The who's who of sixties' comedians were packed into this zany farce about a mad, mad, etc. race to find buried treasure. Spencer Tracy is the detective who watches the likes of Sid Caesar, Milton Berle, Buddy Hackett, Ethyl Merman, Jonathan Winters, Phil Silvers, Mickey Rooney, Terry-Thomas, and many more chase after the loot left by Jimmy Durante, who literally kicks the bucket in this film. Fans of the late, great Dick Shawn *must* see his performance in this one. Of all the mad-cap driving that goes on here, his sprint to save his mama is the best.—MDa

The Italian Job

(1969) This one is so sixties it hurts. Michael Caine is a swinging thief in tight flared slacks who decides to rob the Italian Fiat car maker's bankroll, which for some reason is trucked around in gold bars. So he gets together a gang of race and rally drivers to stage the heist in downtown Turin during the big England vs. Italy soccer match, creating a traffic jam to thwart the carabinieri while his gang escapes through the sewers in rally-prepped Mini Coopers. Problem is, the carabinieri have their own little Alfa Romeo Giulia Berlinas and keep up with the Britishers—except that the Italians can't drive worth a cappuccino and all crash. And that's the way with a lot of the movie's "humor": jokes about stupid Eye-talians in all their stereotypical forms.

But it's the cars we're here to see and there's lots of them in *The Italian Job*. The movie opens with an orange Lamborghini Miura blasting its way through the Italian Alps before crashing into the Mafia's evil bulldozer at the end of a dark tunnel (never fear; you can tell they didn't wreck a real Miura when they roll the car off the cliff). Caine and his gang drive an Aston Martin DB4 cabriolet and two Jaguar E-Types, all of which are senselessly destroyed by the Mafia's merciless bulldozer. For their escape, the thieves leave in a long-wheelbase Land Rover 109 before switching to the three Mini Coopers.

Hitting the highway, the Mini Coopers catch up with the robbers' special bus and drive up ramps into the back; this bus was actually a race team transporter. The final scenes leave the bus stranded in the ultimate cliffhanger ending.

Directed by Peter Collinson, *The Italian Job* also starred Noel Coward, swinging sixties chick Maggie Blye, suave Italian blade Raf Vallone, and Benny Hill as a wacko girl-grabbing computer hacker.—MDr

The Jalopy

(1953) "Meet the Cracked Blocks of Racing!" That's what the ads cried because the Bowery Boys are at it again, and when they go racing, the results are hilarious. Leo Gorcey's (Slip Mahoney) old Model T Ford is unbeatable using Satch's (Huntz Hall) new rocket fuel that he concocted in the back room of Louie's Sweet Shop. Lovely Jane Easton uses all her charms to steal Satch's secret formula. In the big race, this Ford goes at a furious

Former professional baseball player and future TV "Rifleman" Chuck Connors plays the heavy here, trying to shut down the illegal racers in *Hot-Rod Girl.* *American International/ Ron Main Collection*

pace—backwards! It was filmed at Culver City Speedway in California.—RM

Johnny Dark

(1954) *JD* stars Tony Curtis, Piper Laurie, Don Taylor, Paul Kelly, Ilka Chase, and Sidney Blackmer. Curtis designs his own sports racer and enters a road race that runs from Canada to Mexico, where he competes against a former friend. Although the film is largely forgotten now, there's good acting and some good racing footage.

Junkman

(1982) From the same man who brought us *Gone in 60 Seconds*—H. B. "Toby" Halicki—comes an orgy of car action: races, chases, and no shortage of crashes. This epic includes Toby in the cast as well as the director's chair, while costars include country-western singer Hoyt Axton, Lynda Day George, Susan Shaw, and Christopher Stone. Halicki was killed in August 1989 while at work on a sequel to *Gone in 60 Seconds*.—MDa

If you're looking for a groovy shindig with swingers who are with it, check out *Hot Rod Hullabaloo*. Crazy, man. *Allied Artists/ Ron Main Collection*

Killdozer

(1974) In this heavy machinery thriller, a deadly dozer with a mind of its own tries to do in Clint Walker, Robert Urich, and an entire construction crew. The dozer carries the spirit (or whatever you call it) of an alien as it runs rampant against the men. The cast includes Carl Betz, the father from TV's "The Donna Reed Show". Bulldozer fans will also want to check out the big dozers used in films such as *Tremors*, *Lethal Weapon*, *Vanishing Point* (ouch!), and *Fighting Seabees*, which stars the Duke, John Wayne. Under fire from snipers, the Duke drives a bulldozer into a gas tank to touch off a huge fire to thwart some oncoming tanks.—MDa

King of the Mountain

(1981) This film stars Harry Hamlin, Joseph Bottoms, Deborah Van Walkenburgh, and Dennis Hopper. It's about street racing in sports cars on the winding roads in the Hollywood hills (like Mulholland Drive), trying to set the lowest time between two points.

There's a nice silver 1958 Porsche Speedster, a fancy Porsche 911 with wheel flares, a Boss Mustang, and a hot-rodded '65 Corvette coupe with no hood. Bottoms plays the pop songwriter with the Speedster, and Hopper plays the reclusive eccentric who lost it out on Mulholland Drive in his Stingray years ago and spends his time alone philosophizing and growing his hair. "I know what you're thinking man—you beat the mountain. It's not that easy." (And in the flashback scene to his wipeout, the producers dubbed in an audio track that was a recording of a four-cylinder!) The climax involves a race between the Corvette and the Speedster. *King of the Mountain* is interesting because of the sports cars in it. If it wasn't for Hopper and the cars, it would have stunk.

Knightriders

(1981) Here is an excellent movie about a group that travels around performing medieval fairs where knights on motorcycles joust. It was written and directed by George Romero, and stars Ed Harris, Gary Lahti, Tom Savini, Amy Ingersoll, Patricia Tallman, Christine Forrest, Warner Shook, and Brother Blue.

La Strada

(1954) *La Strada* is my pick as one of the best movies of all time—and *the* best road movie. "La Strada" is Italian for "The Road," and the film was created by the eccentric visionary Italian director Federico Fellini and takes place in post-World War II Italy.

The great Anthony Quinn stars as a brutish traveling circus strongman who tours Italy on a three-wheeled motorcycle, setting up his show in the *piazze* of war-torn towns to perform stunts like breaking chains with his chest. For a wife and show companion, he buys a simple-minded waif (played by Giulietta Masina, Fellini's wife) from her mother. The movie turns into a tragic love story that won't leave a dry eye in the house.

Motorheads will want to keep an eye on Quinn's motorcycle. At one point in the movie, Quinn tells Masina that his trusty steed is American made, which makes you think it must be a war-surplus Harley-Davidson or perhaps a prewar Indian. Yet although the cycle is a major character throughout the film, there's never a good shot of the cycle's engine to identify it. At some points it looks like a horizontal single-cylinder Moto Guzzi.

The film also stars Richard Basehart as the Fool, another circus showman. *La Strada* won 1954's Best Foreign Film Oscar, and is backed by a great musical score by Nino Rota.—MDr

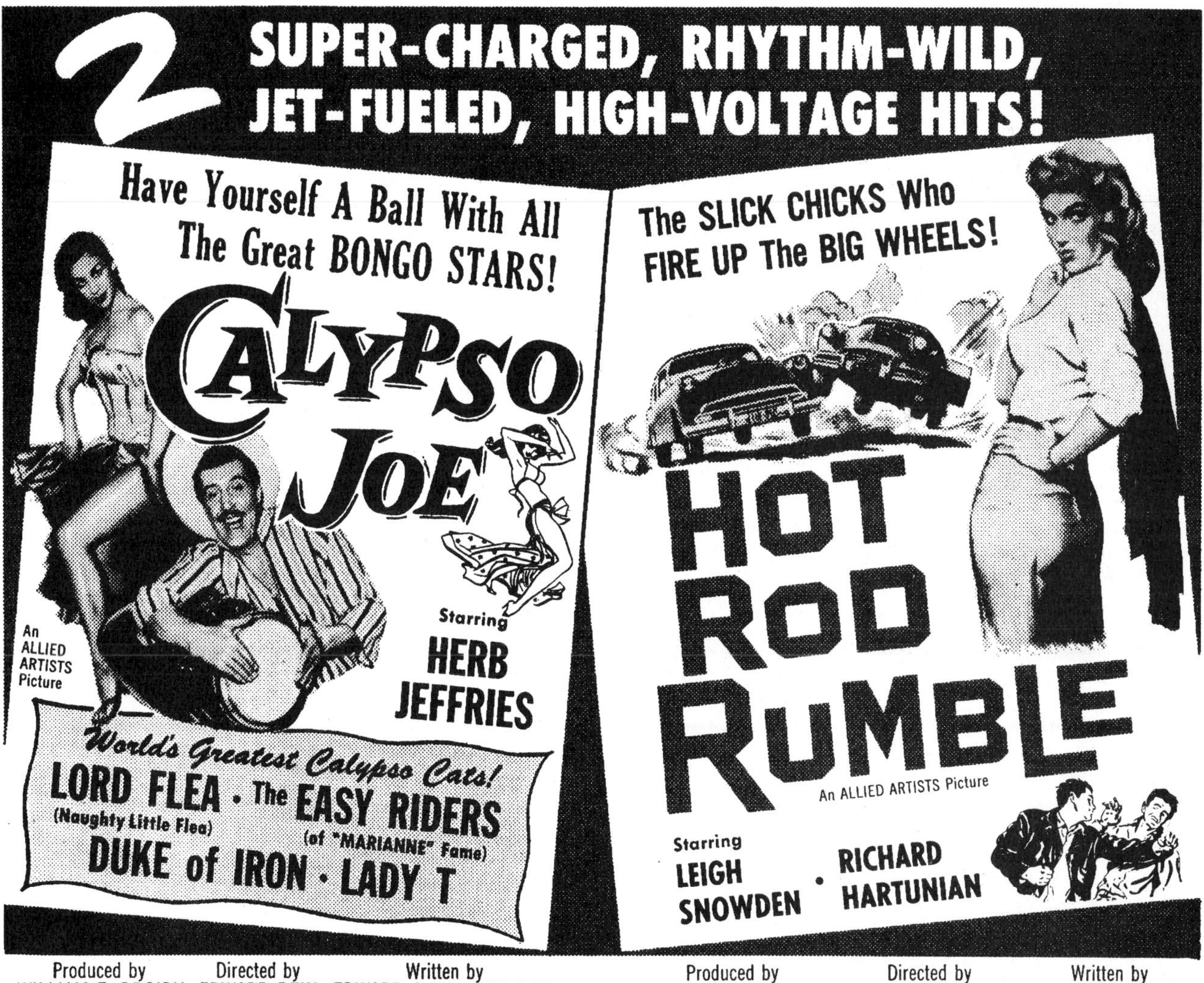

Theaters were probably best served by showing *Calypso Joe* first, followed by *Hot Rod Rumble*, just to avoid inspired movie-goers breaking into melees at the snack counter between features. Maybe we're just nostalgic, but there simply aren't enough car movies these days that are "jet-fueled with that Bongo Beat!" like these two. *Allied Artists/ Ron Main Collection*

The Last American Hero

(1973) This is based on the book with the same name by Tom Wolfe. Both set out to document the life of NASCAR racing legend Junior Johnson. Jeff Bridges does a good job here as Junior, with Valerie Perrine, Art Lund, Geraldine Fitzgerald, Ed Lauter, and Gary Busey in the cast. This movie was shown on television as "Hard Driver".

Some authentic NASCAR racing footage is woven in throughout the picture. In the early part of the movie most of the stock cars are 1963-1967 Chevelles. Later on there is a good cross-section of late-sixties and early-seventies Chevy, Dodge, Ford and Plymouth NASCAR Grand National race cars. The racing coverage is decent but not outstanding.

The movie is a decent tribute to a great man. It's interesting to compare *The Last American Hero* with *Days of Thunder*. This one was done with a small fraction of the budget of the other, and is a lot more believable and representative of stock car racing.

Today, Junior Johnson is still at it, running his own winning team on the NASCAR Winston Cup circuit, with Hut Stricklin driving the McDonald's Ford Thunderbird. Mr. "Cole Trickle" and his entourage went back to Hollywood.

The Last Chase

(1981) Here is a Canadian movie starring Lee Majors, Burgess Meredith, Chris Makepeace, Alexander Stewart, and Ben Gordon. The world ran out of oil in the eighties, and twenty years later Majors digs his old Porsche out of the ground and heads out on what becomes a statement and a chase.

Dwayne Hickman had his 15 minutes of fame as the star of TV's "Dobie Gillis Show". *How to Stuff...* was among the few films in which he starred. *Ron Main Collection*

The Last Ride

(1944) This is the second of two movies about the black market for automotive tires during World War II. It's not the most exciting movie in the book but it's still significant from a historical perspective.

The Last Riders

(1990) With its excellent opening scenes—a thong bikini-clad babe (who is a professional wrestler) kicks the tar out of two bikers with whom she has just conducted a drug deal—this film showed great potential, but it didn't pan out. That's surprising, too, since it has some choice elements such as an all-chick heavy metal band in tight leathers (The Sheila's), and Erik Estrada in the lead role of Johnny, the biker who is wronged by both the cops and his biker gang mates—the Slavers—and has to kill most of them as revenge since they killed his wife and child. After the strong start the film wastes our time by developing characters and a story line. Hey, we want action, like the opening scenes, and the series of vengeance beatings Johnny (Ponch's bad brother perhaps?) dishes out. Lots of chopped Harleys, lots of swearing, no nudity, and too few action scenes.—MDa

The Last Run

(1971) *The Last Run* stars George C. Scott and a BMW 503 roadster, along with Tony Musante, Trish Van Devere, and Colleen Dewhurst. Scott is a driver for the mob, and has one errand to run—he helps a mobster get away from the Spanish police. That's it for the plot, but it's got outstanding photography although it lacks the pace of the better chase movies.

Le Mans

(1971) *Le Mans* is one of the finest racing movies ever made. Steve McQueen plays a race car driver who has had some bad crashes in the past, looking for a win in the annual 24 Hours of Le Mans race. There is excellent coverage of the racing here, with minimal needless "human interest" nonsense thrown in like there usually is. Siegfried Rauch, Elga Andersen and Ronald Leigh-Hunt also act in Le Mans, which was directed by Lee H.

Katzin. The acting, the camera work, and the excitement are as good as it gets. If you think you can do better, every motorsports fan in the world wishes you'd hurry up and release it. (For this film, Steve McQueen built a kit car with a VW powerplant with a turbocharger and nitrous. It was repainted and used in "Herbie Goes to Monte Carlo," and now sits in Guinness Book of Records Museum in Gatlinburg, Tennessee.)—DM

Michael Dregni's review of Le Mans:

This is the kind of movie your date will hate and you'll want to sit in the front row for. Steve McQueen stars as a Porsche 917K driver returning to race at Le Mans after a brutal accident nearly took his life the year before. But you can easily forget the corny storyline and just watch the racing, which was filmed during the actual 24 Heures du Mans in 1971.

The movie is like a documentary of Le Mans, mixing actors with real drivers and race teams, providing some of the best racing footage anywhere, any time. Amidst the smoke and glory of the 250mph Ferrari 512s and Porsche 917s, the most exciting moments are watching British driver Vic Elford in his white 917 long-tail (#25)—Elford wasn't about to let a film crew get in his way of running in the real race!—MDr

Ron Main's review of Le Mans:

This film came from an idea of Steve McQueen's, to actually compete at Le Mans with a camera mounted atop his race car. The year before this film was shot, McQueen had finished second in a Porsche behind Mario Andretti at Sebring, and he won at Holtsville and Phoenix. Even after qualifying at Le Mans, the producers said no, it was just too much to risk, so they rented the course and reshot the race with Steve at the wheel of a 700hp Porsche 917. The film has some real race footage and some of the best camera work ever done, making *Le Mans* one of the finest and most accurate race films ever made.—RM

The Leather Boys

(1963) This British film stars sixties Brit starlet Rita Tushingham as a woman whose husband is a motorcycle enthusiast. The trouble begins when she realizes he cares more about motorcycles than her. Uh-oh! The cast also includes Colin Campbell, Dudley Sutton, and Gladys Henson. As the title might suggest, this one is not for kids. Look for BSA Gold Star Clubmans, Nortons, Triumphs, and other Brit classics in this cult film.—DM

Michael Dregni's review of The Leather Boys:

(1963) This was far from the typical teenploitation biker flicks of the 1960s; instead, here was a sensitive, realistic look at the life of a budding young Rocker in working class England. The story's all too close to the truth: the hero's wife doesn't understand him, his family shuns him, and he's stuck with a BSA when he really wants a Triumph twin. The ending brings in an odd homophobic plot twist, but it leaves our hero to ride the streets alone in the best Western tradition. Scenes filmed live at the famous Ace Cafe will make all Rockers swoon with memories.—MDr

Little Fauss and Big Halsy

(1970) This was a great movie—we all enjoyed it when it was new and it's worth looking at again. Robert Redford is the professional off-road motorcycle racer, and Michael J. Pollard is his mechanic and sidekick. They travel around to various races and have their ups and downs, without there being much more to the story other than Halsy being suspended from racing but going anyway. *Little Fauss and Big Halsy* is no masterpiece, but it's something that every motorcyclist I've asked enjoyed.

The Lively Set

(1964) This film stars James Darren as a guy who quits college to become a professional sports car racer. Among the vehicles in the film is a

With mugs like theirs, Huntz Hall and Leo Gorcey had to be hilarious to become leading men in movies. The Bowery Boys' leaders weren't long on looks, but they knew how to crack up an audience. They also got to try to woo Jane Easton and Mona Knox in *Jalopy. Allied Artists/ Ron Main Collection*

Chrysler turbine-powered car. Ghia of Italy built the body of the car, one of fifty-five Chrysler built, and it was painted white for the movie (the rest were painted Turbine Bronze). The car was later destroyed, as were all but nine of the experimental turbine cars. The cast also includes Pamela Tiffin, Doug McClure, Marilyn Maxwell, Charles Drake, and Greg Morris.

Ron Main's review of The Lively Set:

Thrill to dragster duels powered by a J-47 jet engine. See Chrysler's revolutionary experimental turbine engine car. See Bonneville record cars such as The Challenger 1, owned by Mickey Thompson, who also drives and plays himself here. See Jim (Jazzy) Nelson—Old Leadfoot—who plays himself racing a hyped-up stock car, a 1929 roadster with a 409 Chevy. He races Doug McClure's T-Bucket and the highway patrol wins. This one has lovely Pamela Tiffin and Joanie Sommers for the lonely nights. Get ready!—RM

The Loners

(1988) *The Loners* has Dean Stockwell cast as a motorcyclist who is hassled by a motorist on the highway. He survives by disabling the car and becomes the object of a police chase, hooking up with a buddy and his girlfriend. This one was released on videotape by Bingo Video.

The Long Haul

(1957) Here is another British picture, starring Victor Mature, Diana Dors, Patrick Allen, and Gene Anderson. The original version was 100 minutes and ended up being 88 minutes. It doesn't do nearly as well as the previous several trucking classics. In fact, it's so bad it's laughable. Forget about it.

The gang was crowded around Tiny's Waffle Shop after the big race in *Johnny Dark*, which starred Tony Curtis and Piper Laurie, a veteran of Hitchcock movies and TV's "Twin Peaks". *Universal International/ Ron Main Collection*

The Long, Long Trailer

(1954) Lucille Ball and husband-partner Dezi Arnez star as a couple on a driving honeymoon with an exceptionally large travel trailer in tow. Combine the zany redheaded comedienne with a cumbersome trailer and a curvy mountain road and you've got trouble—and laughs. You'll come away chanting the mantra: "Trailer brakes first, trailer brakes first..."—MDa

The Losers

(1970) This one stars William Smith, Bernie Hamilton, and Adam Roarke. Would you believe that five Hell's Angels went to Cambodia in 1970 with their bikes? Would you believe they were Yamahas?

Races run, friendships strained, romances made and broken. Add it all up and you get *Johnny Dark*, a film that didn't end up atop the list of quality releases for Tony Curtis, who also starred in *Houdini*. *Universal International/ Ron Main Collection*

The Love Bug

(1969) *The Love Bug* was the first of the "Herbie, the Volkswagen that can do anything" series of movies. The cast in this one includes Dean Jones, Michele Lee, Buddy Hackett, David Tomlinson, Joe Flynn, Benson Fong, and Iris Adrian.

This vintage Bug goes through some wild moves, including a harrowing (how do they do it?) two-wheel drive on a curving mountain road. Trivia question: What's the number on Herbie's hood? It's 53.

Our jury is split on *The Last American Hero*. Some jurors love it, claiming it tells the story of a moonshiner-turned-racer—ala Junior Johnson—quite well. Dissenting voices lump it into the *Days of Thunder* category, calling it a failed attempt by Hollywood to tell a great racing story that need not have been botched. *20th Century Fox/ Ron Main Collection*

If you're over 8 years old, you might not get too caught up in the story line. But car buffs will spot lots of interesting classics, including an AC Cobra, Austin Healeys, Corvette and Devin roadsters, and several Ferrari and Jaguar XKE coupes.

The Loveless

(1983) Look out because this one has a gang of bikers on their way to Daytona pulling in to a small town, where there just happens to be some available women, and a bunch of rednecks who don't want them on their turf. Wow! I wonder what happens? This inferior rip-off of *The Wild One* stars J. Don Ferguson, Willem Dafoe, Marlin Kanter, Robert Gordon, Tina L'Hotsky, and Liz Gans, and was directed by Kathryn Bigelow and Monty Montgomery.

Macon County Line

(1974) This one is set in Louisiana in 1954, and is based on a true story. It's not about motorsports, but several people suggested it as one to include here. Two young brothers have two weeks to enjoy before they go into the army, and head out on the highway in their white 1948 Chrysler woody convertible. They offer a ride to a 20-year old girl but soon have problems with the car's fuel pump. They limp into a gas station, where they discover they don't have enough to get a new one, so they pool their money to have the old one patched up. The local redneck cop shows up, asks the mechanic about them and reminds the three that they each have to have at least ten dollars with them or they'll be considered vagrants. After they assure him they'll all be leaving as soon as they can, he and his attitude leave. While they're back on the road that night, the cop's daughter is robbed at their home by a couple of guys. When they realize her dad is a cop they kill her.

Shortly after that, the fuel pump packs it in again, and the three have no choice but to pull over and rest until the next day, and they stop without realizing they're parked right by the cop's house. The stage is now set for a tragic case of mistaken identity. This is not a happy movie but since so many interesting cars are shown it will interest some readers. The movie is full of American cars from the early fifties, including a bullet-nose 1946 Studebaker (driven by the killers) and a T-bucket hot rod shown in the opening. Macon County Line stars Alan Vint, Cheryl Waters, Geoffrey Lewis, Joan Blackman, and Jessie Vint. It was followed by a sequel in 1975, *Return to Macon County*, which has more car chase action.

Mad Max

(1979) Here is a great movie. Mel Gibson plays Max, the soft-spoken highway patrol cop in a future world where the only people who have gas are outlaws and cops. Max drives a Holden police car, which gets fitted with a blown V-8 when the action on the highway heats up. *Mad Max* features a good story, some really good acting from an excellent and diverse cast, and lots of action, excitement, and suspense. In addition to Gibson, the cast includes Joan Samuel, Hugh Keays-Byrne, Steve Bisley, Tim Burns, and Roger Ward.

Mad Max 2—The Road Warrior

(1981) This one has Mel Gibson back as the highway patrol cop fighting the outlaws who are after gasoline, which is scarce. With all of the motorcycles and wild cars, the story, the interesting and diverse cast, the great stunt work, and the quality acting, this is a great action movie. The great cast includes Bruce Spence, Vernon Wells, Mike Preston, Virginia Hay, Emil Minty, and Kjell Nilsson.

Mad Max 3—Beyond the Thunderdome

(1985) Number 3 has less highway action than its two successors, but still qualifies as a motorhead movie. As with all of them, George Miller directed with Mel Gibson as Max. This one also stars George Ogilvie, singer Tina Turner in a saucy role, Angelo Rossitto, Helen Buday, Rod Zuanic, Frank Thring, and Angry Anderson. The whole series is really outstanding, with the first of them, *Mad Max*, still the best.

Mag Wheels

(1977) Phoebe Schmidt, Steven Rose, and the King of the Kustoms himself, George Barris, star in this one. It shows us World War III, and it's the girls in their pickups and the bad boys in their hot vans dragging it out. Barris' whole family got into this one: son Brett is doing chases and stunts, daughter JoJi is jumping a motorcycle into a lake, and lovely wife Shirley plays a housewife.—RM

A Man and a Woman

(1966) This film is one of the finest movies in this book. While it's a love story from France, the plot involves a Formula One driver and his lady. Everything about the movie is outstanding, and it won a pair of Oscars for Best Foreign Film and Best Original Screenplay. The cast includes Anouk Aimee, Jean-Louis Trintignant, Pierre Barouh, and Valerie Lagrange.

The Man With the Golden Gun

(1974) Roger Moore stars as James Bond in this 007 thriller, with Britt Ekland and Maud Adams among the lovely actresses with which he conducts business. The great driving stunts should be considered all the more remarkable since this was virtually an all-AMC production when it came to cars. A Hornet did a barrel-roll jump over a river, and a Matador sprouts wings and flies. Christopher Lee, the legendary horror film star, plays a wonderful villain here, and the late and short Herve Villechaize is also along for the ride.—MDa

The Lively Set* lists among its cast members Mickey Thompson, drag racing star Jim Nelson, sports car champion Bill Krause, and Indy 500 veteran Duane Carter. *Universal/ Ron Main Collection

Maniacs on Wheels

Here's the behind-the-scenes story about the motives and ambitions of the men who race like maniacs. One reason the thrills here are mile-a-minute is the film's authenticity. It was shot on location at Monte Carlo, Mosport, and Monza during actual competitions. Graham Hill, twice world Grand Prix champion, plays himself, and admitted: "I'm somewhat of a kook, you know, a maniac. That's why the title so attracted me!" One would have thought young Italian Giacomo Agostini has enough excitement in his life. After all, he only won the world motorcycle championship six different times! He gets some new thrills in his screen debut, including getting caught with sultry Olinka Berova, the adulterous wife, by Brad Harris. This

Ron Main's Guide to Some Classics

When you are as big a movie enthusiast as Ron Main, you are well qualified to suggest a list of all-time classics. But then again, when you've seen everything from Elvis movies to Zsa Zsa Gabor as the Queen of Outer Space to Tommy Ivo racing in *Dragstrip Girl,* you may have too much to choose from.

We tried to pin Ron down for a list of his faves and his picks as significant car flicks. They include:

• *Hot Rod,* the 1979 version. "One of the coolest racing films ever done," Ron says. Robert Culp, a Willys coupe, a '65 Dodge Hemi, a 442 Olds, great racing, great music, great dialogue, and the need for revenge.

• *The Giant Gila Monster.* "Great teen trash," he said. This 1959 epic includes a big ol' gila monster, rock 'n' roll, "and a '32 Ford hot rod loaded with nitro that saves the world." There's the stupid monster, and footage of models and toys meant to look like real scenery and equipment.

• *Hot Rod,* the 1950 version. "It's the ultimate, grand-daddy hot rod movie," Ron says. It's got hot action on the dry lakes like El Mirage; illegal hot rodders, "and a classic showdown race that ends in tragedy... It shows the way it was in the beginning of hot rodding."

• *Death Race 2000.* "This was the most outrageous car movie. And the uncut version was much sexier."

• *Vanishing Point.* "A milestone car action movie. Legendary."

• *On Any Sunday.* "The greatest motorcycle movie ever made."

• *Bullit.* "The ultimate chase scene ever filmed."

• *Hollywood Knights.* This is a 1980 film starring Tony Danza (in his first feature role), Michelle Pfeiffer, Fran Drescher, and hot rod legend Tony Nancy. It's a movie that didn't wow the critics or score big at the box offices, but Ron says it's a winner. "If this film were made ten years later, it would have been the *Wayne's World* of today. It's got racing, comedy ..." and plenty of the action Ron loves.

• *Harley Davidson and the Marlboro Man.* "Don Johnson is great."

• *Fireball 500*: This one was filmed at the now-defunct Ascot racetrack in Los Angeles, and featured a great Barris-built car, the Thundercharger, which is now a show car.

• *Love in a Goldfish Bowl.* "Fabian, a '32 Ford roadster, and Dick Stritchfield's car. Great!"

• *The Big Wheel.* "This is my favorite racing movie. It's got so much heart and so much excitement." Mickey Rooney drives the final ten laps at the Indy 500 with his car on fire, refusing to give up or stop.

• *To Please a Lady.* This is Ron's top pick among big-budget Hollywood car movies. It's got stars (Clark Gable and Barbara Stanwyck), Indy racer Mauri Rose (who doubled for Gable during driving scenes filmed at Indy), and Joie Chitwood's thrill team. "When they filmed this one, Clark and the real Indy racers were each other's heroes."

• *Burn 'em Up O'Conner:* A most outrageous racing movie in which the hero drives his final race blind. A mechanic runs to the corners and blows a whistle to signal the driver when to turn. Indy winner Sam Hanks did all the driving for the cameras—with his eyes open, we presume.

• *Burn 'em Up Barnes.* A cliffhanger with non-stop peril that involves everything from race cars to motorcycles to boats as the hero fights the bad guys to save a kindly woman's bus company.

Among his favorite actors are Mickey Rooney, who was an intense race car driver in *The Big Wheel,* and Robert Mitchum (*Thunder Road*) and Ryan O'Neal (*The Driver*). "They're very cool," Ron says.

If you're just getting started as a B movie fan, Ron suggests you watch *Hot Rod Girl.* "It's got girls, a lot of heart, and the line, 'We've got to have a chicken race!'" He also recommends *Teenage Thunder* and *Dragstrip Girl.*

role was tailor-made for the kinds of thrills he was used to. So get ready to ride flat out... on the rim of death!—RM

Mask

(1985) *Mask* stars Eric Stoltz as Rocky, a teenager with a very rare disease that has left his face horribly disfigured. Cher plays his mother and Sam Elliott is cast as her boyfriend, who rides a custom Harley-Davidson as do all of their friends. The movie is based on the actual story of Rocky Dennis, and it's a great story and a fine movie. The script was written by Anna Hamilton Phelps. Everyone connected with *Mask* did a fine job and it's highly recommended.

Masters Of Menace

(1990) *M.O.M.* is a *comical*, mediocre, phony, stupid, stereotypical portrayal of motorcyclists as dumb violent bad guys. You may find it funny, but no promises. Worth watching for the few scenes of the Top Fuel Harley-Davidson drag bike—probably the only movie in the book to feature one.

Maximum Overdrive

(1986) This one's a Stephen King thriller that could be considered the predecessor to his *Christine*, with big trucks driving themselves by some unknown force, with deadly results. As the story develops all kinds of motorized vehicles and electrical devices start attacking people. The soundtrack, by AC/DC, is a nice touch to a very bizarre movie.

Megaforce

(1982) This flick uses customized troop carrier van that is now on display at the Miami Beach Police Museum. It also appears in parades. Barry Bostwick stars as the leader of a crime-fighting outfit loaded with what's supposed to be thoroughly modern.

Midnite Spares

(1982) *Midnight Spares* features a monster truck and is called a "demolition extravaganza." The story is based around a former race car driver who finds out his father is missing and that the family's towing business is dealing in stolen parts. Sixty-five vehicles are totaled in the movie, which is available on videotape.

The Miniskirt Mob

(1968) *Mob* stars Jeremy Slate, Diane McBain, Sherry Jackson, Patty McCormack, Ross Hagen, Harry Dean Stanton, and Ronnie Rondell, with Diane McBain playing the leader of another all-girls biker gang.

The Moon in the Gutter

(1985) This one was directed by Jean-Jacques Beineix, who also created the stunning *Diva*. Unfortunately, this flick is painfully pretentious and painfully boring. It's film noir in color, both overwrought and over-long—all this despite Nastassia Kinski and her red Ferrari 250GT California cabriolet.—MDr

Moonrunners

(1974) This film is based on the life of the North Carolina folk hero Jerry Rushing, starring James Mitchum, Kiel Martin, Arthur Hunnicut, Joan Blackman, singer Waylon Jennings, and Chris Forbes. This movie has lots of chase scenes, and was the basis for the popular "Dukes of Hazzard" TV series.—DM

Michael Dregni's review of Moonrunners:

Moonrunners is based on the life of North Carolina moonshine-runner and folk hero Jerry Rushing. Here's a case of art imitating life imitating art, or a celluloid déjà vû: in real life, Rushing drove a hot-rodded car that was complete with all the best James Bond gimmicks. It had owner-installed options such as a twenty-gallon oil dump tank and secret switches that turned off all of the car's running lights. Rushing's car was a Chrysler 300D Letter Series car with specially modified suspension to handle the 'shine and an engine that could power the car to 140mph even fully loaded. The Hollywood version of Rushing's life starred James Mitchum, Kiel Martin, Arthur Hunnicut, Joan Blackman, singer Waylon Jennings, and Chris Forbes.

Moonrunners became the basis for the TV series "Dukes of Hazzard", which featured a whole stunt-car army of stand-in Dodge Chargers painted in fire-engine red as the good ol' Duke boys' General Lee. A bit of trivia: Why was the Dukes of Hazzard's Charger named General Lee? Well, Jerry Rushing's original trick moonrunner car was named "Traveler," which was the name of Confederate Civil War General Robert E. Lee's trusty steed, so why not name the TV show counterpart General Lee?—MDr

Moonshine County Express

(1977) This film stars John Saxon, Susan Howard, the late William Conrad (star of TV's Cannon), Morgan Woodward, Claudia Jennings,

Jeff Corey, Dib Taylor, and Maureen McCormick (Marcia of TV's "Brady Bunch"). When a moonshiner is murdered, his three daughters decide to go up against the competitor they suspect of killing him. There's some good chase scenes and the movie is pretty good.

More American Graffiti

(1979) *"More"* has several segments that were shot at Fremont Raceway in Northern California, with Paul LeMat playing the role of John Milner, a young privateer running his blown small-block Chevy dragster. The parts of the movie that deal with racing feature a good variety of race cars, although the story deals more with his interest in a visiting Norwegian girl than with drag racing. Diamond P Sports/TNN racing commentator Steve Evans appears as the track announcer. The film lacks the excitement and humor of the original American Graffiti, but you'll want to see it if you're a drag racing fan.

Motor Psycho!

(1965) *"Psycho!"* stars Haji, Alex Rocco, Steven Oliver, and Coleman Francis. It's a classic Russ Meyer biker movie, with the bikers setting themselves up for revenge after they commit a murder. And if you're wondering about Haji, let's just say she makes Dolly Parton look "rather malnourished," okay? What else would you expect from Russ Meyer.

Motorcycle Gang

(1957) This is another classic from American International Pictures. It stars Anne Neyland, John Ashley, Carl Switzer, Raymond Hatton, and Edmund Cobb. When an outlaw gang of bikers gets out of control, the law tries to hold them back.

James Darren gets a little help from girlfriend-cum-mechanic Pamela Tiffin in *The Lively Set. Universal/ Ron Main Collection*

Motorcycle Squad

This film stars Kane Richmond and Wynne Gibson. It's about a motorcycle cop who is taken off the force so he can join a gang of crooks.

Moving Violation

(1976) Here's a film that is more squealing tires, with a plot based around a young couple being chased by a sheriff. The cast includes Stephen McHattie, Kay Lenz, Eddie Albert, Lonny Chapman, Will Geer, and Jack Murdock.

Mr. Kagle and the Baby Sitter

(1956) Talk about buried treasure! I've wanted to see this one ever since I read about it in *Rod and Custom* way back in '56. It was one of the first times Norm Grabowski's T ("Kookie Car") was used in films. He got fifty bucks per day and has been star-struck ever since. In the story, Charles Coburn, who is about 90, decides to elope with Fay Holden. He is so overwhelmed with romantic intentions that he takes his grandson's hot rod and storms away to the closest justice of the peace, but gets nailed for exhibition of speed by the local sheriff. Norm told me that Coburn couldn't handle his 300+ horsepower, 1,500lb rocket, so they had to make a 12ft tow bar. They shot him in close-up while the car was being towed around. The rest is hot rod history! I wonder how many dreams this hot rod film inspired?—RM

Mr. Roadrunner

(1950) This was a British movie that included among its stars a fabulous Vincent Rapide big twin motorcycle.—MDr

Munster, Go Home

(1966) America's funniest family in their first film. Fred Gwynne, Yvonne DeCarlo, Al Lewis, Butch Patrick, and—making her film debut as the niece—pert Debbie Watson. The cross-country race is the highlight of the film, but "car" is hardly the word for Herman's ride. "Dragula" is a dragster like no other, and WOW! does it move! It goes from O to over 150mph in a matter of seconds. To stop, you are braked to a halt by a parachute. It looks like a coffin on wheels. The casket is powered by a 500hp Ford engine. The engine's exhaust pipes are metal organ tubes that are, believe it or not, tuned! The sound is out of this world. Dragula was created by George Barris, the kustom kar king of North Hollywood who also built the family car called "The Munster Koach," which is a ghoulish version of a Beverly Hillbillies type of family hauler. The enclosed section of the Koach contains a laboratory for Grandpa Munster. The road-race, interspersed with a fox hunt, is hilarious. A four coffin rating!—RM

My Own Private Idaho

(1992) This one was a good but uneven movie by new-wave director Gus Van Zant, who also created *Drugstore Cowboy*. We'll disregard the eccentricities of the plot here but just mention that a major episode centers around the two heroes (the late River Phoenix and Keanu Reeves) stealing a dazzlingly beautiful yellow Dunstall Norton and riding it two-up(!) across half of Washington and Idaho(!). This portion of the film is so realistic that there's even a scene that centers around the duo having the usual trouble kickstarting the beast.—MDr

Naked Angels

(1969) This is a 1969 release produced by someone you've never heard of and starring people never heard of since. Equal parts sex, violence, nudity, bug eating, and getting whupped with pool cues. Guys with names like Mouse, Mother, and Jesus take chicks that look like Nancy Sinatra and head for a rumble in Vegas. J.D. flips out in the desert and tries to make Marlene provide service

We doubt whether modern-era drivers like Nigel Mansell would agree to appear in a movie called *Maniacs on Wheels.* In the loosey-goosey sixties, though, World Champion Graham Hill was comfortable enough with his image that he welcomed the chance to appear in the movie, even saying that the title appealed to him because he considered himself something of a maniac. *Cinemation Industries/ Ron Main Collection*

for the gang. It climaxes with a pointless fight and just sort of ends. Worth the two buck rental? No,

Look out, man, it's another Russ Meyer release, *Motor Psycho,* which gave Russ the chance to mix his favorite theme—buxom women—with motorcycle gang action. Excellent combo, Russ. It's hard to find fault with a movie that bills itself as "cycle maniacs assaulting and killing for THRILLS!" Far out. *Eve/ Ron Main Collection*

but partially redeemed by a great fuzz guitar soundtrack.—SG

Night on Earth

(1991) While this isn't particularly a car enthusiast's movie, its characters are filmed almost exclusively in their cars, in this case, five taxi cabs in different cities around the globe. Jim Jarmusch directed this film, which is mostly a comedy but also has its touching points. Winona Ryder, Gena Rowlands, and Rosie Perez are among the best-known cast members, but some of the others really shine, particularly when Armin Mueller-Stahl (portraying a New York City cabby) has Giancarlo Esposito as his fare. Their exchange on their names is classic. Cabs include Ryder's massive Caprice wagon and a Volvo sedan that carries drunks through Helsinki on a cold winter's night.—MDa

No Limit

No Limit is a light-hearted thirties British romp starring George Formby and Florence Desmond, and directed by Monty Banks. It deals with the antics of George Shuttleworth, "Speed Demon," as he attempts to race his "Shuttleworth Snap" at the Isle of Man TT. Shuttleworth's racing credentials are vague to non-existent (his occupation is chimney sweep's assistant). His bike is a heavily disguised twenties AJS side-valve. On the ferry boat the movie reveals itself to be a musical of sorts when Shuttleworth whips out a ukulele and leads the crowd in "Riding in the TT Races." Once on the island he sets a lap record by virtue of his throttle jamming open (this features a few good driver's eye views); steals his factory-ride opponent's girl, ("Riding on a Rainbow"); does a blackface routine ("In My Garden"); gets a factory ride (a disguised Ariel Red Hunter); and wins the TT in a race full of zany crashes and a lot of nerfing. He an Miss Desmond live happily ever after ("Walking Together").

This is a difficult movie to categorize. With only four songs, it isn't quite a musical, though credit does go to Ord Hamilton and his 20th Century Band for backup. As a romantic comedy it has Desmond as a brash, spunky, resourceful sort of a gal, but perplexes us with Formby, who is unattractive, slow-witted, and talks like Joey Dunlop. Its most frustrating failure is, unfortunately, as a bike movie. Obviously made by people who neither knew, nor liked, bikes, it was intended for a like-minded audience. A big slice of pre-war TT racing or bike week atmosphere would have been great, but Monty Banks appeared to have only stuck in a bike where absolutely necessary. Watching it, I was reminded of the Elvis-Nancy Sinatra epic, *Speedway*: Romance, a few songs, but little for the stock car historian. *No Limit* has even less for bike enthusiasts. Recommended only for fans of light musical comedy. Availability unknown.—SG

No Man's Land

(1987) This one is a "must see" for Porsche fans. Charlie Sheen, D.B Sweeney, Lara Harris, Randy Quaid, Bill Duke, R.D. Call, and M. Emmet Walsh star in the story of a young cop who gets assigned to gather evidence. The target is a murder suspect who is a car thief that specializes in exotic Porsches, which usually get chopped up and sold for parts. Like most movies, this story suffers from being compressed into a couple of hours. There are several exciting chase scenes that feature fast driving and good photography, with the camera occasionally mounted outside the door and close to the ground. One particularly good chase scene has the cop and his target driving a stolen Porsche while being chased by a rival gang in a Lincoln Continental and a late Camaro. *No Man's Land* is no masterpiece but it's one of the better movies of its kind, largely due to Charlie Sheen's performance as the thief and the picture's technical qualities.

No Time to Be Young

(1957) Too old to be teenagers, too young to be adults, Robert (*Man from U.N.C.L.E.*) Vaughn, Roger Smith (of *77 Sunset Strip*), and Tom Pittman (of *High School Big Shot*) star in this mile-a-minute story of teenage love, robbery, car chases, murder, and death. The beauties in tight

Lou Russoff wrote the screenplay for *Motorcycle Gang*, one of dozens of Hollywood pieces for which he served as most capable wordsmith. He loved to dish up the action at a fever pace. *American International/ Ron Main Collection*

sweaters include Dorothy Green, Mary Anders, and Kathy Nolan (Kate on TV's "The Real McCoys").—RM

The Northville Cemetery Massacre

(1976) This massacre was directed by William Dear and stars David Hyry, Carson Jackson, J. Craig Collicut, and Jan Sisk. When a non-violent motorcycle gang is falsely accused of attacking someone, they fight back against the sheriff and the people of a small town.

The Notorious Gentleman

(1945) This is a British film about a race car driver who's a playboy. The stars are Rex Harrison and Lilli Palmer. This movie was also released under the title *The Rake's Progress*.

Nowhere to Run

(1993) Action flick stud Jean-Claude Van Damme is an escaped con on the lam who gets around on a motorcycle, occasionally parking it long enough to stomp bad guys all in the name of helping a young widow/mother in need. Van Damme's scripts should consist of minimal dialogue and lots of instructions such as "kick the hell out of three guys," and "disable and cripple four bad guys who jump you." This plot stinks, and there's not as much action as hoped for, but it's a giant leap more watchable than the rot that overfed, overhyped, alleged action hero Steven Seagal puts out.—MDa

On Any Sunday

(1971) *On Any Sunday* was the original motorcycle racing documentary directed by Bruce Brown, which was followed ten years later by *On Any Sunday 2.* This one shows lots of off-road riders playing on the desert, including famous riders like Mert Lawwill, Steve McQueen, and Malcolm Smith. There are some hilarious shots of riders competing and kidding around. *On Any Sunday* is

Motorcycle Gang was released on a twin-bill with _Sorority Girl_, which was loaded with nasty, nasty college girls. Yeow! Unfortunately, double features at theaters have gone the way of double headers in major league baseball. Today, they're a memory and a dream. _American International/ Ron Main Collection_

The late Fred Gwynne was as much of a gentleman as was kind-hearted Herman Munster. In real life, Gwynne was also a veteran of the Broadway stage who lived in Connecticut and enjoyed a lively game of tennis. He sometimes shooed kids from courtside by turning and yelling "Boo!," but he wasn't the sort to hurt a flea. *Universal/ Ron Main Collection*

highly recommended for the whole family. More than twenty years later, it's still The One.—DM

Steve Gray's review of On Any Sunday:

Everyone should see this one. Nominated in 1971 for a best documentary academy award, this was a labor of love for write/producer/director/cameraman Bruce Brown assisted by Steve McQueen, Malcolm Smith, and Mert Lawwill. It was a less complex world then. You could motocross, desert race, hill climb, and cow trail on the same bike. The national flat-track title was being contested by guys who would drive three days straight in a Econoline to duke it out with Harleys and BSAs, riding with busted legs, ribs, and noses. When desert racing one had to watch out for those goofy turtles. The "widowmaker" was *the* hill climb venue, with Malcolm Smith freaking out the crowd by riding DOWN the hill after his run. (He was also a trials expert.) A heck of a fun movie, 90 minutes long with a perky "5th Dimension" type soundtrack. Available at some video rentals, also can be bought mail order.—SG

On Any Sunday 2

(1981) "2" was directed by Ed Forsyth and Don Shoemaker, unlike the first which was the work of Bruce Brown. While it didn't match the original for excitement and laughs it's still a worthwhile look at off-road motorcycle racing.

On Her Majesty's Secret Service

(1969) This film featured George Lazenby (who?) as James Bond; Sean Connery had left for other roles. All in all, even though it's not one of the early classics in the same league as *Goldfinger*, this may be one of the most exciting Bond movies ever. There are car chases, ski chases, luge chases, and more. Telly Savalas is the baddy in his best

Oh, the dream life of the star playboy-racer in *Out of Sight*. Here's a groovy California beach pad, right next to some bitchin' sets of waves, perfect for surf action, and room for his rod to sit inside. The workbench not only has a fine tool collection, but it's also well-stocked with cases of Pepsi. *Universal/ Ron Main Collection*

form (disregarding TV's "Kojak"). And Bond is back behind the wheel of an Aston Martin, although Q has traded in the DB5 on a new DBS. Good flick.—MDr

On The Beach

(1959) This film stars Gregory Peck, Ava Gardner, Fred Astaire, and Anthony Perkins. The focus of the story is the aftermath of the third world war, where the survivors know they're going to die anyway from radiation.

This is one of the many movies in here I haven't seen. A still photo from it shows a scene about a sports car race, where there is a Jaguar XK-120 and an early Austin Healey on the track. A stellar cast that includes dancer Astaire doing a good job in his first true dramatic role.—DM

Michael Dregni's review of On the Beach:

Here is an end-of-the-world movie that takes place in Australia where the evil radiation cloud is blowing south to wipe out life as we know it. The film version of Nevil Shute's novel focuses on the emotions of Gregory Peck, Ava Gardner, Fred Astaire, and Anthony Perkins who all know they are about to die. Since there's nothing left to live for, one character risks it all by going sports car racing and there are some good—albeit short—scenes of Jaguar XK-120s and Austin-Healeys battling it out on the racetrack. A great film, you'll probably enjoy it more for the doomsday story than for the cars.—MDr

Once a Jolly Swagman

(1948) This Jack Lee-directed oldie stars Dirk Bogarde as Bill Fox, motorcycle racer. In fact, he's a speedway racer, making this a hard-to-find film that covers a subject rarely touched in motorcycle movies. Bonar Colleno, Bill Owen, and Renee Asherson (uh-oh: dame trouble!) also star. Available from Clyde Earl Vintage Videos.

Out of Sight

(1966) This was the first teenage-beach party-hot rod-secret agent-rock 'n' roll musical. This film made hot rod history with the crazy dual Buick-engined roadster ("ZZR") built by—who else?—the king of the kustoms, George Barris. The car is so crazy that you have to see it to believe it. It has gizmos that can cover you in tar and feathers, flames shooting out of the fenders, assorted weapons, and, yes, both engines running at once. The movie features the Girl from F.L.U.S.H., Billy Curtis, Gary Lewis and the Playboys, the Turtles, and Freddie and the Dreamers. This one is truly outta sight!—RM

The Pace That Thrills

(1952) This film starred Bill Williams as a test rider for a motorcycle company. He becomes involved with a woman who's writing a story about riding. Like all early motorcycle movies, the daredevil angle of the picture makes it worth seeing.

Palm Springs Weekend

(1963) So much fun, so little time. This is from a time when cars had fins, girls had flips, and guys had ducktails. Frankie and Annette lived in swimsuits here. We have Spring Break with Troy Donahue, Connie (hubba hubba) Stevens, Stefanie (love bunny) Powers, Robert Conrad, Ty Harden, and Jerry Van Dyke as team nerd Biff. Will cool Conrad with his T-Bird convertible get Connie in the back seat? Lots of fun in the sun and after dark, too!—RM

The Peace Killers

(1971) *"Killers"* stars Clint Ritchie, Jesse Walton, Paul Prokop, and Darlene Duralia. All there is to this one is a group of bikers pulling in to a commune and tearing everything up. It's total violent garbage.

Pee-Wee's Big Adventure

(1985) This zany flick has a scene with some bikers, and Pee-wee actually rides a Harley-Davidson in this one so here it is. The story begins with Pee-wee on his beloved old Schwinn bicycle from the fifties (which has a knee-action sprung fork, in case anyone ever asks). Pee-Wee's bike gets stolen, and all through the movie he tries to find it. The movie stars Paul Reubens as Pee-wee Herman, and Elizabeth Daily, Mark Holton, Diane Salinger, Tony Bill, Cassandra Peterson, James Brolin, and Morgan Fairchild, and was directed by animator Tim Burton.

Pink Cadillac

(1989) *Pink Cadillac* has Bernadette Peters playing the mistreated wife and mother who takes off in her husband's '59 Cadillac convertible, with Clint Eastwood cast as the bounty hunter sent to hunt her down and bring her in. This is a quality movie that's well done and fun.

Planes, Trains & Automobiles

(1987) This sounds like it should be a star in this book, but it's here almost solely because of some production notes. The word is that the film-makers asked the major auto makers to supply them with a vehicle for a particular scene. The car makers read the script and turned the movie makers down. So the film people chose a car at random—a Chrysler K car convertible—for use in the scene where the car gets completely burned up. Overall, it's a funny and somewhat touching film starring two greats, Steve Martin and the late John Candy.—MDa

The Pom Pom Girls

(1976) It's kind of the "Rebels with a cause meet the swinging cheerleaders." (Where were these girls when I went to high school?) Laurie (who could ever forget those pom poms?) Roxanne, billed as being 36-22-34, stars in this one. Her partners include Judy of the beach party where everything came off; Sue Anne, the backseat bingo winner; and Sally, who did everything she could for the team! How can anyone forget their stealing the fire truck? "I'll bet we had every cop in the county on our tail!" There's Johnnie in his hot '55 Chevy (who would have thought he would ride it all the way?), and Jessie in his hot rod roadster getting ready for another night's racing. Robert Carradine, Michael Mullins, Lisa Reeves, and Jennifer Ashley star. Originally released with an R rating, but edited to a PG later.—RM

Private Road

(1988) *Private Road* has a motorcycle rider in it. For just once in the movies, the motorcyclist is not a bad guy. So the producers have him get hit by a car instead. (Makes sense to me.) And the car is a Ferrari, driven by a beautiful, single, available, interested young woman whose extremely rich father is building an exotic race car. And they have a

Here's the publicity photo for *Out of Sight* put to use in a lobby card. Gary Lewis and the Playboys and Freddie and the Dreamers were among the musicians providing music for the film. *Universal/ Ron Main Collection*

spare room in their house for the motorcyclist to recover from his accident in, a room in the big house at the end of the Private Road. Oooh!

Psychomania

(1971) This one is a British biker movie, with the members of a motorcycle gang rising from the dead after selling their souls to the devil and tearing across the country raising hell. George Sanders, Nicky Henson, Mary Larkin, Patrick Holt, and Beryl Reid star, directed by Don Sharp.

Quadrophenia

(1979) *Quadrophenia* chronicled the Mod-Rocker Wars of the mid-1960s in England with motorized juvenile delinquents battling it out for the two-wheeled rule of the roads. Just like a good old-fashioned Western, you could tell the good guys by their white horses and the bad guys by their black steeds; in *Quadrophenia*, the Mods galloped along on "Italian Hairdryers"—Vespa and Lambretta scooters with lots of mirrors and driving lights—whereas the brutish Rockers rode working-class British iron including BSA and Triumph motorcycles straight from the Ace Cafe. Among the Mod set was Sting as a sensitive guy caught up in the two-stroke turmoil.

A gasoline opera staged to the sounds of The Who with Pete Townshend's Rickenbacker and Hiwatt turned to 10, *Quadrophenia* is the quintessential scooter flick.—MDr

Race for Glory

(1989) *Race for Glory* is one of the best motorcycle racing movies ever made (which isn't saying much!). Available on HBO Video, it has a plot that is somewhat similar to the 1980 British film *Silver Dream Racer*. Working on the familiar "buddy" movie theme, a pair of rural American nobodies try to put themselves on the map in the world of Grand Prix motorcycle roadracing. One is a talented rider named Cody Gifford, played by Alex McArthur. His buddy is a gifted fabricator and mechanic named Chris Washburn, played by Peter Berg, who has built up a very strong 500 Grand Prix roadracer.

The picture begins with the two stars and some of their friends preparing a street course around their small town before dawn. (These guys are some serious street racers. They weld the manhole covers shut first!) When the roads are ready, Cody goes for some hot laps and rides his heart out. After some "discussion" with the powers that be, the pair end up on a real racetrack against some world-class competition.

The race starts off with the heroes' bike failing to fire up, and Cody almost gets run over by some of the other riders. Chris runs over to help, slugs an official who was pointing out that mechanics don't belong on the racetrack, and pushes their bike until it fires. Cody catches everyone, and is dicing with the leader when he runs into more trouble. After bumping with his main competition, Kroeter, the star rider for the big-buck Samurai Corporation factory team, both riders go down hard. When the sliding stops, the insults start flying and a bitter rivalry is born.

Cody's hard riding style catches the attention of the Samurai talent scout, who asks him to ride one of their RZ-500 team bikes. From that point, the story is built around the ups and downs between Cody and Chris, the Samurai team, Kroeter, and Cody's girlfriend and family.

There's enough good roadracing in *Race for Glory* to make it worth watching, and enough obligatory personal drama to give you lots of opportunities to head for the kitchen. There is far more swearing here than necessary though, which keeps it from being something for the whole family. That's unfortunate.

You could say that *Race for Glory* is motorcycling's equivalent to *Days of Thunder*, in the sense that Hollywood set out to make a modern motion picture that captures the action, excitement, friendships, and struggles that are all part of professional racing. Of the two, *Race for Glory* is the less unbelievable, less predictable and far less "glamorous". There is also a better use of music, suspense, and tension. This one is worth watching.

A Race for Life

(1913) Here's a silent movie starring Indy Car champion Barney Oldfield, who has to race a train to rescue a woman chained to the tracks.—RM

Race for Life

(1954) *Race for Life* is a classic British car racing film, this time about an American who's competing on the European tracks. His wife's urging him to stop racing makes the movie drag in parts, but there's some very good racing footage that makes the picture worth your while if you can find it. The cast includes Richard Conte, Mari Aldon, George Coulouris, Peter Illing, Alec Mango, and Meredith Edwards.

Race With The Devil

(1975) Here is another movie with Peter Fonda, this one following a horror and suspense theme, involving Satan worshippers racing around in hot cars. The cast includes Loretta Swit (of TV's *M*A*S*H*), Warren Oates, R.G. Armstrong, and Lara Parker.

The Racers

(1955) *The Racers* is about the lives of Grand Prix race car drivers in Europe. Despite the cast that includes Kirk Douglas, Gilbert Roland, Bella Darvi, Lee J. Cobb, and Cesar Romero, the movie is not one of the greats due to the story line. Sports car enthusiasts will want to see it regardless for some of the vintage race cars that appear in the film. The car that Kirk Douglas races in *The Racers*, a British-made 1949 HMV, is the first Grand Prix car that Stirling Moss ever raced.

Racing Fever

(1964) Bill Grefe wrote, directed, and produced this outrageous film. It was filmed on weekends in Miami during the Gold Coast Speed Boat Marathon. The idea came from a real-life tragedy that Bill had witnessed at the Orange Bowl Regatta. Famed Italian racer Enzio Selva's supercharged race boat got airborne and flipped. He fell out and the hydro fell down right on top of him, crushing him to death. Grefe later incorporated footage of that incident with all its blood and gore into *Racing Fever*. Now for the good: You will see and hear the thunder of 3000hp hydros trailed by 50ft rooster tails throwing tons of water. Pit crews and 150ft cranes are working at top speed behind the scenes. Bill is a stickler for realism. All the racing was filmed during the running of the annual Grand Prix races from Miami to West Palm Beach and back. Lovely Barbara Biggart heads the voluptuous

Oh, how we long for the days when racetrack disputes weren't settled by appeals boards and attorneys but, rather, were settled with tire irons out behind the transporters. The racers in the film *Pit Stop* preferred a big axe as their weapon of choice, but thumbs up regardless because of their attempt to settle things on the spot. *Rio Pinto/ Ron Main Collection*

beach babes, and Joe Morrison and Charles Martin are the hunks. Gerry Granahan also stars and sings the title song. In breathtaking color.—RM

The Rain People

(1969) *The Rain People* stars Shirley Knight as a bored and pregnant Long Island house mouse who leaves her husband and heads out on the road, where she meets up with a football player on a motorcycle, played by James Caan. Directed by Francis Ford Coppola; cast includes Robert Duvall.

Rebel Without a Cause

(1955) Soon after the success of *The Wild One*, B movies really started to take off in 1955, with *Rebel Without a Cause*. James Dean knocked America out with his talent, his anger, and his look. The 1949 Mercury two-door sedan reached popular celebrity status along with Dean, and the popularity of both lives on today. This movie captured an era with unprecedented accuracy and emotion, dealing with the social pressures of teenagers, their family problems and friendships in a new light. It's worth another look if you haven't seen it for a while.

When Dean was killed on a California highway in September of 1955 in his Porsche, the nation lost someone whose potential was never reached. Today, his old 1955 Triumph 500 Trophy twin, which he had bought that January, rests in the Fairmount Historical Museum in Fairmount, Indiana, having been traced through its serial number and restored to the way it was when he rode it.

Some Dean notes: James Dean drove a '49 Merc in the film, but off-screen favored European wheels, as he owned an MG roadster, two Porsches (a Speedster and the Spyder that he was driving at the time of his fatal accident) and a Triumph motorcycle. He did, however, drive a '49 Ford of his uncle Marcus' in high school, and he towed his race cars with a Ford station wagon. In 1955 he was driving from L.A. to Salinas to compete in the third race of his career when he crashed.

(This car was seemingly jinxed: After being hauled from the crash site, it reportedly slipped off the tow truck and broke a mechanic's leg. It was displayed in a safe driving exhibit that was shown at car shows, etc., and it reportedly fell off its platform at one show and broke a teenager's hip. Transported to the next show on a flatbed truck, it was reportedly hit in the rear by another driver, who was thrown from his vehicle and killed when the Spyder fell on him. In Oregon, the transporter's brakes failed and it ended up in a storefront, and then the car supposedly broke apart while on display in New Orleans. It vanished while being shipped back to L.A. on a train.)

The previous May, in a car club race at Palm Springs, he drove well. In his first race ever, he won a prelim event and finished third in the Speedster and first in his class (cars under 1500 cc's; (Ken Miles drove his Flying Shingle MG to the win ahead of Cy Yedor). Dean saw *East of Eden* released, but died before *Rebel* and *Giant* were released.

Rebel Rousers

(1967) This one stars a great cast that includes Cameron Mitchell, Jack Nicholson, Bruce Dern, Diane Ladd, and Dean Stanton. Big Jack is back and he steals the show again. This time the plot involves two guys arguing over a girl, so they have a drag race to settle ownership, fair and square.

The Reivers

(1969) When they said, "Steve McQueen as you've never seen him before," they weren't kidding. This film was released the year after *Bullit*, the movie that made McQueen the biggest screen star of the time. Don't look for any high-action chases here, though. McQueen plays Boon Hogganbeck, a klutzy screw-up, in this film based on a Pulitzer Prize-winning William Faulkner novel. The story has McQueen and some mates enjoying a fling in the big city of Memphis around the turn of the century. The vehicle that carries them on their adventure is a bright yellow 1905 Winton Flyer, a car built by Von Dutch (a good friend of McQueen's), who gave the car a Crosley engine. The film was produced by McQueen's Solar production company, and it created quite a stir when the superstar was on location in Carrollton, Mississippi. Will Geer, Rupert Crosse, and Diane Ladd also star. This is a movie worth seeing, especially if you want to see McQueen in a role beyond his normal tough-guy persona. (Also highly recommended is the biography *McQueen*, by Penina Spiegel, 1986, Doubleday & Co.)—MDa

Reckless

(1984) *Reckless* has Aidan Quinn (who's also in *Avalon*) playing a wild punk on a motorcycle, chasing after Daryl Hannah, who finds him exciting but wants to save him. The plot is disappointing but James Foley's directing adds a lot to the movie. Kenneth McMillan, Lois Smith, Cliff DeYoung, Adam Baldwin, and Dan Hedaya also star.

Red Ball Express

(1952) This film deals with truckers delivering supplies to the front lines during World War II. Lots of action and a good cast that includes Jeff Chandler, Alex Nicol, Sidney Poitier, Hugh O'Brian, and Jack Kelly make this movie of the better ones of its kind.

Red Line 7000

(1965) Here is another movie about stock car racing that could have been a lot better than it was, but it has its place. Directed by Howard Hawks, it stars James Caan, Laura Devon, and Charlene Holt. Good ol' boys out on the track doing a little trading paint, NASCAR-style.

Red Surf

(1990) *Red Surf* is more about drugs than anything else, but since one of the characters rides a Harley-Davidson chopper, it's included here. He and his surfer friends have been making deliveries for a violent cocaine dealer but they decide to get out while they can. The biker wants to take his share of the money and buy into a shop that works on vintage Harley-Davidsons. George Clooney, Doug Savant, and Dedee Pfeiffer are the stars in what turns into a grim story. By the way, the bike is referred to as being "a '67", but it's actually a Panhead (which were made from 1948-1965). There's barely enough here to qualify it as a motorcycle movie. If you're only interested in the bikes you can skip the first 45 minutes.

Rendezvous

(1965) What a Sunday drive! This short is based on a simple premise: strap a movie camera loaded with one film canister into the passenger's seat of a Ferrari 275 GTB and drive across Paris at full speed filming all the way. The film was made on a bet by French New Wave director Claude Lelouch, who also created *A Man and a Woman*. The man behind the steering wheel is the famed French Grand Prix racer Maurice Trintingnant, and the ride will French fry the most subdued couch potato. It's a Sunday morning drive across Paris that's pure aural and visual sensation, swooping around early morning buses, racing onto the sidewalk to miss a garbage truck, and using pedestrians as corner apexes. If you don't blink you can spot the Paris Opera and the Place de la Concorde, a valuable aid in vacation planning. The ride lasts about ten minutes before the film runs out with the rendezvous at the end.

These were in the old days before film credits reassured you that no animals had been hurt during the filming of this movie; in *Rendezvous*, many a Parisian pigeon meets an untimely demise on the Ferrari's grille.—MDr

Repo Man

(1984) A wild comedy with dashes of sci-fi about a young buck (Emilio Estevez) who yearns to become a car repossesser and learns at the foot of a classic repo man (Harry Dean Stanton) about cars *and* life. It gets a little zany at the end, but is basically a fun movie. While the cars aren't collector models, there is some funny car action, especially when Estevez has to move quickly to make his getaways. It's nice to see Estevez putting his energy into a decent comedy rather than some of the other trash he made.—MDa

Return of The Rebels

(1981) *"Return"* has a group of old friends that used to belong to a motorcycle club getting back together again and dusting off their old Panheads after many years to help out one of their members. It's corny but it's harmless fun, starring Barbara Eden ("I Dream of Jeannie"), Don Murray, Christopher Connelly, Michael Baseleon, Patrick Swayze, Robert Mandan, Jamie Farr ("Clinger"), and DeAnna Robbins.

Return of The Rebels, Angels Die Hard (from 1970), and *Mask* are perhaps the only three movies in this book that portray motorcycle club members who ride Harley-Davidsons as being decent human beings, for which I hereby award them all the Golden Pushrod Cover Award ("show-chromed for extra class").

Return to Macon County

(1975) This flick has something for everyone: violence, murder, sex, and drag racing. Don Johnson and Nick Nolte are the drivers here, but they're probably not too proud of the script they had to work with. *Return to Macon County* was directed by Richard Compton.

been harassing Reinhold torch the car and it's toast. Dafoe splits, wanting to avoid further trouble, but returns in time for the big annual roadrace. Dafoe's piloting a hot '55 Chevy that's poised to beat the perennial champs in their '57 Chevy. The big race is on, and for the reigning champs, anything goes, including blasting a shotgun at Dafoe to slow him down. The winner? We won't spoil it for you.—RM

Roadracers

(1958) This is a movie that's about closed-wheel sports car racing. The movie includes cars running on a road course, cars along the lines of the Jaguar Type C and A.C. Bristol, but that's not really what they are—they look like they've been customized by the studio, unless they're based on kit cars from the late fifties. They're all running steel wheels, only one of the five cars has a roll bar, and one of the cars has a USAC (United States Auto Club) sticker.

The Roar of the Crowd

(1953) This was a low-budget racing film that is now not often seen on TV. The cast includes Howard Duff, Helene Stanley, Louise Arthur, Harry Shannon, Minor Watson, and Don Haggerty. A trivia note: 1953 was also the birth of the era of stereo movie soundtracks. While it has nothing to do with any of the other films in this book, *The Robe* was the first stereo movie that was released to theaters, and also the first to be released in CinemaScope.

Roar of the Iron Horse

(1951) This *"Roar"* is another early movie about motorcycle riding, available from Stokey's Serials (see the appendices). 1951 was also the year that Wally Parks founded the National Hot Rod Association (NHRA), to provide thousands of hot rodders with a drag racing sanctioning body.

The Roaring Road

(1919) Wallace Reid stars as "Toodles," the car salesman who dreams of being a race car driver. There is plenty of action-packed actual race footage from the Santa Monica roadrace in this silent film.—RM

Roaring Speedboats

(1937) This film was also released as *Mile a Minute Love*. William Bakewell is the all-American boy with a supercharger that will revolutionize boat racing. However, the evil count, Duncan Renaldo, the European champion, frames our boy—but William's not done yet! Lots of flying fists and roaring action.—RM

Roger and Me

(1989) *Roger and Me* was a controversial sensation at film festivals that received considerable critical acclaim before being released to neighborhood theaters.

Michael Moore is a native of Flint, Michigan. He sees the disturbing decay around Flint as more and more employees of the General Motors plant there are left without jobs, as GM shifts much of its manufacturing to plants in Mexico and overseas. He spends much of the time in the film chasing after the president of General Motors and documenting the attempts of the local leaders to salvage the local economy. Parts of Flint look like a ghost town, with the area residents split between the very rich and the hungry. There are is a mixture of sadness and humor in Roger and Me that, when combined with its account of GM's diminishing presence in the world marketplace, results in a powerful picture.

Whether you have an interest in the automotive industry, the nation's economy, management, or sociology, see this film. It's funny, but it shouldn't be. For that matter, it shouldn't have been necessary. But it was, and it looks like it's going to continue to be relevant to all North Americans.

Go see the movie. And think about it.

Rollerball

(1975) James Caan stars in this futuristic film as a professional athlete playing an ultra-violent sport called Rollerball, in which player/gladiators on motorcycles try to chase down opposing team players who are on roller skates. It's violent and only mildly interesting and entertaining. It's the kind of film you won't feel compelled to seek out for a second look. John Houseman and Maud Adams also star.—MDa

Rolling Vengeance

(1987) This is a story of multiple murder resulting in revenge on wheels. The surviving member of a slaughtered family modifies his truck to help him get even and heads out on the highway looking for the killer. As you can imagine, there's lots of action, including the mandatory Hollywood explosions. Lawrence Dane and Ned Beatty are the stars. This is not a happy picture, or for kids.

Roman Holiday

(1953) Here is a classic fifties Hollywood fairy tale with the magic carpet ride taking place on a Piaggio Vespa motorscooter. Gregory Peck stars as a dashing American journalist in Rome with his sidekick the wacky photographer played by Eddie Albert with a glue-on beard. Peck spots Italian princess Audrey Hepburn at a palazzo press conference and they make eyes. See, Audrey has spent her whole life cooped up in the palace and yearns to truly live—throw lire in the Trevi fountain and so on. So she runs away to fall into Peck's waiting arms and they tour Rome on their Vespa just like real people. In the end, Audrey must return to the palace, but Gregory—and the motorscooter—have opened her eyes to the world.

Directed by William Wyler, *Roman Holiday* is chock full of great scenes of Rome in the 1950s and great shots of a fifties Vespa! The story will touch your heart almost as much as the cool scooter.—MDr

Rome Adventure

(1962) This romantic film truly sparked a bond: Costars Troy Donahue and Suzanne Pleshette got married for real two years after making the movie. Hoping to recapture the chemistry that made *Roman Holiday* a great film, the producers of this one put Americans in Italy for romance and cavorting about the countryside on scooters. It's fun to see the young (and sassy) Angie Dickinson and young Chad Everett, but this one's a distant second-best to the classic, *Roman Holiday*.—MDa

Apparently the title *To Please a Lady* wasn't attracting enough car lovers to the theaters, so the Clark Gable/Barbara Stanwyck film was rereleased as *Red Hot Wheels. MGM/ Ron Main Collection*

The Rookie

(1990) This cop flick stars Clint Eastwood (who also directed) and Charlie Sheen (the rook), Raul Julia, Sonia Braga (who torments Clint), and Tom Skerritt. Along with plenty of police action (chases, shooting, skirmishes), including a great freeway crash scene, the movie includes motorcycles such as a Norton, Triumph, and some Harleys. The Harleys present some difficulties since they won't start at one point. (Art imitating life?) So when Charlie speeds home on a finally-resurrected Harley to save a girlfriend, he has to ride it through the door to save time.—MDa

Rough Riders

If you judge a video by its cover—which in this case was two young ladies in leisure togs stepping on a guy's head and wrapping a chain around his neck while holding a gun on him—you'd say, "wow, another crappy biker flick." Not in this case, however. Producer Al Adamson has truly gone the extra mile to elevate *Rough Riders* above the norm. Take the opening sequence: One of the girls is being manhandled by a couple of louts when her "sisters" show up. They are dispatched with the usual gouging and knees in the groin, but just to ice the cake, Margo (Vicki Volante looking tough in white lipstick) works the guys over royal with a bullwhip.

A bit later "Speed" (Ross Hagen) is having the usual long, pointless string of fist fights when he has to mix it up with a guy waving a broken bottle. Sure, there were pistols, shotguns, whips, rocks, sticks, and pool cues, but how often do you see any decent work with broken bottles? Speed then takes the guys (Slim, Preacher, Turk, etc.) on the Desert Run. "Swell," you say, "and they probably swill beer and fall off their bikes and pass out all

Next page
Make no doubt about it, *Red Line 7000* is a Howard Hawks film. The legendary director gets top billing, and the cast gets listed as costars, leaving even rock-jawed, square-shouldered young James Caan without star status in this 1965 racing classic. *Paramount/ Ron Main Collection*

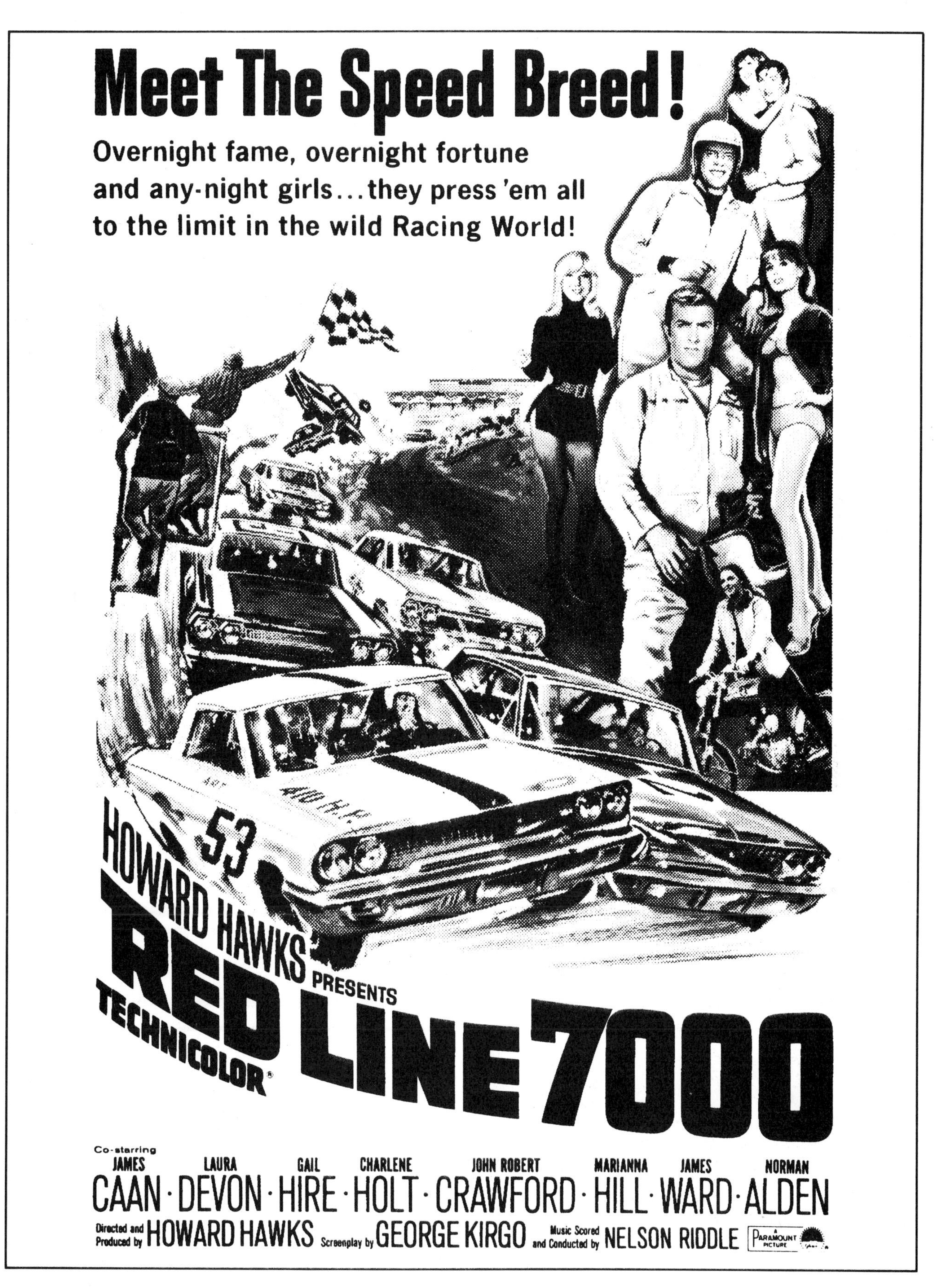
Meet The Speed Breed!
Overnight fame, overnight fortune and any-night girls... they press 'em all to the limit in the wild Racing World!
53
HOWARD HAWKS' PRESENTS
TECHNICOLOR
RED LINE 7000
Co-starring
JAMES CAAN · LAURA DEVON · GAIL HIRE · CHARLENE HOLT · JOHN ROBERT CRAWFORD · MARIANNA HILL · JAMES WARD · NORMAN ALDEN
Directed and Produced by HOWARD HAWKS
Screenplay by GEORGE KIRGO
Music Scored and Conducted by NELSON RIDDLE
A PARAMOUNT PICTURE

over the place." True, but these guys do it so well, and they do get urinated on to wake 'em up again!

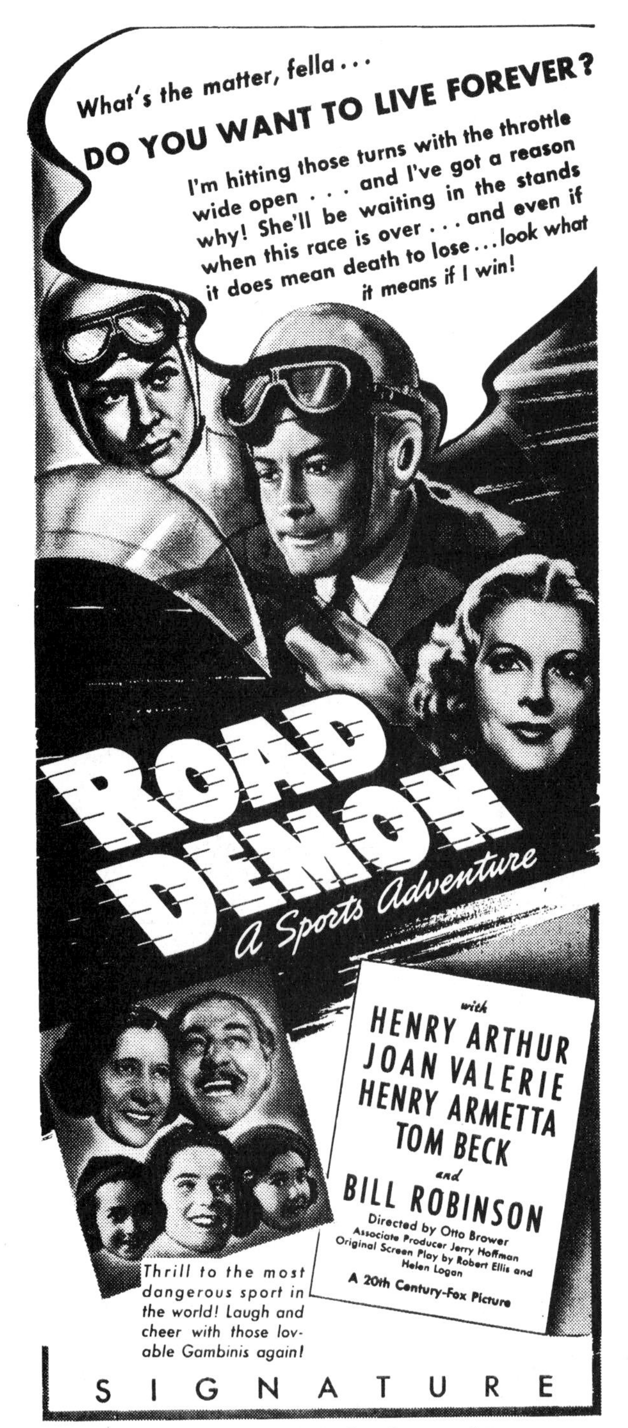

After seeing several ad slicks for the *Road Demon*, we've gone sleepless. We're haunted with the visage of Papa Gambini's contorted, shaking, laughing face. Until somebody correctly labels this as a horror movie, we're too scared to look. At least warn us when somebody's about to crack a joke in Papa's presence. *20th Century Fox/ Ron Main Collection*

Are the women just sitting around pining for the bros to return? Not quite. In an amusing bit of turnabout, the women waylay an innocent farmhand and force him to, well, entertain them. They eventually arrive at the "Movie Ranch" commune for a bout with bad acid and ritual sacrifice. The boys return from the desert just in time for the inevitable big brawl which the bad guys escape from in a Falcon wagon pursued by Speed on his Triumph. Can Speed be avenged by merely shooting Tex and The King or maybe running them off the road? Of course not! He hurls his Triumph through their windshield, which causes the Falcon to explode off the face of the earth. Not a movie with a lot of nudity, violence, or plot development, but a good soundtrack and good camera work, adequate acting, and a few Brit bikes make *Rough Riders* worth the two bucks.—SG

Roustabout

(1964) This film and *Viva Las Vegas* were both Elvis Presley movies released in 1964. The King of Rock 'n' Roll plays "Wheels on My Heels" while he's sitting on a scooter in this film, which stars Barbara Stanwyck, Leif Erickson, Joan Freeman and Sue Langdon. As "Charlie Rogers," he rides up to the carnival on his Honda with a guitar and a big load of bad attitude strapped to his back. Carnival boss Stanwyck puts him to work to tey to straighten him out. The highlight of the film is when he finally takes the wall of death rider's dare and jumps on the bike to try riding the dangerous wall. Dangerous, schmangerous for the King. He's up on the wall and running full throttle in the blink of an eye. He's portrayed as a mortal, however, when he brings the bike back down to the base of the wall and lays it down when he's practically at a dead stop.

Rubber Racketeers

(1942) This is the first of two movies made about the hardships endured by motorists who needed new tires during the Second World War. With most of the available rubber (and metals) going toward the war effort, a black market was developed by sleazy *Rubber Racketeers*. While this movie is a drama, it dramatizes something that actually happened.

Rumble Fish

(1983) This film stars a cast that grew up to achieve considerable Hollywood fame, including Matt Dillon, Mickey Rourke, Diane Lane, Dennis Hopper, Diana Scarwid, Vincent Spano, Nicholas

Cage, Christopher Penn, and singer-songwriter Tom Waits, and was directed by Francis Ford Coppola. It's the story of a teenager who wants to be like his older brother, "The Motorcycle Boy," played by Rourke. The fine cast does well with an interesting story and although there isn't much of the motorcycle in the movie the result is something to make a point of seeing.

Run, Angel, Run

(1969) Look out! This flick stars William Smith as Angel, a member of the Devil's Advocates M.C. in California. He has done an expose on the club for "LIKE" magazine. The club chases after him and his old lady, played by Valerie Starrett, through most of the movie, and that's the whole plot. Angel's bike is an orange XLCH Sportster with an extended front end and a teardrop gas tank (but in two scenes where Angel has to jump something with it, the bike magically turns into a silver two-stroke Bultaco motocross bike).

About the only part of the movie that provides some relief from the gloomy story centers around the partial restoration of a 1917 Harley-Davidson JD that belongs to a man who gives him a job and a new life. Aside from that, *Run, Angel, Run* is a disappointment.

Safari 3000

(1982) "The race that drove Africa wild!" That's how they billed this one starring David Carradine, Stockard Channing, and Christopher Lee. A former Hollywood stuntman has to overcome the damnedest adversaries in this international

You can guess that American-International Pictures was playing up the romance angle of *Roadracers* to the hilt since the star getting top billing wasn't a he-man racer, but instead was actress/bombshell Sally Fraser. This lobby card *did* play up the film's race action and spills angle, however. *American International/ Ron Main Collection*

race (which includes several vehicles created by kustoms king George Barris).—RM

Satan's Sadists

(1970) Here is another violent movie about outlaw bikers. It stars Russ Tamblyn, Scott Brady, Kent Taylor, and John Cardos. This was the first movie made by Independent-International Pictures, and Russ Tamblyn's first biker movie role. By the way, *Satan's Sadists* was made for $50,000, and has grossed over $10 million so far.—DM

Ron Main's Review of Satan's Sadists:

Warped women, and sick, savage motorcycle maniacs. You knew this one was destined to become a cult classic from the very start, which is when Russ Tamblyn looks into the camera and says, "You're right, I'm a rotten bastard!" To pass time, the gang kills and rapes college girls after putting LSD in their coffee. (Hey, so the gang had a little extra time on their hands.) Scott Brady, Kent Taylor, and Regina Carroll ("The Freak Out Girl") also star. Viewers today still can't believe how crude, sadistic, and dumb this movie is. It's great for parties (not including the rape scene).—RM

American International released *Roadracers* on a twin bill with *Daddy-'O'*, which presented a swingin' view of the hip life. *American International/ Ron Main Collection*

The Savage Seven

(1968) This film stars Robert Walker, Larry Bishop, Joanna Frank, John Garwood (Gabe De Lutri), Adam Roarke, Max Julien, John Cardos, Beach Dickerson, Gary Littlejohn, Penny Marshall, and Duane Eddy, and was produced by Dick Clark. It's another American International Pictures biker flick, in some ways better than most, with sleazy businessmen setting the bikers up to slug it out with the Indians.

Scream Free

(1968) This film might also have been released as *Free Grass*. This biker-drug film is virtually unknown, and some say it played only in Waco, Texas. Russ Tamblyn is our biker, Richard Beymer is the hippie, and Lana Wood (yes, Natalie's sister) is his love child. Beymer hires Tamblyn and his biker gang to smuggle drugs, but when he objects to murder, Russ puts LSD in Beymer's drink and sets him on fire! Well, that's one way to settle a conflict. If you find this one, let me know.—RM

Sex Kittens Go to College

(1960) You might not appreciate or be able to sit through this attempt at wacky comedy, but you *will* get to see a gorgeous Norm Grabowski hot rod as well as see Norm—who's billed as "Woo Woo" Grabowski—act. B movie goddess Mamie Van Doren is a college science professor, but—uh-oh!—her background includes time spent as a stripper. This, as you might expect, leads to trouble. You wish the movie were funnier, but it's really poorly made, so your ability to stick it out is in question. Mamie's an eyeful, as always, as are some of the young kittens on hand. The zany cast also includes young Tuesday Weld, lovely Mijanou Bardot (Brigitte's sister!), Pamela Mason, Marty (*Route 66; Adam-12*) Milner, kookie Louie Nye, and nutty Jackie Coogan.—MDa

Sgt. Pepper's Lonely Hearts Club Band

(1978) Didn't think we'd include this one? It's here only so we can mention that it includes a stretched station wagon, a monster Checker with four doors on each side of the car. Also, if you just get a kick out of bad movies, this one's about as big a waste of film as you can find.

Shaker Run

(1984) *Shaker* (not stirred) *Run* stars Cliff Robertson, Leif Garrett, and Lisa Harrow. Robertson is an American stunt driver who has been performing in New Zealand. Harrow plays a government scientist who hires Robertson and his 1982

Pontiac Firebird stunt car to transport lethal virus in a hurry to keep it safe from government agents. There's nothing here to recommend.

She-Devils From Hell

This is the only thing this movie could have been legitimately titled. Consider the plot: a gang of wild biker chicks straddling everything from Harley-Davidsons to a Honda Cub (that sounds like a Harley) go through the ritual make-out scenes and rumbles with boy gangs moving in on their territory. The She-Devils snarl like Hells Angels in panty hose and strike tough girl poses that should have won a flock of B flick Oscars.

In the end, you realize the whole plot has been written so the director can film a cool decapitation stunt where the She-Devils behead a bad guy boy biker at speed by stringing a wire across the road. If this wasn't such a cheesy sexploitation flick, you'd swear it was a motorized manifesto for women's lib.—MDr

She-Devils On Wheels

(1968) This flick stars Betty Connell, Pat Poston, Nancy Lee Noble, Christie Wagner, and Ruby Tuesday as members of a motorcycle gang that dominates the men who get in their way. The movie was made by Herschell Gordon Lewis, who got a friend of his who had been a truant officer to get some real bikers to star in the picture—they were members of the Iron Cross motorcycle club, Female Cut-Throats Division.

Sidecar Racers

(1975) Ben Murphy stars in this Australian-made film whose cast includes Peter Graves, the star of TV's "Mission: Impossible". Murphy overcomes the odds to win the world sidecar racing title

The Sidehackers

(1969) First released as *Five the Hard Way*, this film features Diane McBain, one of the most beautiful blondes in movies, costars with Ross Hagen and Mike Pataki. Be prepared for a new thrill. This film brings to the screen sidehacking, a sport much better known in European racing circles than in the United States. Sidehacking involves a motorcycle and a form of a sidecar, a three-wheeled vehicle with two men defying death at every turn. Their motto is, "Let it all hang out!"—RM

Signal 30

This might also be seen under the title *Wheels of Tragedy*. This is in here because it's an example of the classic driver's education films you were forced to watch years ago. It starts out with actual footage of incredible mutilation and mangled victims from accidents, then switches to actors to show you how the accidents happened. At the end, Mansfield, Ohio, is seen with no people because 43,000 people die in traffic accidents each year, and that was the city's population. Oh, well, it was fun to watch the girls get sick in class.—RM

Silver Bullet

(1985) This film has the residents of a small town being terrorized by a motorcycle-riding werewolf. The movie is based on the Stephen King's novel "Cycle of the Werewolf," and stars Gary Busey, Corey Haim, Megan Follows, Everett McGill, Terry O'Quinn, Leon Russom, and Robin Groves.

Silver Dream Racer

(1979) This film is a "must see" for motorcycle roadracing enthusiasts. Yes, it's corny, and others have called things like "hackneyed" and "boring". But these guys were critics, not motorheads.

This is one of only a few movies made that features motorcycle roadracing. Real racing footage has been added to make it fairly convincing at that. The racing scenes were filmed at the Brands Hatch, Donnington Park, and Silverstone circuits in England.

British rock singer David Essex played Nick Freeman, a British roadracer who is struggling with his race bike. Essex also sings a couple of songs in the picture.

Beau Bridges plays Bruce McBride, the highly-motivated and arrogant American roadracer who does very well on the track. Until he faces the Silver Dream Racer.

The hand-built prototype bike that the movie is named after belonged to Nick's brother Greg, a fellow competitor who dies while playing around on a dirt bike. Greg had an engineering background and had created the bike in his shop. The Silver Dream Racer motorcycle was actually designed by Barry Hart, and is very similar to the factory Grand Prix bikes of today.

Early in the film there is a scene where Nick is going through Greg's garage. Just before he uncovers the bike the movie is named after, we are given a glimpse of several vintage British bikes, including a fine old Norton roadracer. Other than a couple of brief scenes that feature dirt bikes, all of the motorcycles in the film are modern roadracers.

You may wish this movie had less personal drama and more hard racing footage, but that's the way most movies are. There is still enough riding here to make it worth your while. *Silver Dream Racer* does a good job of documenting the way privateers are confronted with such overwhelming odds when they square off against the budgets, technology, and equipment of the big boys. I won't promise that you'll enjoy it as much as I did, but for what it is, it's one of the best.

Six-Pack

(1982) Burp. *Six-Pack* has Kenny Rogers cast as an unsponsored professional stock car driver making a return to racing. Shortly after the movie begins he gets "adopted" by some orphaned kids who have been supporting themselves by stealing. They travel around together to various short tracks, where the kids get him into some crazy situations. Diane Lane and Erin Grey (of TV's "Happy Days") costar in some harmless entertainment.

In the world of movie bad guys, the line starts with second place, right behind the impossible-to-match rotten nature of the bikers in *Satan's Sadists*. The ads for the film even proclaimed that it was "A sick story of savage lust!" And that was an understatement. *Ron Main Collection*

Sleeper

(1973) This zany Woody Allen comedy used The Sleeper Car, which also appeared in several commercials and *Back to the Future Part II*.

Sleazy Rider

(1988) Two sleazy girls sell a kilo of pork sausage and make a hitchhiker sniff spray paint in this black-and-white, all-female *Easy Rider* take-off. Karen Black is shown in the graveyard scene from the original (*Easy Rider*), plus there are biker movie clips and a bit of hard-core sex. What more could you ask?—RM

Slither

(1973) This film is about a going out on the road, with trailers in tow, looking for some hidden loot. There are some laughs and good chase scenes in *Slither*, which has a strong cast and stars James Caan, Peter Boyle, Sally Kellerman, Louise Lasser, Allen Garfield, and Richard B. Shull.

Smash-Up Alley

(1972) *"Alley"* was also released under the title of *43: The Richard Petty Story*. The King of stock car racing plays himself in this look back at the lives of Richard and his father Lee Petty. Edward Lasko directed, with a cast that includes Darren McGavin in the role of Lee Petty, along with Kathie Browne, Noah Beery, Jr., Pierre Jalbert, and L.Q. Jones.

By this time the tastes of the American public had begun its move away from the juvenile delinquent formula, and for the most part another era came to an end. That's not to say B movies and exploitation weren't made any more—they're still being turned out today. But the new ones, that are supposed to be funny, or dramatic, don't come close to the originals.

Smash-Up on Interstate 5

(1976) Here is a strange one. Would you believe it's a "commuter exploitation movie"? Well, it is. Robert Conrad stars as a highway patrol cop who is confronted with a number of highway traffic situations that eventually lead to a catastrophic wreck.

There is almost nothing of interest here, with no particular cars or good chase scenes to be found. The movie has been included in the book because the producers realized the story was pretty lame, so they stuck in the inevitable biker gang to add some interest. The bikers ride Triumph choppers mostly, and get in trouble when one of their

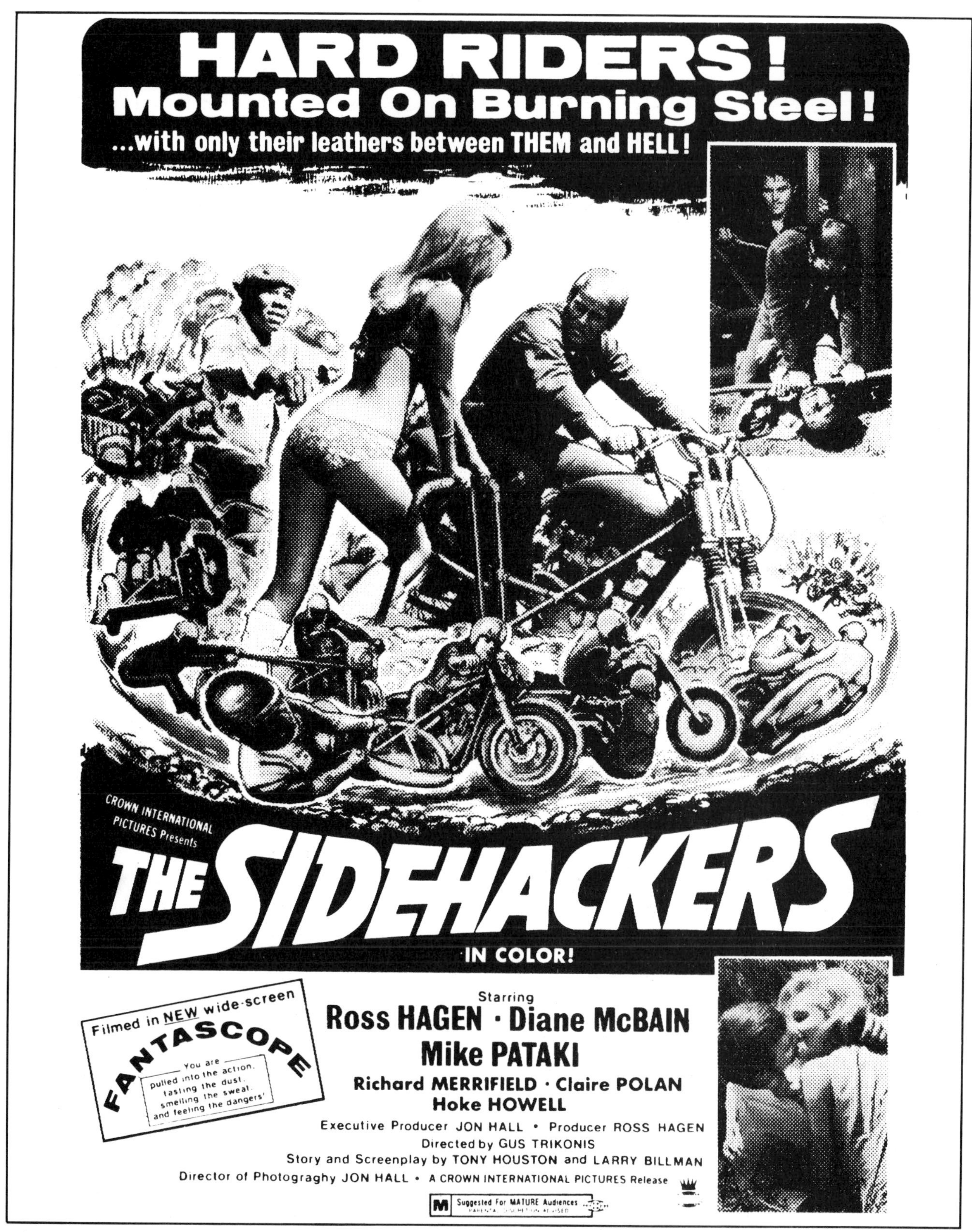

After seeing the ad photos for *The Sidehackers,* it's obvious to us why sidecar racing is on the decline: Not enough bikini-clad women involved in racing. There's way too much emphasis today on safety gear. When your local track unveils its "bikini-, halter top-, or tube top-clad rider class," give us a call. Until then, we're home watching MTV. *Crown International/ Ron Main Collection*

Smokey and the Bandit
CB
"What we have here is
a total lack of respect for
the law!"
Burt Reynolds
"Smokey and the Bandit"
Sally Field · Jerry Reed and Jackie Gleason
as Sheriff Buford T. Justice
Screenplay by JAMES LEE BARRETT and CHARLES SHYER & ALAN MANDEL
Story by HAL NEEDHAM & ROBERT L. LEVY · Music by BILL JUSTIS and JERRY REED
Directed by HAL NEEDHAM · Produced by MORT ENGELBERG · Executive Producer ROBERT L LEVY
A RASTAR Production · A UNIVERSAL Picture · Technicolor®
PG PARENTAL GUIDANCE SUGGESTED
SOME MATERIAL MAY NOT BE SUITABLE FOR PRE TEENAGERS
Original sound track available exclusively on MCA Records & Tapes

Previous page
Perhaps the best of all the movies with "Smokey" in the title was one of the originals, *Smokey and the Bandit,* with Burt Reynolds, Academy Award winner Sally Field, and Jerry Reed. This 1977 film also had some sterling directing by Hal Needham, and the little man–big man combo of Paul Williams and Pat McCormick (a former staff writer for "The Tonight Show Starring Johnny Carson"). *Universal/ Ron Main Collection*

women pulls a lady out of her car for a present for one of the members. A passing trucker notices the lady calling for help and screeches to her rescue, whereupon she melts with gratitude. The bikers are all jerks, the plot stinks, and the movie was essentially a mistake.

Smokey and the Bandit

(1977) This film stars Burt Reynolds as a driver who's been hired to race through the South carrying some illegal beer, resulting in a movie that's almost one continuous chase scene. The cast includes Sally Field, Jackie Gleason, Jerry Reed, Mike Henry, and Paul McCormack. There were more movies in the *Smokey* series released in 1980, 1981 and 1983, but this one was perhaps the best of the series. It was also the first movie directed by the master stunt man Hal Needham.

Smokey and the Bandit 2

(1980) "2" was the second in the series, with Burt Reynolds, Jackie Gleason, Jerry Reed, Dom DeLuise, Sally Field, Paul Williams, Pat McCormick, and John Anderson. The story involves trucking an elephant and doesn't have much action. It's included here because the rest of the series is.

Smokey and the Bandit 3

(1983) "3" was the last of the four Smokey movies, and by this time they seemed to be running out of angles to try. Jackie Gleason is the redneck sheriff again, chasing Jerry Reed.

Smokey and the Hotwire Gang

(1979) Hard-drivin' and free-lovin'—whew!—grand theft auto was never like this! Stanley Livingston (I presume), Tony Lorea, and Carla Ziegfield (as "Hotwire") star here. The mob is after Billy the Kid, and who shows up but—who else?—George Barris, the kustom car king!—RM

Smokey Bites the Dust

(1981) This was the third in the *Smokey* series, with Jimmy McNichol starring as the kidnapper of a girl whose sheriff father chases him throughout much of the movie. Other actors include Janet Julian, Walter Barnes, Patrick Campbell, Kari Lizer, and John Barrymore.

Son of Flubber

(1963) Here is the sequel to *The Absent-Minded Professor*. Not as good as the original, it features the same 1915 Ford Model T phaeton with magical flying power. The cast includes Fred MacMurray, Nancy Olson, Keenan Wynn, Tommy Kirk, Elliott Reid, Joanna Moore, Leon Ames, Ed Wynn, Charlie Ruggles, and Paul Lynde.

The Sorcerer

(1977) This is a remake of the critically-acclaimed 1952 picture *Wages of Fear*. Starring Roy Scheider, Bruno Cremer, Francisco Rabal, Amidou, Ramon Bieri, and Peter Capell, *The Sorcerer* is suspenseful and recommended like the original.

Speed

(1936) *Speed* stars James Stewart as a test driver and race driver who builds an engine and then uses it in a car in the Indy 500. It's a great picture

The ads for *Speed Crazy* were a subliminal message analyst's dream come true. We were so captivated by the 50ft tall woman with the checkered flag that we almost missed the fact that Slick Slavin sings "Speed Crazy" in the movie. *Allied Artists/ Ron Main Collection*

for fans of racing, the automotive industry, and Stewart. He cranked out seven other movies in 1936, which probably compelled him to drive even faster during the racing scenes. The other stars include Wendy Barrie, Ted Healy, Una Merkel, and Ralph Morgan.

Speed Along

(1927) A "Mirthquake Comedy," this silent film features a farmer getting a race car for his birthday. Since it's silent, some of the action is hard to follow, but it's a fast-moving farce with three race cars in a once-peaceful farm area. They speed around the livestock, bump into farmers, and chase each other endlessly.—RM

Speed Crazy

(1959) This is the story of a crazy drifter who's obsessed with sports cars. The stars include Brett Halsey, Yvonne Lime, Charles Wilcox, Slick Slavin, Jacqueline Ravell, Baynes Barron, Jackie Joseph, a 1954 Austin Healey roadster, and a 1954 Porsche roadster. If bad movies are your bag, you've stumbled upon a beauty here.

The Speed Lovers

(1968) This film had real-life NASCAR champion Fred Lorentzen in his first starring role. This film was unforgettable, especially for Fred! He should have sued them. Actually, he's not too bad, but the story is too silly. Try to stay awake for the actual race footage of the NASCAR gang with that

The ads for *Thunder Alley* didn't portray it as a typical Annette movie, but it was actually full of harmless fun, not the debauchery this ad seems to promise. Fabian plays a stock car racer who doesn't have what it takes, which leads to his being suspended from driving. Yes, you can bet that everything works out in the end. *American International/ Ron Main Collection*

wild 427 tearing up the tracks at Charlotte, Atlanta, and the Daytona 500. David Marcus, Peggy O'Hara, and some go-go girls complete the cast.—RM

The Speed Merchants

(1972) Michael Keyer's highly acclaimed documentary details the race for the 1972 World Sports Car Championship. The factory Ferrari and Alfa Romeo teams battle for the championship over the last of the true roadrace circuits. They race on actual roads, not the current "street circuits" or parking lot layouts. Mario Andretti, Vic Elford, and Brian Redmond tell us in their own words what it's like to be out there. Can you believe Mario was talking about retirement in this film made some 20-plus years ago? You'll be amazed by the in-car camera shots, which were very sophisticated for the time. They zero in on the old 14-mile Nurburgring track in Germany, and the real street circuit of the Targa Florio in Sicily, where Mario made his amazing finish. This film offers more excitement than any video game and is highly recommended as a valuable addition to any racing film library!—RM

Speed to Spare

(1948) Here is the story of a retired stunt driver who wants to settle down. He becomes long-distance trucker for the National Express Company. A jealous coworker sabotages his rig to cause him trouble on the job. The plot takes an unusual twist when he volunteers to haul a load of acid which has to remain below freezing. Richard Arlen, Jean Rogers, Richard Travis, and Pat Phelan star in this corny but entertaining picture.

Speed Zone

(1989) *Speed Zone* is another alleged comedy in the *Cannonball Run* mode, this time shot in Canada (which explains why the cast features lots of *Second City TV* alums). The cast includes the late John Candy, Peter Boyle, Donna Dixon (Ellie Mae of TV's *Beverly Hillbillies*), Joe Flaherty, Matt Frewer, Mimi Kuzyk, Eugene Levy, Tim Matheson, Jamie "Klinger" Farr, Melody Anderson, Shari Belafonte, The Smothers Brothers (Dick really *is* a race car driver), Lee Van Cleef, and, apparently mistaking the film for a Bob Hope TV special, Brooke Shields. The cars in the film include a Bentley Corniche convertible, a Jaguar XJ-12, and a Lamborghini Countach.

Despite all of the talent involved it ends up being something so incredibly bad it ought to be an embarrassment to everyone that was involved with it, although it still was popular in some circles. The videotape's liner notes say "6 cars, 17 stars. A million laughs." Maybe it was a typo and was supposed to say "and a milli-laugh."

Speeding Along

(1927) This is one of the silent films listed in this book, this one being about old-time race cars blasting down country roads. It is available by mail order, sometimes with *Teddy at the Throttle* on the same tape for a total running time of 63 minutes. As an interesting side note, it was around this time that some of the great silent film stars also became notorious street racers, screaming down Hollywood Boulevard in the middle of the night. There was Clara Bow in her hot Kessel roadster, Rudolph Valentino in his French 1925 Avion Voison phaeton, and mean Jean Harlow in her ground-pounding black V-12 Cadillac.

Speedtrap

(1977) This flick stars Tyne Daly, Joe Don Baker (Buford Pusser of the *Walking Tall* movies), Richard Jaeckel, Robert Loggia, Morgan Woodward, and Timothy Carey. The story involves a pair of cops (Daly and Baker) trying to catch a car thief, and it stinks.

Speedway

(1968) *Speedway* is another Elvis Presley movie, with him playing Steve Grayson, a singing NASCAR Grand National stock car driver. There's some NASCAR racing footage, with cameo appearances by Cale Yarborough, Buck Baker, Richard Petty, and the boys. It's great to see all those old stock cars running at Charlotte, even if much of the racing footage looks like it came from TV coverage of a race in about 1966. The token plot carries on the tradition of all the Elvis movies and is, well, a plot. Costars include Nancy Sinatra as a tax official (Hey, audit me!), the late Bill Bixby, and Gale Gordon.

Spinout

(1966) *Spinout* stars Elvis Presley as Mike McCoy, the leader of a rock band and a racer who pilots a white 427 Shelby Cobra. Like all of the Elvis movies, it was essentially a vehicle to cash in on his singing popularity. The band goes on the road in a 1927 Duesenberg phaeton that's towing the the Cobra on a trailer. There's some road racing in the movie, but most of the story concerns Elvis and the three women chasing the King. (And don't worry about the opening scene, which has Elvis dumping the Cobra in a river—it's not actually a Cobra! It was an Austin-Healey frame with a Chevy engine and a fiberglass Cobra-replica body.) The cast includes Shelley Fabares (of TV's "Coach", Diane McBain, Deborah Walley, Cecil Kellaway, and Una Merkel.

The Spy Who Loved Me

(1977) Roger Moore joins forces with a seductive Russian agent (the lovely Barbara Bach—Mrs. Ringo Starr) to crush Curt Jurgens' plan for world destruction. You're going to love the 7ft, 2in Richard Kiel with his steel dentures. But the most memorable aspect of the film is the Lotus Espirit. It was chased by everything from car to helicopter, but film history was made when it plunged into the Atlantic Ocean and sprouted fins. Perry Submarine (a Bahamas company) gave the car four electric motors, a ballast tank, and a life support system for the driver. This auto-sub was for real!—RM

State Fair

(1962) Here is a musical that stars Pat Boone as a sports car racer and Ann-Margaret as the love interest. This elaborate production has the star rac-

Sort of a biker version of the old Rat Pack-in-Vegas classic, *Ocean's Eleven, Hell's Angels '69* was to a great extent the work of star Tom Stern. He developed the story, produced the film, and starred in it–along with real members of the original Hell's Angels Oakland Chapter, the best-known biker gang in the nation. *American International/ Ron Main Collection*

ing against a field of mid-fifties sports racers in a brief scene. Boone's car is a special along the lines of a Devin roadster (an early fiberglass kit car). The racing segment features lots of sports roadsters, including a first-generation Austin Healey, a 1957 Corvette, a Jaguar XK-120 roadster.

Steel Arena

(1973) This one was directed by Mark Lester, who also did *Truck Stop Women* in 1974. *Steel Arena* is based on the story of Dusty Russell, the great stunt driver whose team of daredevils was an American institution. *Steel Arena* is a low-budget picture, made for $150,000. The actual members of Dusty's stunt team are shown in the movie, which shows him work his way up the ranks from competing in demolition derbies to having the team that toured across the States. In addition to Dusty Russell, the cast features Gene Drew, Buddy Love, Ed Ryan, Laura Books, Nancy Walton, Eric Nord, and the guy with the coolest name in the book, Speed Sterns. It's hard to find but see it if you get the chance.

Steel Cowboy

(1978) This film was made for television. The story here involves a trucker who's got money problems. He takes a job hauling stolen livestock and manages to end up a winner. James Brolin, Rip Torn, Strother Martin, Jennifer Warren, Melanie Griffith, and Julie Cobb star. Sounds like a made-for-TV-quality cast.

Stingray

(1978) High-speed hi-jinx climaxed by a wild car chase (that includes a car going into the Mississippi River) highlight this comedy adventure. Starring Christopher Mitchum, Les Lannom, and Sherry Jackson, who played the smart aleck daughter in TV's "Make Room for Daddy". She plays the beautiful but tough gangster who rides a motorcycle, operates a bulldozer, and crashes through a hot dog stand in a car. (So now I suppose it's "Make Room for Sherry," especially if she's driving that bulldozer!) Mitchum and Lannom buy a Corvette, not realizing it's loaded with stolen money and dope that belongs to Jackson, who pursues them with vigor. Filmed in the St. Louis area, this film introduces perky Playmate Sondra Theodore (Miss July 1977). Veteran stunt coordinator Carey Loftin, well known for his reckless driving, crashes, and nail-biting near-misses, choreographed the spectacular jump off Eads Bridge into the Big Muddy! Loftin used four identical red Corvettes as stunt doubles (Hey, sometimes cars need them, too.) Get it on!—RM

Stingray

(1985) This made-for-television and was the pilot for the TV series, with the same plot about the mysterious man who shows up in his black 1966 Corvette coupe and helps people out when they are in trouble. It stars Nick Mancuso, Susan Blakely, Robyn Douglass, Gregory Sierra, Michael Fairman, Wendell Wright, and Lee Richardson.

St. Louis Kid

(1934) This film stars James Cagney as a truck driver who gets messed up with a strike and the scabs who cross the line and then gets falsely accused of killing a union activist. Cagney's performance is outstanding as always. This is one to look out for. The cast also includes Patricia Ellis, Hobart Cavanaugh, Allan Jenkins, and Robert Barrat, with Ray Enright directing.

Stock Car

(1976) *Stock Car* gives us a look at the NASCAR Grand National (now called NASCAR Winston Cup) competition in the mid-seventies. It's not a very good movie, and it's seldom talked about, but they tried and it's worth watching if you're a NASCAR fan and you come across it. It shows up on Prime Sports affiliates about once a year. The cast includes Nick Adams, Jeanine Riley, Norman Alden, Vaughn Taylor, Daxson Thomas, and Robert Broyles.

Stone Cold

(1991) *Stone Cold* stars former pro football player (washout) Brian Bosworth as a cop who goes undercover to expose a motorcycle club. *Stone Cold* has enough Harley-Davidsons and action to make it worth watching for entertainment. It's better than many modern motorcycle movies, but ask yourself how much that's really saying. This time all of the motorcyclists aren't just portrayed as violent and dumb, they're murderers, pimps, and dope dealers, too.

Well isn't that special.—DM

Steve Gray's review of Stone Cold:

Columbia Pictures serves up action with a capital A in this star vehicle for football great and all-around renaissance man Brian Bosworth. On suspension from the Alabama cops for being such a wild man, Bosworth's character, Stone is trapped by the FBI to infiltrate "the Brotherhood," an unbelievably violent bike gang based in Mississippi.

How violent? For laughs, they shoot beer cans off each other's heads and shoulders with large caliber pistols.

The Brotherhood was planning to spring one of the boys out of a high security courtroom as a brother just did not *do* time, man. (He had shot a minister point blank while doing a baptism.) As Stone gains the gang's confidence we see a few of the biker movie staples: the biker hospital visit, the biker funeral (Viking style), and the big bike chase.

The producers of *Stingray* made sure that they introduced young actress Sondra Theodore, but that was her career's only shot at the spotlight. *Avco Embassy/ Ron Main Collection*

All of this is a warm-up for the big event, the courtroom breakout. While it would've been noble to bust the gang in time to prevent a massacre, it better suits a true action movie to be a little too late to a potential blood bath. *Everybody* dies. The judge, lawyers, deputies—even the governor. Like a Consumer Report's test of hand-held automatic weapons.

Then, with all the good guys dead, Stone can show up to waste the bikers, who are blasting down the marble halls of the state house on their hogs, killing anyone they met. The bikers all meet pointless deaths (like trying to run over a weapon the size of a mailbox, or playing chicken with the National Guard), and Stone, bloody but all in a day's work, strolls out of the scene.

As an action movie, *Stone Cold* followed all the rules like, "any vehicle shot shall explode," and "any person, when shot, shall contrive to fall a great distance." But as a bike movie, something was missing. They didn't pay any attention to the bikes! Just a bunch of factory customs, they rode 'em around, but the camera never settled on them, no one ever talked about them, and worse: How can a biker say something like, "I'll peel your skin off with a knife dipped in s—," then follow up by poking the starter button with their pinkie and motoring away? Is that sort of nancy, or what? That's how my mom starts her microwave. There's only one way for a biker to punctuate a threat: by lighting the iron with one hard kick. And what's with the clowns who made the damn movie giving "special thanks" to the rather Frenchy sounding "Credit Lyonnais Bank Nederland N.V." for financing? You never saw American International kissing a banker's ass!

The recommendation? Bad music, no sex, and precious little nudity.—SG

A Strange Adventure

(1956) A rare and seldom-seen film, but it's a great hot rod epic about hot rodders who get involved in a hold-up. "Hey, it costs money to go fast," they note. It stars Nick Adams and Marla English.—RM

Streets Of Fire

(1984) This one could be considered a remake of a B movie from the fifties. It has a violent motorcycle gang kidnapping a girl who's a rock musician, with her boyfriend trying to get her back. But the story is the weak point of the movie—the visual effects are outstanding and the music includes The Blasters and Ry Cooder. The cast includes Michael Paré, Diane Lane, Rick Moranis, Amy Madigan, Willem Dafoe, Deborah Van Valkenburgh, Elizabeth Daily, Lee Ving, Marine Jahan, and Ed Begley, Jr.

Streets of Justice

(1985) This film was another pilot for a proposed TV series, but nobody picked it up. The story is along the lines of the *Death Wish* series, with a gang of bikers wiping out a family, and the surviving member out for revenge. Christopher Crowe directed it, with John Laughlin, Lance Henriksen, Jack Thibeau, John Hancock, Douglas Dirkson, Cristina Raines, and Robin Gammell. More negative biker stereotyping and way too much violence make this one best forgotten about.

Stroker Ace

(1983) *"Stroker"* stars Burt Reynolds and Loni Anderson along with Ned Beatty, Jim Nabors, Parker Stevenson, Bubba Smith, John Byner, and Frank O. Hill. Reynolds is a stock car driver, Beatty is his sponsor and Anderson is the lady he hassles (but it paid off, huh Burt?). His sponsor is in the chicken business, so Burt keeps him happy by racing in a chicken suit. This is a low-budget movie that is of historical interest only unless you're a fan of the *Dukes of Hazzard* school of comedy.

John Brinkley not only starred as Frank in *T-Bird Gang*, but he was also a co-writer of the screenplay with Tony Miller, who played Raymond. The movie was distributed on a double bill with *High School Big Shot*. *Ron Main Collection*

The publicity staff at Howco International must have been working on a typewriter with tiny letters. Readers with magnifying glasses could read the poster blurb that says, "CHICKEN is not just a word... it's MURDER!" ***Howco International/ Ron Main Collection***

Super Van

Mark Schneider, Katie Saylor, and George Barris, the king of the kustoms, star in this one. George is the creator of the outrageous solar-powered super van, and the competition spends the bulk of the movie trying to steal it.—RM

Take This Job and Shove It

(1981) This film features an appearance by one of the early Bigfoot Ford monster trucks, which gets put to work doing a bit of getting even. There are appearances by Lacy J. Dalton, Johnny Paycheck, David Allen Coe, and Charlie Rich in the movie. This one still shows up on TV now and again. An example of a movie made only because its title was the same as that of a huge hit song (originally recorded by Paycheck).

Tango & Cash

(1989) No great shakes in this film starring Sylvester Stallone and Kurt Russell, but there is a good action sequence featuring our heroes launching a beefed-up mini-pickup that looks like a stadium racer during a prison break-out.—MDa

Taxi

(1953) Dan Dailey, a fine actor, and Broadway star Stubby Kaye star in this comedy about New York City hack Dailey trying to help promote romance for a woman friend. Constance Smith and John Cassavetes are also in this film, which comes from an era of no in-car cameras, but plenty of shots of actors seated in front of backdrops onto which street scene footage is projected.—MDa

Taxi Driver

(1976) Not much of a car movie, really, but star Robert De Niro *does* put in some time in his Checker cab, including a scene where his fare is Director Martin Scorsese. Intense, thrilling, and violent, this film is a classic, yet it's disturbing enough so you might never be compelled to see it a second time. Harvey Keitel is brilliant, and (a very young) Jodie Foster, Cybil Shepherd, Peter Boyle, and Albert Brooks all contribute excellent performances. This is why people in Manhattan sometimes decide, "On second thought, I guess I'll walk."—MDa

T-Bird Gang

(1959) *"Gang"* stars John Brinkley, Ed Nelson, Pat George, Tony Miller, and a 1958 Ford Thunderbird convertible. This is another teen exploitation flick, with a gang of punks out to revenge a murder.

"Fast cars, fast girls, and no place to go!"

Teddy at the Throttle

(1917) This is among the earliest feature films made about cars. It is still listed in some video guides, along with *Speeding Along* from 1927 which is listed below. Although many film libraries have access to it, this is fairly esoteric stuff so don't expect to find it too easily. *Teddy at the Throttle* stars Gloria Swanson along with Teddy the dog. The picture makes fun of chase movies, with Gloria stalling the car at a railroad crossing, only to be saved by Teddy who jumps on the gas pedal.

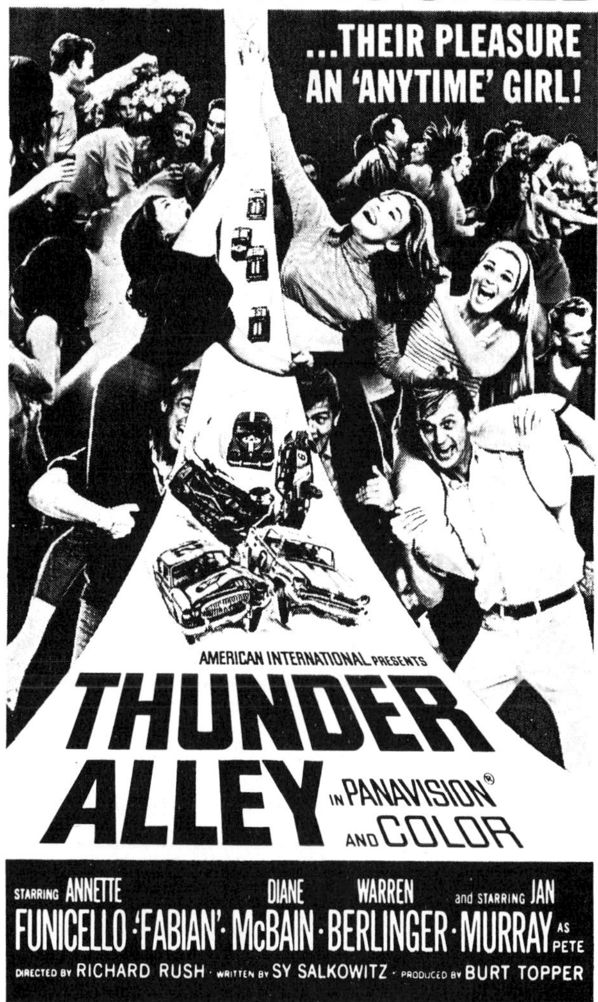

Thunder Alley* starred Annette Funicello and Fabian, but don't forget that it also featured TV funny man and stand-up comic Jan Murray. The American International release was produced by Burt Topper, who made several classic car films. *American International/ Ron Main Collection

Teenage Crime Wave

(1955) After the lead of *Rebel Without a Cause*, movies like *Teenage Crime Wave* soon followed to cash in on the success of it and *The Wild One*. In Columbia Pictures' *Teenage Crime Wave* a gang of teenagers commit a robbery and then raise hell with a family of farmers, with lots of tasteful tire squealing. *Teenage Crime Wave* stars Tommy Cook, Sue English, Molly McCart, Frank Griffin, James Bell, and Ray Riehl. The promotional poster for it says: "Cool Kid In A Hot Car! Stolen cars, stolen guns, stolen thrills! Out of the sidewalk jungle...the terrifying story of our teenagers gone wrong!"

A note at the bottom of the poster headlined "Crime Of Our Times" reads: "Over 25% of the crimes committed in this country are perpetrated by teenagers. Only an aroused public can put an end to this. We hope this picture will open your eyes."

Teenage Cruisers

(1977) This was another teen movie with rock 'n' roll and hot rods.

Teenage Doll

(1957) Here is another squealing-tire juvenile delinquent exploitation picture, better than most. June Kenney, Fay Spain, and John Brinkley star in the story of a girl who knifes a member of a rival gang.

Teenage Mother

(1966) *"Mother"* has the kind of title that just says "quality entertainment for the discriminating viewer". There's some good drag racing in it, including a scene that has a shootout between a pair of blown 1941 Willys coupes.

Teenage Rebel

(1956) This film stars Ginger Rogers as the mother of a spoiled and rebellious daughter named Dorothy, played by Betty Lou Keim. Warren Berlinger is cast as Dick, the kid next door with the hot rod, who eventually goes to the drags with Dorothy's name written on his car for good luck.

The car is a fenderless Model A roadster with a 1932 frame and grille and a hot flathead with four Stromberg carbs. An hour into the movie there is a scene that shows lots of early hot rods, mostly Ford roadsters with no fenders or hoods, all with painted steel wheels. The big Silver Trophy Dash is held at a real old-time drag strip, where the cars run three at a time. *Teenage Rebel* is not nearly as wild a movie as the title might lead you expect—it's pretty wholesome stuff.

Teenage Strangler

(1964) "Hot Rods! Hot Songs! And Hot Girls!" This obscure cheapy has it all: drag races, teen dancing, and rumbles. Don't get me wrong, it is cheap, cheap, cheap! But somehow it all works. This rare one about a mad killer in high school was done in pure fifties style with Bill Bloom, Stacy Smith, and Rick Harris starring. It's a must-see for lovers of teen schlock. The ad said, "Budding Young Teeny-Boppers Were the Bluebeard's Prey! See Dismemberment and Death!" In color.—RM

Ten Laps to Go

(1938) Rex Leash is our cocky hero: "Why, I am the greatest driver in the world!" But sleazy fellow driver Duncano Renaldo makes sure Rex won't finish the next race. After the crash, Rex's car and nerves are shattered. He becomes a bum and learns humility before regaining his self-confidence. This is old-time melodrama at its best. It's fast-moving, with action featuring the famous Householder white #2 Offy racer.—RM

Terminator 2—Judgment Day

(1991) *T2* was the highest-grossing movie of 1991, starring Arnold Schwarzenegger and Linda Hamilton. In the opening sequence, Arnold borrows a black 1991 Harley-Davidson Fatboy, which he rides throughout most of the movie. Spectacular stunts and special effects add a lot to *T2*, which is said to have cost $100 million to make. Among the stunts is a Kawasaki police motorcycle being ridden through the upper-story windows of an office building so the rider can hijack a police helicopter hovering nearby. Although it's more violent than it had to be, it's a great action movie, highly recommended.

Thelma & Louise

(1991) A hugely popular film that has two women hitting the road because of a totally justified shooting of a rapist. It's a terrific movie with Susan Sarandon and Gena Davis tearing up the highway and down the dusty road in a '66 Thunderbird, finding romance, conflict, adventure, danger, and perhaps less satisfaction or happiness than they hoped. In the end, the Bird flies. It also stars Brad Pitt and Harvey Keitel.—MDa

Then Came Bronson

(1969) This was the pilot for the TV series with

Hey, Little Buddy, isn't that Alan Hale, Jr., who went on to play the Skipper in TV's "Gilligan's Island", co starring in the 1960 release, *Thunder in Carolina*? You can bet it's the wayward Skipper because he—and his father before him—were versatile character actors who appeared in a wide variety of films. *Howco International/ Ron Main Collection*

the same name, made before Charles Bronson was signed on. This one stars Michael Parks as Bronson, along with the popular and talented actress Bonnie Bedelia. *Then Came Bronson* starts out with Parks as a reporter called to talk a friend out of suicide. When he fails to convince him not to jump, Parks heads off to clear his head on his dead friend's Harley-Davidson Sportster. On the highway he meets up with Bedelia, who is running from a marriage she doesn't want any more. It's not a happy story but it's worth watching. For motorcycle enthusiasts, things get interesting about halfway into the picture, when Parks and Bedelia pull into a motorcycle hill climb. Parks takes on the competition, which includes some serious, scratch-built race bikes. On his second try he clears the hill, on a Sportster that's stock except for a sissy bar! If you look closely at the scene of the bike making it over the top, it's actually something like an Ossa or Bultaco 250 motocross bike with a sissy bar.

They Drive By Night

(1940) *They Drive By Night* stars Humphrey Bogart as one of a pair of brothers struggling with their boss. Some good acting helps make this a classic trucking film, although the first half of the picture will likely provide the most interest.

The cast includes George Raft, Ann Sheridan, Ida Lupino, Gale Page, Alan Hale, Sr., and Roscoe Karns.—DM

Michael Dregni's review of They Drive By Night:

This film starred Humphrey Bogart as one of a pair of straight-dealing, truck-driving brothers battling against the odds and their crooked bosses. This is classic forties melodrama with all of the

Clark Gable (right) was a no-nonsense racer in *To Please a Lady,* a film that was later rereleased as *Red Hot Wheels. MGM/ Ron Main Collection*

fabulous tough-talking dialogue that Bogart flicks became famous for.

The acting is perfectly in keeping with the melodrama, and the cast includes George Raft, Ann Sheridan, Ida Lupino, Gale Page, Alan Hale, and Roscoe Karns. Both the original black and white and a computer-colored version are available.—MDr

Thieves' Highway

(1949) This one stars Richard Conte, Valentina Cortese, Lee J. Cobb, and Jack Oakie. It's the story of truckers in California hauling produce, with mobsters trying to move in on them. This is one of the best of the trucking movies.

This Stuff'll Kill Ya

(1971) This film was produced by Herschell Gordon Lewis, starring Jeffrey Allen as preacher whose church is actually a front for a moonshine operation. In his last role before his death, Tim Holt played a federal agent sent in to investigate. There's the usual car chase action here, with Gloria King also starring.

The Thomas Crown Affair

(1968) Steve McQueen is cool as they come as he plots the perfect bank robbery, and he's matched by as-cool Faye Dunaway, who has designs on catching him in the act. Among the vehicles McQueen drives is a Corvair-powered dune buggy built by Bruce Manx. It was a Manx dune buggy with custom bodywork, a low windshield, and modest side windows. This is a movie worth seeing, and not only because it contains the first French kiss between two stars in a mass-market-released film. (The kiss between McQueen and Dunaway—the only kiss in the movie—lasts for more than a minute straight.) Among the movies he made, this was McQueen's favorite because he worked so hard to make himself convincing as the smooth, educated, polished robber; he considered it a stretch from his true background and personality, and was proud of his work. It was directed by Norman Jewison and includes 1968's Oscar-winning song, "The Windmills of Your Mind."—MDa

Those Daring Young Men in their Jaunty Jalopies

(1969) *TDYMITJJ* stars Tony Curtis, Susan Hampshire, gap-toothed comedian Terry-Thomas, Eric Sykes, Gert Frobe (Goldfinger), Peter Cook, a young Dudley Moore, and Jack Hawkins. Set in the twenties, this is a comedy about the people who have entered a 1,500-mile car race to Monte Carlo.

Thunder Alley

(1967) This one stars Annette Funicello, Fabian, Diane McBain, Warren Berlinger, Jan Murray, and Maureen Arthur. Fabian plays a NASCAR stock car driver who gets suspended from racing because he keeps passing out on the track.

Thunder and Lightning

(1977) *"T & L"* stars David Carradine, Kate Jackson, Roger C. Carmel, Sterling Holloway, Ed

The poster for *Vanishing Point* told movie goers would "hear the supercharged sounds" of performers such as Mountain, Delaney & Bonnie & Friends, Jerry Reed, and our favorite, Big Mama Thornton. *Ron Main Collection*

Barth, and Ron Feinberg. Moonshiners, car chases, screeching tires, and crashes.

Thunder Boat Row

(1989) This film was made for TV, with Chad Everett, Jason Adams, Nicki Corri, Robert Estes, and Anthony Jones starring. It's about dope smugglers in Florida being chased by cops with muscle boats.

This is one of the few movies in the book to feature high-performance boats, which in this case are offshore powerboats along the lines of the famous Cigarette and Scarab designs. (Another movie with high-performance boats is called *Racing Fever*, from 1964.)

Hot Car Girl and _Cry Baby Killer_ made for an outstanding double-bill of teenage exploitation in 1958. _Cry Baby Killer_ was Jack Nicholson's first feature film. He also made several biker flicks in the sixties before scoring big at decade's end in the 1969 release _Easy Rider_. _Allied Artists/ Ron Main Collection_

Thunder in Carolina

(1960) This flick was also released under the title of *Hard Drivin'*. It stars Rory Calhoun, Alan Hale, Jr. (the Skipper from "Gilligan's Island"), Connie Hines, and John Gentry. The Southern 500 at Darlington, South Carolina is the scene for this story about a guy chasing a girl. The plot is redundant but there's some good old NASCAR racing footage here from one of America's great paved and banked oval tracks.

Thunder Road

(1958) *Thunder Road* stars Robert Mitchum in a very good bootlegging movie. Mitchum gives a fine performance here as Luke, the son of a moonshiner. He's the driver, using a series of hot cars through some good chase scenes which are set in rural Kentucky. The first car he runs is a 1950 Ford coupe that looks stock but has a hot engine and some features that help keep the cops at a distance. In a scene where he's being chased by a cop in a 1957 Ford he pulls a lever on the dash to pour oil on the road, just before a turn on a mountain road. Later in the movie he gets his own 1957 Ford which is also tricked-up a bit. It's supposedly based on some actual events. In the closing credits, we read:

"We gratefully acknowledge the factual cooperation of the Alcohol and Tobacco Tax Division, Internal Revenue Service, Treasury Department."

The movie has good use of suspense, and any car enthusiast is bound to get something out of it. The ending is not happy, but *Thunder Road* is a classic documentation of an undeniable part of the roots of modern stock car racing. It also stars Gene Barry, Jacques Aubuchon, Keely Smith, and James Mitchum. Robert Mitchum also wrote and sang the title song, and helped write and produce this movie.

Thunderball

(1965) This film featured the return of the famous Aston Martin DB5 (as well as Sean Connery as James Bond). The fourth Bond flick, this one set the style for things to come with gadgets galore and more action than plot. There's missing nuclear warheads, squealing Dunlop tires, high-stakes casinos, girls in bikinis, an underwater frogman war, and even more accessories added to the DB5 by techno mastermind Q. Always worth catching on a late-night rerun.—MDr

Timerider—The Adventure of Lyle Swann

(1983) Here is a science fiction story about a an exceptional motocross racer. While he's competing in the Baja 1000, he becomes transported back to the year 1877, in the Old West. Nobody can believe the sight of his bike—in fact they're all terrified of it and of him. *Timerider* will be of interest to science fiction fans but it has little to offer

Silent and, Most Likely, Unseen

There are many other films that include great car and motorcycle action that aren't listed in this book. Unfortunately, chances are that you'll never be able to see many of those films. In fact, no one will.

Many old films—especially those made up into the twenties and thirties—were not stored properly, and thus have degenerated to a state which precludes their ever being projected again. It's no one's fault in particular. Major studios weren't always aware of how their stored film was decaying. Once the decay was discovered, the money and interest to save every film simply wasn't there.

The good news, however, is that film preservation techniques are improving every year, meaning that any existing print has at least a chance of being transferred and saved. Thanks to video tape and modern film preservation approaches, it's safe to say that the loss of old films won't happen again.

Among the old films that might not have survived are many silent films that featured terrific car chases, crashes, and motorcycle action. The majority of these now rare, perhaps unobtainable films, were silent films. (The first "talkie" with its own soundtrack was the 1927 film *The Jazz Singer*, starring Al Jolson. By the early thirties, production of silent movies had pretty well ended.)

Soundtracks hardly mattered to movies involving the Keystone Cops, early Laurel & Hardy movies, and action flicks such as Tom Mix's *The Speed Maniacs*. The foundation of these films was their action, and it was enough to have a movie-house organ or piano provide accompaniment while the cars, trucks, buses, street cars, and motorcycles on screen wove their ways through an endless series of miraculous near-misses.

If you get the chance to see some silent films with their particular brand of chase scenes, jump at the chance. Consider that these old movies were made with equipment that was primitive by all standards compared to today. The cameras were less numerous and were mounted on less forgiving perches (such as trucks rolling down cobblestone streets ahead of the chase); the cars, trucks, and motorcycles were not the smart-handling vehicles they are today, making stunt maneuvers less predictable; and the stunt crew's safety equipment was practically non-existent.

Video stores don't normally carry many of these old movies, but be sure to ask for them and look at the titles in the "action," "comedy," and "silent movies" sections. Many are short films, so your commitment of time might be only 20 or 30 minutes to watch an old classic. Probably the best place to find these movies is in video catalogs. With its emphasis on car and motorcycles titles, Main Attractions is a good starting point.

A word of caution: Hollywood recycles movie titles, so you might find the 1951 version of *Excuse My Dust* instead of the 1920 version. Or you might seek the 1919 *Greased Lightning* but only find the 1977 movie starring Richard Pryor. And there's truly a fifty-year generation gap between the *Dead Man's Curve* of 1928 and the 1978 version based on the Jan & Dean song.

Titles to look for include: *Across the Continent* (1922), *Cyclone Rider* (1924), *Checkered Flag* (1926), *Catch My Smoke* (1922), *Crack O'Dawn* (1925), *Fast and Furious* (1927), *The First Auto* (1927), *High Speed* (1920), and Louis B. Meyer's *In Pursuit of Polly* (1918).

There's also: *Lizzies of the Field* (a 1924 Mack Sennett film), *Love, Speed, and Thrills* (a 1915 Keystone production), *Lucky Devil* (1925), *The Married Flapper* (1922), *Mind Over Motor* (1923), *Perils of Pauline* (1914), *The Race* (1916), *The Roaring Road* (1919), *The Racing Fool* (1927), *Racing for Life* (1924), *A Racing Romeo* (1927), *Race for a Life* (1913), and *The Road Demon* (1921).

The Keystone productions of *Speed Kings* (1913) and *Speeding Along* (1927) were wild, and there's also great action in: *Skip Proof* (1923), *Soiled* (1924), *The Speed Classic* (1928), *Speed Crazed* (1926), *The Speed Spook* (1924), *The Speeding Venus* (1926), *Sporting Youth* (1929), *Thirty A Week* (1918), *Too Much Speed* (1921), *Two-Edged Sword* (1916), *Wife and Auto Trouble* (1916), and *What's Your Hurry?* (1920).

motorcycle enthusiasts other than the novelty of the story line. The cast includes Fred Ward, Belinda Bauer, Peter Coyote, Ed Lauter, Richard Masur, Tracey Walter, and L.Q. Jones, and was produced and directed by former Monkees guitarist Michael Nesmith.

Tire Trouble

(1924) This was another silent film, this time from the Our Gang comedy series. The vehicle the Gang has trouble with is a Model T bus.

To Please A Lady

(1950) *"To Please"* features Clark Gable (as Mike Brannan) playing the driver of an open-wheel race car, with Barbara Stanwyck as a reporter begging him to quit. It's not a great picture. To those of you who only know Stanwyck as the tough matriarch from TV's "Big Valley", this is a chance to see her as a Hollywood leading lady, which she was in the fifties. Indy winner Mauri Rose doubles for Gable in driving scenes filmed at Indianapolis, and California racer Bud Rose doubled as Gable's driver during filming at Arlington Downs, Texas, site of a 1-mile oval.

Tomboy

(1985) This is a movie that takes the familiar roles and switches them around to get a story about a young lady who's a car nut, out to win races and a cute guy. It could have worked, but the result is clearly aimed at giggly kids struggling through puberty. The racy racer is played by Betsy Russel with Jerry Dinome playing the hunk.

Tommy

(1975) *Tommy* is a rock opera that may seem out of place here, but it does as good a job as any movie in portraying the Mods in England and their culture that includes customized Vespa and Lambretta scooters.

Very simply put, the story involves a kid who has problems with a girl and his scooter. *Tommy* was directed by Ken Russell, with a cast is made up of over a hundred British teenagers.

Track of Thunder

(1968) *"Track"* stars Tom Kirk, Ray Stricklyn, and H.M. Wyant. It's another movie about stock car racers and the scrapes they get into on and off the track.

Truck Busters

This one is based around the fight between the independent drivers and the big trucking companies. It's a poorly done movie that has lots of violence. The cast includes Richard Travis, Virginia Christine, Charles Lang, Ruth Ford, Richard Fraser, and Frank Wilcox. The script was written by Robert Kent and Raymond Schrock, directed by Reaves Eason.

Truck Stop Women

(1974) Here is a sexploitation flick starring Claudia Jennings, Lieux Dressler, Jennifer Burton, and Dennis Fimple that obviously deals with those dangerous truck stop babes. It's well-done and although there's lots of violence, it's recommended, but not for kids.

Tucker—The Man and His Dream

(1988) *Tucker* is one of those rare and special movies that combines fine acting, excellent sets and props, with a fascinating story. Jeff Bridges plays Preston Tucker, the humanitarian automotive visionary who set out to take on the big boys.

The story begins in Ypsilanti, Michigan, in 1945. Tucker has been spending time with his long-time friend, legendary Indy Car builder Harry "Ak" Miller. He arrives at his home in his 1941 Lincoln convertible and presents his family with the plans for a revolutionary car of the future, the Tucker Torpedo. Nothing like this has been built before. An air-cooled engine, in the rear. The first car to fully address the issue of safety, with seat belts, a built-in roll bar, a pop-out windshield, and a fully padded interior. This was incredible thinking back in the mid-forties. Everyone who sees his vision is justifiably amazed.

An investor is invited over to see if he would put up the money to finance the project. When Tucker is turned down, he takes the family out for some ice cream. While at the ice cream parlor, he picks up a magazine and sees something new being written about inside. When someone asks him what he thinks of it, he says that the product might not even exist. The response is "So what? It says so in the magazine!" And so another idea is born—to promote the Tucker Torpedo in the press before it has actually been built, to raise money for its production.

An article is published in a popular magazine that tells of Tucker's visionary ideas. The public starts to line up for a car that exists only on paper, and in the mind of Preston Tucker. From here on, Tucker's life becomes a series of ups and downs that I'll leave for you discover.

Tucker is a Lucasfilm production, produced by

George Lucas, directed by Francis Ford Coppola and released by Paramount in Dolby surround sound. Besides Jeff Bridges, the cast includes Joan Allen as his wife, Martin Landau as the financier, along with Frederic Forrest, Mako, Dean Stockwell, Lloyd Bridges, Elias Koteas, Nina Siemaszko, Christian Slater, Corky Nemec, Marshall Bell, Don Novello, Peter Donat, Dean Goodman, and Patti Austin.

Tucker is a real masterpiece that set a new standard for accuracy and attention to detail in automotive movies. It is highly recommended, for the whole family, without reservation. This one is about as good as they get.

'Twas Henry's Fault

(1919) This film poked fun at the "Tin Lizzie" Ford Model T, its reliability and its impact on society. It was a very popular silent comedy in its time, starring Elinor Field and Harry Deep. Although *'Twas Henry's Fault* made fun of the Model T, it was a sensation that only added to the car's legendary popularity.

Two-Lane Blacktop

(1971) This film enjoys cult status to this day, and airs occasionally on A&E (Arts and Entertainment). This movie got a lot of publicity in magazines like *Car Craft* and *Hot Rod* in its day. James Taylor starred as the owner and builder of a wild street racer. He and his mechanic buddy support themselves by roaming around American highways looking for people to race for money. The car is a 1955 Chevy two-door sedan with a roll bar, no chrome, radiused rear wheelwells, a one-piece flip front end with a huge hood scoop, a lift-off trunk and American Racing 200-S 5-spoke aluminum wheels. They don't say much about the powertrain, but it's got a four-speed and is powered by a big-block Chevy with dual quads, a tunnel-ram

Sign of the apocalypse: In the old days, one-name stars were people like Elvis, and Fabian, who starred in *The Wild Racers*; these days, we're stuck with drips like Madonna and Fabio. Fabian, please come back. ***American International/ Ron Main Collection***

and home-built headers. When our heroes encounter a mouthy "bad actor" with a 455-powered 1970 GTO, he accepts their challenge to race all the way to Washington, DC for pink slips.

In addition to singer-songwriter James Taylor, *Two-Lane Blacktop* stars a most impressive Warren Oates, Laurie Bird, Dennis Wilson (of the Beach Boys), David Drake, and Richard Ruth. It includes a cameo by Harry Dean Stanton and was directed by Monte Hellman.

V-four Victory

This is an oddball, not a Hollywood theater release, but we're including it anyway. A good, clean, fun movie is *V-four Victory*, an account of Joey Dunlop's 1983 Isle of Man T.T. win. The first half of the tape is filler, racing shots, interviews, etc. The second half is the meat and potatoes, a full 37 mile fast practice lap of the island by Dunlop on his 850 Honda. The squeamish should not watch, and anyone who thinks they have it figured out should, as Joey Dunlop shows why he's a roadracer and you're not. Most things that happen are long gone by the time you notice them. If you've been reading about the T.T. for years, as most of us have, then you should watch this video to really put it in perspective. The tape must be listened to several times to understand Dunlop's commentary, which, due to his Irish accent, is truly unintelligible. Another absolute must-see. For sale or rent at some bike shops.—SG

The Van

(1976) *The Van* is a movie about California youth culture and cruising vans. Stuart Getz plays a kid who buys a fancy custom van to impress girls. The cast also includes Deborah White, Danny DeVito, Harry Moses, Marcie Barkin, Bill Adler, and Steven Oliver. It's entertaining and harmless.—DM

Ron Main's review of The Van:

Stuart Getz, Deborah White, and introducing Danny DeVito as "Andy." Shy Getz has no luck with the ladies until George Barris, the king of the kustoms, builds him an outrageous yellow van. Then Getz has fun trucking, drag racing, and using it to seduce the girls. All goes well until he meets the "Killer" van with the big-block Chevy.—RM

Van Nuys Blvd.

(1979) This is a movie about Southern California youth culture, starring Bill Adler, Cynthia Wood, Dennis Bowen, Melissa Prophet, and David Hayward. Adler plays a kid from a small town who takes on the big boys at the drag strip and the disco.

Vanishing Point

(1971) Here is a classic car chase movie with Barry Newman trying to deliver a 1971 Dodge Challenger to San Francisco, from Denver, in fifteen hours. That's about all there is to the plot, but it's a motorhead classic. The cast includes Cleavon Little (as the radio DJ whose broadcasts tip Newman off about the cops' locations), Dean Jagger, Paul Koslo, Robert Donner, Severn Darden, Gilda Texter, and Victoria Medlin. Heavy machinery fans will enjoy the ending.

Viva Knievel!

(1973) *"Viva"* stars Evel Knievel, Gene Kelly, Lauren Hutton, Marjoe Gortner, Red Buttons, Eric Shea, Leslie Nielsen, Cameron Mitchell, Frank Gifford, Albert Salmi, and Dabney Coleman. It sounds good so far, but it turns out to be an unintentional comedy that puts the famed stunt rider at the mercy of some thugs who tail him to Mexico so they can kill him and smuggle dope into the States in his coffin. Well hey, it's possible, right? There's some good stunt riding in the picture, including a scene where Evel rides his Sportster stunt bike around a stadium and through the grandstand with a lady reporter on the back. Some of the dialogue is classic. Too bad about the plot, though. It's painful.

Viva Las Vegas

(1964) Among the Elvis movies, *Viva Las Vegas* has some of the most interesting vehicles, mostly sports cars from the early sixties. The Las Vegas Grand Prix racing segment only lasts about five minutes, but it includes several Corvette coupes, a pair of Cobras, a Mercedes 300SL gullwing, a pair of Jaguar XK-150 coupes and a red E-Type roadster, several Austin Healey roadsters, and a beautiful old Ferrari that gets rolled and smashed in one of several crashes. To help you get over it, you'll also see the fantastic Ann-Margaret in her white Triumph TR-3 roadster. She also sings songs such as "My Rival is a Baby Blue Racing Car." The King, who plays racer Lucky Jackson in this film, belts out the rockin' title track as well as good songs such as "I Need Somebody."

The Wages of Fear

(1952) *The Wages of Fear* was made in France and Italy. It tells the story of four truckers who haul loads of nitro through South America. *Wages of Fear* has been given extremely high praise by critics. Beware, though. The film originally ran 140 minutes, and this is the version to hunt for. Several later, edited-down versions can leave certain aspects puzzling. The long version is recommended; the shorter is still worth watching. Yves Montand, Charles Vanel, Peter Van Eyck, Vera Clouzot, Fol-

Now these were movie ads! Rather than today's retouched photos of weak stars, we want mug shots with individual profiles like these that appeared in the *Wild Rebels* ads. You know you're dealing with a must-see classic when you can read that a character like Banjo is "savage, sadistic, brutal!" or that the film stars "Linda: their mama...never satisfied!" *Crown International/ Ron Main Collection*

VIOLENT STORY OF
WILD BIKE RIDERS
VS
DUNE BUGGY BOYS!
THE ORIGINAL CALIFORNIA GANG!
They Wreck Each Other's Wheels
and Steal Each Other's Girls!!
WILD
WHEELS
HEAR 5 NEW TUNES
COLOR
Starring DON EPPERSON · ROBERT DIX
Co-starring CASEY KASEM · DOVIE BEAMS · TERRY STAFFORD · JOHENNE LEMONT · And introducing BRUCE KIMBLE as "BOOMER"
Produced by BUDD DELL · Written by KENT OSBORNE and RALPH LUCE · Directed by KENT OSBORNE · Released by FANFARE FILM PRODUCTIONS, INC.
R
RESTRICTED – Persons under 16 not admitted unless accompanied by parent or adult guardian

Previous page
Oh, man, we're glad we aren't in California, where the "wild Bike riders" clashed with the "dune buggy boys" in *Wild Wheels.* They not only "wreck each other's wheels," but they "steal each other's girls!!" *Fanfare Films/ Ron Main Collection*

co Lulli, and William Tubbs star.—DM

Michael Dregni's review of The Wages of Fear:

This film tells the tale of four truckers racing against the clock to haul loads of nitro across half of South America to put out an oil well fire. This film is so suspenseful and believable that the scenes of them crossing mountains will make your jaw muscles ache with clenched teeth. When one of the trucks blows up, you'll be in tears.

Beware, however. There are several cuts of this classic French-Italian movie; the original 140-minute version, although tryingly long, is the one to hunt for. The later, edited version will leave you guessing and scratching your head about the storyline. The film was directed by H. G. Cluzot and starred French actor Yves Montand as well as Charles Vanel, Peter Van Eyck, Vera Cluzot, Folco Lulli, and William Tubbs.

The ending is typical French existentialism. The sole surviving driver is on his way back home with his pay in his pocket and his goofy girlfriend awaiting his return. She is dancing with happiness back home while he is singing and swerving his truck with joy when all of the sudden, on that same mountain pass, he... —MDr

Wall of Death

Lewis Gilbert directed this film that starred Maxwell Reed, Susan Shaw, and Lawrence Harvey. The film tells the story of some thrill show riders who take their lumps on and off their bikes, and some of their troubles are courtesy of Miss Shaw. Doggone dames!—MDa

War of the Roses

(1991) This was not a true motorhead movie—or even a truly good movie at all. Its sole redeeming moment was when Mrs. Rose (Kathleen Turner) trades in the family Volvo station wagon for a monster truck, which she then drives over Mr. Rose's (Michael Douglas) Morgan. You can skip the rest of the flick.—MDr

Wayne's World

(1992) This was perhaps the only movie ever to feature an AMC Pacer as a the star car.—MDr

Wayne's World 2

(1993) The old Hollywood formula seems to be "once is never enough," and the formula for Wayne's World cooked, so we get this sequel, in which our hard-rockin' heroes find themselves promoting a rock festival—Waynestock—which features their mega-idols, the rock band Aerosmith. The band arrives in the film's ultimate star: a 36-foot-long Pacer limousine.—MDa

The Weird World of LSD

(1967) "Drag Racers on LSD!" Hey, it got me to buy it! This no-budget documentary tries to show you what an LSD trip is like. Men go crazy, a hand is cut off, a lonely 350lb art dealer eats an entire turkey buffet, faces mutate (thanks to rubber masks), girls lust for men, and one woman cuts her clothes off with a scissors. There's no nudity, but it sure has great women's underwear fashions. Finally, a sports car nut thinks he's Don Garlits and we see smoke-filled runs of top fuel dragsters. All in all, it's pretty tame except the erotic dance in underwear.—RM

Werewolves On Wheels

(1971) This is another classically bad B movie, this time with werewolves on Harley-Davidsons! Sound like fun? Stephen Oliver, Severn Darden, D.J. Anderson, Deuce Berry, Billy Gray, and Barry McGuire star in a movie about a high priest who puts a spell on the bikers.

White Lightnin' Road

(1965) This film was made by June and Ron Ormond, the popular and highly imaginative creators of *Mesa of Lost Women, Untamed Mistress, 40 Acre Feud, Girl from Tobacco Row,* and the classic *Please Don't Touch Me!*

White Lightning

(1973) Here's a movie with Burt Reynolds starring as a moonshiner constantly trying to out-race the law. The cast also includes Jennifer Billingsley, Ned Beatty, Louise Latham, and Bo Hopkins. The sequel to *White Lightning* is *Gator.*

White Line Fever

(1975) *"Fever"* has an Air Force veteran getting into the trucking business and not liking the corruption he finds. There are some good stunts in the film, which stars Jan-Michael Vincent, Kay Lenz, Slim Pickens, and L.Q. Jones. Pickens is a hoot, as usual, doing what almost amounts to a down-home sheriff version of his famous role in *Dr. Strangelove.*

The Wild Angels

(1966) This film stars Peter Fonda (whose character's name here is "Heavenly Blues"), Nancy Sinatra ("Monkey"), Bruce Dern ("Loser"), Michael J. Pollard, Diane Ladd, Lou Procopio, Coby Denton, Marc Cavell, Gayle Hunnicutt, and several members of the Hell's Angels. It was made by American International Pictures and written by Charles Griffith, whose original script for *The Wild Angels* was less than 120 lines.

"Somebody call the art department. It seems like all of our graphics people are tripping too hard to generate any truly creative graphics for our new movie, *The Weird World of LSD.*" *Americana Entertainment Assoc./Ron Main Collection*

This is a classic movie because of the cast and the riders in it—until *Easy Rider* was released three years later this was thought to be the definitive outlaw biker movie. This one was rough and striking, and broke new ground at the time. You know it's special when Leonard Maltin says it's "OK after about 24 beers."—DM

Wild Angels

(Editor's note: This is a different movie than *The Wild Angels* featuring Peter Fonda, Nancy Sinatra, and Bruce Dern.) This one summed it up pretty well. A late-sixties movie that had enough spent on it to make it good without being overblown. John Cassavetes was well cast as Cody, leader of the Skulls; he's smooth, mature, cynical. The movie had a message: survival of the individual, of the gang in a world where you could not control the rules. The movie opens to that masterpiece of fuzz-tone repetition, "The Wild Angels Theme" as the Skulls roll into the clubhouse. Plenty of brew, reefer, and Nazi regalia. Their problem? Due to accident and arrest, the Skulls have dwindled from 200 to twenty-six in five years. On the advice of member Bob, they decide to pack up for a final run to that place of cowboy mythology, the "hole in the wall," where they would be secure to party into eternity.

On that road they venture into Anytown, USA. Turned away from the campground, they wander into that staple of trouble-waiting-to-happen: the small town carnival. Hoping to avoid a confrontation, the thin-lipped townspeople forge a compromise that gets the Skulls out of town and camped by the river, where they explore that other staple of trouble, messing with local teenage girls. Cody is jailed on a trumped-up rape charge, then released by the sheriff, who is still trying to avoid the inevitable showdown. Cody has had enough trouble; he wants the gang to get to Hole-in-the-wall. The gang feel they've been jerked around—they want vengeance, and they've already sent for the Stompers, 200 strong, to help them get it.

They take the town captive and hold a "biker's trial," where justice is served. As things slide towards big violence, Cody makes one last plea to pull out and head for "Hole-in-the-wall." "No such place. I made it up," says Bob. Even Cody's woman is having too much fun trashing the town to leave. Cody pulls off his colors in disgust and throws them in the dirt, lights his bike, and rides into the credits alone.

An all-around good movie with good photography and enough decent bikes (mostly Harleys).

When the Stompers showed up 200 strong, they didn't have to screw around with two-strokes to pad the number out.—SG

The Wild Guitar

(1962) OK, OK, so it's an absolute stinker, but it rates because the exploited rock 'n' roller (the film's star, Arch Hall, Jr.) rides a motorcycle throughout the movie. Apparently, producers and director Ray Dennis Steckler hadn't seen enough bad rock movies from the Elvis factory, and they went ahead and released this one.

The Wild One

(1954) *The Wild One* is another classic, the first movie about motorcycle outlaws. It got so much attention it changed the direction of fifties film into one of a new type of sensationalism—the era of the angry teenage rebel. *The Wild One* represents several firsts in the movies. It was the first real juvenile delinquent/teen exploitation picture. And it was Hollywood's first big movie that portrayed all of the people in it who rode motorcycles as being Bad.

Most of the bikes in *The Wild One* are Triumph twins, which range from stock to stripped-down. There are a few other British bikes, including an AJS, and a handful of Harley-Davidsons—a stripped-down 45 and a 74, as well as a couple of Big Twin police bikes.

The movie begins with the warning: "This is a shocking story. It could never take place in most American towns—but it did in this one. It is a public challenge not to let it happen again."

In case you don't already know what inspired *The Wild One*, here is a very condensed version of the story. On July Fourth, 1947, about 4,000 motorcyclists gathered in Hollister, California, for a club's annual bike rally. People partied and things got pretty rowdy. LIFE magazine, very popular at the time, ran a story about the event, complete with a picture of a guy sitting on a stripped-down

It's easy enough to see why the race cars were flying off the track as shown in this ad. If you were taking a corner and saw a couple making out like the hot couple shown here—whew!—you'd be craning your neck and doing endos through the sand pit, too. *Ron Main Collection*

Harley-Davidson Knucklehead with a springer front end. At his feet lay a pile of empty beer bottles, and each of his hands held full ones. He was smiling at the camera and looked proud of himself. His picture and the accompanying story alarmed the nation—even though the photo was actually staged by the LIFE photographer. In 1951, producer Stanley Kramer read a fictional version of the incident that was written by Frank Rooney. Kramer saw the box-office potential of the story, and set about the creation of what was to become a milestone in cinema.

Marlon Brando plays Johnny, leader of the Black Rebels Motorcycle Club. Lee Marvin plays Chino, leader of the Beetles Motorcycle Club. Brando rides a stock rigid-frame Triumph, and Marvin's ride is a rigid-frame Panhead. At one point an outsider asks Brando, "What are you rebelling against, Johnny?"

"What have you got?"

This line, and much of the slang in the movie, was compiled when the producers spent some time hanging around some genuine California motorcycle nomads back in 1953. Although the motorcyclists portrayed in *The Wild One* are essentially non-violent and really just want to be left alone, the image projected in the film led Columbia Pictures to insist that Kramer add an announcement at the end of the picture, assuring viewers that the doers of evil deeds shown herein were all brought to justice. Columbia also axed Kramer's original title for the film, *Hot Blood*.

The impact of *The Wild One* on society was twofold. The masses, the squares, learned to resent motorcyclists. And Brando's cool look and restless, angry attitude inspired a nation of teenagers who wanted to belong. Because of this, *The Wild One* joins *Rebel Without a Cause* as being more than old movies. These are pieces of history.

Wild Ones On Wheels

(1962) This "Wild One..." stars Fancine York, Robert Blair, and Ray Dennis Steckler. It's the tale of a sports car gang who kills a crook and makes his wife tell them where he had buried the loot.

The Wild Racers

(1968) This film was another attempt at getting Fabian to act, this time with Mimsy Farmer, Judy Cornwall, and David Landers. Still a race car driver, Fabian has girl trouble this time. The movie did poorly in theaters and was his last one.

Wild Rebels

(1967) Starring here is Steve Alaino, who plays a stock car driver that ends up helping the police battle a four-member motorcycle gang called Satan's Angels.

The Wild Ride

(1960) This flick stars Jack Nicholson, Georgianna Carter, and Robert Bean. Nicholson plays a murdering hot rodder in this poor, low-budget picture.

Wild Riders

(1986) *Wild Riders* is available as a 91-minute videotape. It's standard biker movie fare. "Two ladies...one lonely, both lovely. Two bikers, both deadly!" "...forbidden passion, rape and brutality!"

Wild Youth

(1961) Here is an J.D. exploitation flick (not to be confused with the Japanese look at American youth culture with the same name) starring Robert Arthur, Robert Hutton, and Carol Ohmart. A gang of delinquent teenagers fight over some dope, with Carol Ohmart cast as a junkie killer. The poster for *Wild Youth* shows an MG-TD roadster in the background, with a punk terrifying a young girl.

Winners Take All

(1986) *"Winners"* stars Don Michael Paul, Kathleen York, Robert Krantz, and Deborah Richter. The story is about a teenager from California who loves motocross and enters an AMA Camel Pro Supercross race in Dallas, Texas. You'll find some good riding here, with professional riders such as Broc Glover and Brad Lackey.

Winning

(1968) *Winning* stars Paul Newman in the role of a professional race car driver named Frank Caprua. Joanne Woodward is cast as his girlfriend, Richard Thomas plays her son, and Robert Wagner is cast as his teammate, along with David Sheiner and Clu Gulager. Most of the race cars in the early part of the movie are Ford stock cars and open-cockpit Can Am cars, including a 1967 McKee Can Am racer that Newman drives in some of the racing scenes. Later on, Newman arrives at the Indianapolis Motor Speedway to compete in the Indy 500. *Winning* has some fine acting and realistic racing scenes.

One thing about this movie seems unusual today. *Winning* was made in the era when it was not unusual for a car manufacturer to supply virtually every car and truck used in a movie or TV show. In this case it was Ford, and even the Indy Cars in the picture are Lotus chassis that are Ford-powered.

The Wraith

(1986) This film stars Charlie Sheen, Nick Cassavetes, Clint Howard (brother of actor-director Ron), Randy Quaid, and Griffin O'Neal and is about a gang of thieves with hot cars coming up against an outsider in a really hot car.

W.W. and the Dixie Dancekings

(1975) Back in 1957, sweet-talking W.W. lived in a custom '55 Olds, and he loved bubble gum, robbing gas stations, country music, and a gal named Dixie—not necessarily in that order. Don't let the title scare you. Why, this is the film that started the whole *Smokey and the Bandit* craze. Burt Reynolds is W.W., the world's most lovable con man who tries to outrun the law (Art Carney) in his black and gold Rocket 88.—RM

The Yellow Cab Man

(1950) If what we see in the movies were real, the cab drivers from which we could choose would include Robert De Niro (*Taxi Driver*), Mr. T (*D.C. Cab*), and Red Skelton, from this film. (I think I'll walk.) The legendary funnyman plays a bright but accident-prone inventor who ends up driving cab in hopes of selling the company on his latest invention, Elastiglass.—MDa

The Yellow Rolls-Royce

(1965) This one is about an old Rolls and the experiences of its several owners. It stars Rex Harrison, Ingrid Bergman, Shirley MacLaine, Omar Sharif, and George C. Scott.

You Only Live Twice

(1967) "*Y.O.L.T.*" took Sean Connery as James Bond to Japan to fight the baddies. Unfortunately he couldn't bring his Aston Martin DB5 so as a stand-in, the producers found the most exciting Japanese sports car of the time: a beautiful Toyota 2000GT, in perhaps its sole film role ever. (Also look for a rocket-launching BMW motorcycle.)

By this time, Bond flicks were productions in the most grandiose sense of the word. Explosions were larger, tire squeals were louder, and the bad guys were badder. *You Only Live Twice* teeters on the edge of being too much of a good thing, although car buffs can never get enough of watching the Toyota 2000GT.—MDr

Young and Wild

(1958) *Young and Wild* is a good example of the sensational teen exploitation pictures that followed the formula. It was directed by William Whitney and stars Gene Evans, Scott Marlowe, Carolyn Kearney, and Robert Arthur. They're a gang of teenagers who steal a car and get out of control with it.

The Young Cycle Girls

Lornine Ferris, Daphne Lawrence, Deborah Marcus, and Lonnie Panse star in this girl-biker action flick. Who said only boys could do it? A girl can be a dirtbag, too, as these girls are out to prove.—RM

The Young Racers

(1963) *The Young Racers* stars Mark Damon, William Campbell, Patrick Magee, Luana Anders, and Robert Campbell. A former race car driver begins to write a book about another driver but ends up losing his resentment. The promotional poster for *The Young Racers* reads: "A little death each day...a little love every night! They treated beautiful women as if they were fast cars—rough!" This one was produced and directed by Roger Corman, who said, "This was really just an excuse for a lot of us to go to the Grand Prix races." The sound man for the film? A young Francis Ford Coppola.—DM

Ron Main's review of The Young Racers:

"A little death each day... a lot of love every night." What more could you want? This one was filmed on location and in color at Europe's best Grand Prix circuits. Scenes were shot at Aintree, England; Spa, Belgium; Rouen, France; and the glamorous Monte Carlo, Monaco, in 1962. It stars Mark Damon, William Campbell, Luana Anders, and four international playgirls, but better than that is a hot racing trio who appear in real-life roles for this film: Jim Clark, Bruce McLaren, and Trevor Taylor. Clark was a three-time Grand Prix winner that year, and his triple win and those of McLaren and Taylor are featured in this film.—RM

The Young Runaways

(1968) *The Young Runaways* stars Richard Dreyfuss, Brooke Bundy, Kevin Coughlin, Lloyd Bochner, Patty McCormack, Lynn Barri, and Norman Fell (of "Three's Company" fame!). This is a classically bad film, with troubled teens running from their parents right into the arms of bikers and car thieves.

APPENDIX I

WHERE TO FIND BOOKS AND MAGAZINES

There are several ways to obtain copies of the movies listed in this book. In my opinion, in order of quality, the best sources are satellite TV, laserdiscs, mail-order, your local TV station, video rental stores, and cable TV.

Satellite TV

Satellite TV offers by far the greatest selection of movie channels as well as the many networks and superstations that regularly broadcast all kinds of movies. Satellite TV also offers the best picture quality. That's right—a good satellite system, with a good video monitor and top-quality audio equipment, with everything set up optimally, in a good room—will outperform some modern theaters. You can get yourself an excellent satellite system anywhere in the United States for around $3,000 and up. If I sound too enthusiastic it's because I have had a satellite dish for years, and it has brought a whole world of programming into my home.

There are dozens of satellite TV channels specializing in movies. Here are most of the American ones:

ABC can be found in many different locations on two Telstar satellites, T1 and T2. You can usually find an unscrambled feed. The ABC network has feeds for both the east and west time zones.

A&E—Arts & Entertainment is on the powerful Galaxy 5 satellite, on channel 23.

AMC—American Movie Classics shows lots of movies from the thirties and later. They can be found on Satcom C4, channel 1.

Bravo shows movies that are generally somewhat unusual and artistic. They can be found on Satcom C4, channel 7.

Caribbean Super Station is never scrambled and shows movies every night. They're on the Galaxy 6 satellite on channel 22, evenings and weekends.

CBS, like ABC, can be found in many different locations on two Telstar satellites, T1 and T2. You can often find an unscrambled feed. CBS has feeds for both the east and west time zones.

Channel America is never scrambled, and can be found on channel 5 on the Spacenet 2 satellite. They usually show several classic movies a day.

Cinemax has feeds for both the east and west time zones. They are on the Galaxy 1R satellite on channel 19 and on Galaxy 5 channel 16.

Cable Video Store pay-per-view shows only recent box-office hit movies. CVS is on Telstar 303 channel 9.

The Disney Channel has feeds for both the east and west time zones. Their main feed is on Galaxy 5 channel 1, with additional feeds on Galaxy 1R channels 4 and 24.

Flix is a scrambled movie channel on Satcom C3, channel 19.

Fox Network—Fox Classic Theater is unscrambled and can be found on Satcom C1 channel 19. You have access to lots of classic movies here, several a day. (This channel is different from the regular Fox Network feeds, Fox east and Fox west, which are on Telstar 303 channels 18 and 23.)

HBO—Home Box Office has feeds for both the east and west time zones. They are on the Galaxy 5 satellite on channels 8 (west coast feed) and 15 (east coast feed).

Keystone is never scrambled and has classic movies every night and on weekends. They're on the Satcom F2 satellite.

MSTV—Main Street TV is never scrambled, and has been on the air since February, 1992 on the Spacenet 2 satellite, channel 7. Nostalgia programming is the focus here, with the network showing lots of movies from the twenties through the sixties.

NBC is almost always unscrambled. This network has feeds for the east, central and west time zones on the Ku-band Satcom K2 satellite, and an eastern time zone feed on the (more common) C-band Satcom C1 satellite (which some people still call F1 because that's the satellite that used to be in that location).

Nostalgia Television is never scrambled. They are on channel 22 on the Galaxy 1R satellite.

Prime Network and some of their affiliates occasionally show classic motorsports-related movies. Keep watching their listings.

Republic Theater is never scrambled. They are located on channel 20 the Telstar 301 satellite.

Showtime network has feeds for both the east and west time zones. They are on Satcom C4 channel 20 and Satcom C3 channel 15.

TMC—The Movie Channel has feeds for both the east and west time zones. They are on Satcom C3 channel 17 and Galaxy 5 channel 14.

TMT—The Movie Network is from Canada, broadcasting on the Anik E2 satellite on channel 4. TMT used to be called First Choice, and is only available to subscribers in Canada.

TNT—Turner Network Television, channel 17 on the Galaxy 5 satellite, shows a variety of classic movies.

TBS—Turner Broadcast System, also on the Galaxy 5 satellite on channel 6, shows a variety of classic movies.

TVN—Touchstone Video Network has ten pay-per-view movie channels on the Telstar 303 satellite.

Viewers Choice has pay-per-view movie channels that are found on Satcom C1 channel 19, Satcom C4 channel 18 and Satcom C3 channel 3. They all show recent movies.

VTC Movie Greats Network is never scrambled. They show movies twice (or more) a day on Telstar 301 channel 21.

Satellite channel locations change relatively often. The above listings were accurate when this edition went to press in 1994.

Satellite TV viewing guides are one of the best sources for locating movies. The weekly guides tend to be more accurate than those published monthly. *Satellite TV Week* is the best one, in my opinion.

Laserdisc

Laserdiscs are generally second only to satellite in terms of fidelity, and they *can* surpass it. While few of the movies listed in this book are available in this format, it's worth looking for them. An excellent way to learn more about the medium (and film and satellite TV) is to read *The Perfect Vision*.

Local TV

A good outdoor antenna and a rotor, properly set up, can sometimes outperform cable TV in terms of audio and video quality. If you live within fifty miles of a major city, it's worth your while to look into this.

Video Rental Stores

Video rental stores can help you by ordering a copy of a film for you to buy. Most of them will also have some of these titles in stock for rent. If you have the choice, support a dealer who already stocks a good variety of classic and cult films, as opposed to the retailers who are "Top Ten" oriented.

Cable TV

Cable TV offers some of the channels available on satellite, with audio and video quality that is inferior to your own good satellite system.

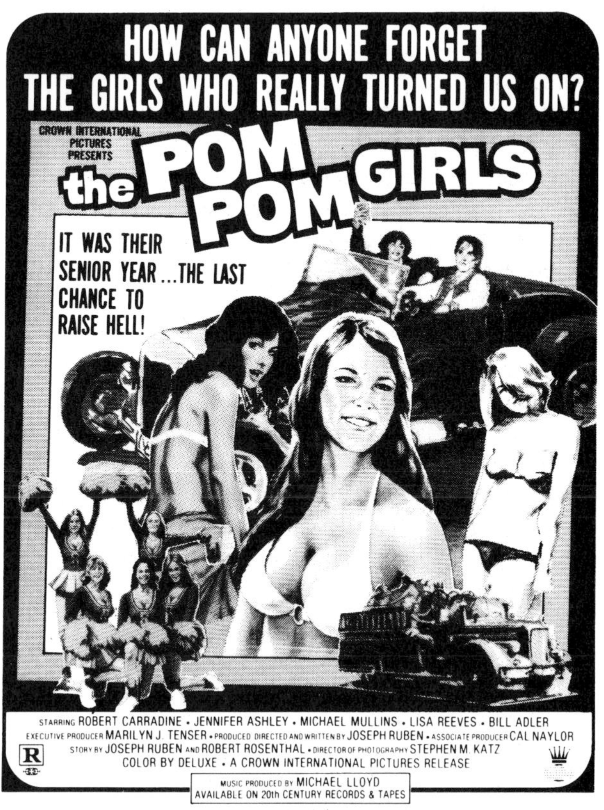

Yikes! *The Pom-Pom Girls* promised to tell the wild and saucy truth about what is for many young men a taboo fantasy: high school cheerleaders. This film was originally released with an R rating, but was later toned down enough to qualify as PG material. *Crown International/ Ron Main Collection*

Mail Order

Mail-order suppliers offer great selection, at varying degrees of quality. Consider that many old movies were not preserved with a lot of care, so it's lucky that some of them are still available at all. Some sources for ordering specific titles are listed below. Virtually all of them can also supply other movies as well, so request catalogs or movie lists. Films listed here are available in VHS only.

Main Attractions
P.O. Box 4923
Chatsworth, CA 91313-4923
Ron Main is a long-time film and memorabilia collector who is the co-author of this book and the operator of Main Attractions. The M.A. catalog has a large list of great movies, most of them perfect for car and motorcycle enthusiasts, B Movie fans, and people looking for movies involving beach action, rock 'n' roll, hot rods, motorcycle gangs, teen troubles—you know, all the most important things in life. Ron's catalogs are a blast to read, and his films are on video after having been transferred from original film reels through a modern process that enhances the quality of the picture and the color.

Clyde Earl Vintage Videos
10619 Felton Ave.
Inglewood, CA 90304
A great collection of motorcycle movies, including Hollywood productions, factory product films, and lots of great race footage, some of it from really old and really interesting events (hillclimbs, trials, etc.).

Easyrider
P.O. Box 1025
Agoura, Hills, CA 91301-1025
Easy Rider and *The Wild One*

M. Longley
2712 N. 60th Street
Milwaukee, WI 53210
414/871-0737
Hot Car Girls

Nostalgia Family Video
P.O. Box 606
Baker City, OR 97814-0606
503/523-9034
Date Bait, High School Caesar, Hot Rod Girl, Motorcycle Gang, Teenage Crime Wave, and *The Wild Ride*

Ormond Films
2925 Sharon Hill Circle
Nashville, TN 37215
The Burning Hell and *White Lightnin' Road*

Shock-Toon Video
Rd 4, Box 136-A
Boonton, NJ 07005
The Ghost of Dragstrip Hollow

Sinister Cinema
P.O Box 4369
Medford, OR 97501-0168
503/773-6860
Motorcycle Squad, Teenage Crime Wave, Teenage Mother, Wages of Fear, Wild Ones On Wheels, and *Wild Youth*

Stokey's Serials
P.O Box 426
Selden, NY 11784-0426
Burn 'Em Up Barnes, Daredevils of the Red Circle, Roar of the Iron Horse, and *Speeding Along*

Video Finders
1770 North Highland #721
Los Angeles, CA 90028

Videomatica
1855 West 4th Avenue
Vancouver, BC
Canada V6J 1M4
604/734-5752
FAX: 604/734-8867

© 1967 American International Pictures

Appendix II

Bibliography of Books and Magazines

To follow up on some of the information provided in (or left out of) this book, there are several other books in particular that can be helpful. All of the following were used as research material in the preparation of this book. Unfortunately, some of them are now out of print.

Fit for the Chase—Cars and the Movies
by Raymond Lee

Most of these early movies in this book, and the information about the cars in those films, came from Raymond Lee's fascinating book, which was published in 1969. It's now out of print, but a copy may turn up in a used book store. Its Library of Congress catalog number is 68-27198. *Fit for the Chase* is filled with rare photographs of cars that were used in the movies from the 'teens to the sixties. There is a lot of information that was not available anywhere else.

Road Movies—The Complete Guide to Cinema on Wheels
by Mark Williams

This book was published by Proteus Publishing in England in 1982 and is now out of print. It features detailed descriptions of 109 movies that generally fit the theme of going on the road. This is an interesting book that goes into detail about the story lines of the movies, but it says virtually nothing about the vehicles involved. Had it not been for Mark's complete lack of humor and his dry, pedantic style of writing, I would not have said the following: If this guy knows anything about cars and motorcycles, it sure doesn't show in his book. According to the back cover of his book, he has seen *Two-Lane Blacktop* six times. Mark, if you're out there, the real star of *Two-Lane Blacktop* was a '55 Chevy, not a "57 Chevvy," as you called it in your book. In fact, if you really want to know what it is, read about it here.

The Films of Roger Corman—Brilliance on a Budget
by Ed Naha

Probably long out of print, this 1982 book from Arco Publishing is a gem, containing descriptions, photos, and behind-the-scenes information about the career and films of master film maker Roger Corman (*Deathrace 2000, The Wild Angels, Angels, Hard as They Come*, etc.). If you find it in a used bookstore, scoop it up.

Movie & Video Guide (updated each year)
by Leonard Maltin

This reference book was one of several of its type used to find descriptive information about some of the movies in this book. This one stands out as being the most complete available, with listings for over 19,000 movies. Leonard Maltin sure isn't much of a motorhead, though.

Movies on TV and Videocassette, 1991-1992
by Steven H. Scheuer

With listings for more than 19,000 movies, this book also proved a great help here. As with Maltin's book, the listings are extensive and to the point, although somewhat fewer actors are usually mentioned. The date on the cover is a bit optimistic though—for example, the "1992-1993" edition doesn't list *Terminator 2*, the largest-grossing movie of 1991. This book still has more movies described than almost any other. But Steven Scheuer is not much of a motorhead either.

FILMFAX

FILMFAX calls itself "the magazine of unusual film and television." In FILMFAX, the B-Movie is treated with appreciation and respect. The focus here also includes biker, exploitation, and J.D. (juvenile delinquent) movies. You will find a wealth of information about all kinds of classic and cult movies in FILMFAX. The articles tend to be written by true devotees of the genre whose knowledge can be amazing. Even the letters from readers often provide good information. The ads alone can be worth the subscription price, since you'll discover many sources to mail-order copies of classic movies from. If you love B-movies, this is the magazine.

FILMFAX
P.O. Box 1900
1042 1/2 Michigan Avenue
Evanston, Illinois 60204-1900
708/866-7155

Main Attractions

Ron and Vanessa Main's *Main Attractions* catalogs aren't the size of some of the movie guides listed here, but their pages are filled with rich descriptions of choice movies for B Movie buffs and car enthusiasts. Whether you're looking for racing documentaries or the worst of the worst of B Movies, *Main Attractions'* catalog probably includes an entertaining listing for your movie.

Main Attractions
P.O. Box 4923
Chatsworth, CA 91313-4923

INDEX/FILM LIST